PUBLIC SECURITY IN FEDERAL POLITIES

Public Security in Federal Polities

EDITED BY CHRISTIAN LEUPRECHT,
MARIO KÖLLING, AND TODD HATALEY

UNIVERSITY OF TORONTO PRESS
Toronto Buffalo London

utorontopress.com

ISBN 978-1-4875-0267-6

Library and Archives Canada Cataloguing in Publication

Public security in federal polities / edited by Christian Leuprecht, Mario Kölling, and Todd Hataley.

Includes bibliographical references.
ISBN 978-1-4875-0267-6 (cloth)

1. National security – Case studies. 2. Globalization – Case studies. 3. Federal government – Case studies. I. Leuprecht, Christian, 1973–, editor II. Kölling, Mario, editor III. Hataley, Todd Steven, 1963–, editor

UA10.5.P83 2019 355′.03 C2018-902368-6

The Forum of Federations, the global network on federalism, supports better governance through learning among federal experts and practitioners. Active on six continents and supported by nine federal countries, it manages programs in established and emerging federations and publishes scholarly and educational materials.

Secrétariat
aux affaires
intergouvernementales
canadiennes

The Forum of Federations acknowledges the financial support from the Government of Québec.

University of Toronto Press acknowledges the financial assistance to its publishing program of the Canada Council for the Arts and the Ontario Arts Council, an agency of the Government of Ontario.

Canada Council for the Arts
Conseil des Arts du Canada

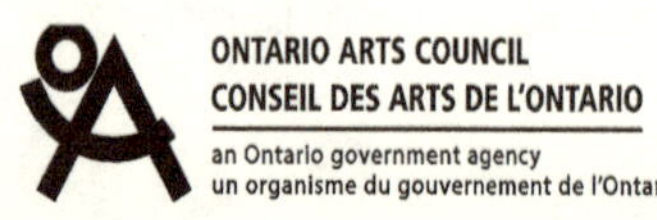

Funded by the Government of Canada
Financé par le gouvernement du Canada

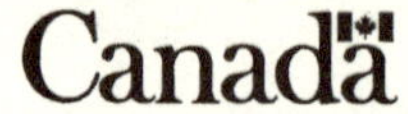

This volume is dedicated to my sunshine Meghan,
and to Montse, Lara, and Anna,
and to Todd's wife Joy, who makes all things possible

Contents

A Note from the Forum of Federations

The current volume *Public Security in Federal Polities* is part of the Forum of Federations' ongoing commitment to shaping comparative research on federalism. It follows the Forum's work on structural issues of federalism published as a seven-volume set as part of the Global Dialogue Program, as well as multi-country studies on capital cities, oil and gas, internal trade, metropolitan regions, political parties and intergovernmental relations, courts, education, and health care.

In several of the Forum's partner countries, the rise of transnational crime and terrorism has challenged existing security and enforcement arrangements. Federal countries have a plethora of agencies and institutions at different levels of government tasked with enforcement and security functions. Typically, federal governments have the following types of agencies:

1 Armed Forces
2 National or Federal Enforcement Agencies – Customs, Coast Guard, Federal Police
3 Security and Intelligence services
4 Criminal Investigation agencies
5 Militia and paramilitary forces

Provincial and municipal governments are likely to have at their disposal their own:

1 Civilian Police Services
2 Special police or Militia

While these organizations were established with specific mandates in mind, assignment of responsibilities is not quite as clear-cut as envisaged. Overlapping mandates, mission creep, and different institutional cultures often lead to inter-service competition rather than cooperation. This in turn creates operational problems and hinders effective public security management.

The rise of drug crime and terrorism underscores the need for closer coordination between agencies and across orders of government. As a result the ever-expanding domestic security agenda has shown that no level of government or no one agency is equipped to confront these challenges on its own. Furthermore, except for federal police and investigative agencies specially established for the prosecution of federal crime (United States, Australia), or as institutions for intergovernmental coordination (Germany), federal security and intelligence agencies are traditionally oriented towards confronting external threats (including customs). Given the international dimension to both drug crime and terrorism, federal or central agencies are increasingly being called on to take up domestic security and enforcement mandates – such as calling out the Armed Forces to deal with drug crime or gang violence.

Clearly there are some functions that the federal level is better equipped to perform, whereas others are better left for local entities. Without innovative modes of intergovernmental and interdepartmental cooperation federal agencies risk dissipating federal governments' energies, while eroding the value added and flexibility contributed by local entities.

The challenge becomes particularly acute when communities encounter security challenges that transcend the community's ability to cope internally, that is, which require outside assistance. A possible point of friction is that outsiders may not share the community's values and thus misunderstand the community's security needs, but they may also end up being perceived as a threat. The source of such challenges at the community level may be a genuine security problem. However, it may also be a function of inadequate funding and/or intelligence sharing and/or inter-agency cooperation by higher levels of government, thus putting subnational and/or municipal forces in the sort of quandary which conjures up a security problem that subsequently provides the rationale for federal intervention. So, we want to identify not only the nature of the security challenges but also obstacles to confronting them.

In order to reflect on these challenges the Forum brought together a group of experts to offer comparative perspectives rooted in their own national experience. We are grateful to Kai Michael Kenkel, Klaus Stüwe, Ajay K. Mehra, Edgar Mohar, Nico Steytler, Lukas Muntingh, Markus H.F. Mohler, Rainer J. Schweizer, and Richard J. Kilroy Jr for their contribution to this volume.

I would also like to thank the editors Christian Leuprecht, Mario Kölling, and Todd Hataley for their skilled creation of this important work and patience in bringing it to fruition. They worked with us to conceptualize the project, in shaping the template and editing this vast piece of research. Thanks are also due to the Giminez Abad Foundation in Zaragoza for hosting the authors' conference for this volume. I would be remiss if I didn't thank my colleagues at the Forum, Philip Gonzalez and Felix Knuepling, for managing this project at its inception, and John Light for seeing its conclusion and walking it through the publication process. Finally, thanks are due to our publisher, the University of Toronto Press, for their tireless work on this important and unique volume.

Rupak Chattopadhyay
President and CEO, Forum of Federations

PUBLIC SECURITY IN FEDERAL POLITIES

1 Introduction

CHRISTIAN LEUPRECHT, TODD HATALEY, AND MARIO KÖLLING

This is the first book to offer an overview of the federal structures and processes that reconcile domestic security with fundamental democratic norms. It offers a broad comparative review of constitutional, institutional, and legislative frameworks that underpin security across nine federations, and the implications that follow for institutional design, public administration, and public policy. Two desiderata motivate this book. One is how institutional structure and attributes, such as heterogeneity and unitary past, affect whether the state takes a top-down or a bottom-up approach to security, and how that affects the performance of security policy. The other is a relative rebirth of policy, administrative, and institutional innovation, because domestic security policy and the state's monopoly of force have been neglected as fields of rigorous comparative research. The systematic and methodical link between a set of nine federal polities on the one hand, and a select policy area on the other thus holds out considerable promise for new – or at least better – approaches to a core mandate of the modern state: security.

How to ensure that security becomes a positive-sum security dilemma for all involved, rather than a zero-sum? Ultimately, this is the research problem that underlies this book: how can (and do) federations overcome the fallacy of composition in the provision of security for their citizens, their sub-state units, and the state as a whole? The answer is *not* self-evident. In fact, it may well be the ultimate challenge that confounds federal countries: security is fundamental to democratic governance, social harmony, social development, and prosperity. Security is a necessary but, as even a most cursory survey of countries readily shows, hardly a sufficient condition for democracy. Federalism, of course, is neither a necessary nor a sufficient condition for democracy. Democracy, however, is a necessary but insufficient condition to ensure that the synthesis of federalism and security advances freedom, equality, and justice for all citizens across a federation's sub-state entities alike. Such is the aim of this book: to identify more (and less) optimal approaches to harness synergies between federalism and security to enhance democratic norms, values, outputs, and outcomes for citizens across sub-state entities.

The Forum of Federation's Global Dialogue series[1] has been making significant comparative inroads along an array of policy fields. However, most of those had antecedents. By contrast, the novelty of this book is twofold: begin to fill a void in the comparative study of security in federations while, in the process, contributing to the nascent field of comparative security studies. In contrast to the maturity of the field of comparative federalism (Watts 2007), comparative security studies has yet to emancipate itself methodologically and substantively as a sovereign field of study (Collins 2016). The findings are intended not only to inform decision-making in the select subset of nine federal case studies that form the basis of this book, but also to enhance conflict resolution through improved prospects for institutional design and power sharing in fledgling federations and proto-democratic regimes, such as Iraq and Ethiopia, in illiberal federations such as Russia, as well as in deeply conflicted societies for which a federal arrangement holds out the sole genuine alternative to fragmentation and disintegration, as in Yemen and Libya.

As a result of global supply and transportation chains, the interconnectedness of social media, population growth of 3 billion additional people on the globe concentrated in some of the least sustainable parts of the world, pernicious effects of climate change, and diffusion of power,

1 The program has thus far examined nine themes:

1: Constitutional origins, structure, and change in federal countries
2: Distribution of powers and responsibilities in federal countries
3: Legislative, executive, and judicial governance in federal countries
4: The practice of fiscal federalism: Comparative perspectives
5: Foreign relations in federal countries
6: Local governments and metropolitan regions in federal systems
7: Diversity and unity in federal systems
8: Intergovernmental relations in federal countries
9: Political parties and civil society in federal countries

to name but a few trends, the emergent challenges to the security environment are prone to persist. The end of the Cold War, globalization, and the concomitant trans-nationalization of deviance, and the aftermath of 9/11 as a tipping points for transnational terrorism have engendered rapid changes in domestic, regional, and the global security environments. These developments challenge the institutionalized security claim of the modern state: to renew, deepen, and expand control over risk phenomena that are ultimately impervious to state control.

Since security involves some of the most basic yet potentially coercive powers of the machinery of the modern state, how best to reconcile freedom and security is among the most prominent issues of the day. Striking the appropriate balance is complicated by the changing nature of risks that transcend a specific geographic location, whose consequences are in principle incalculable, and with fleeting control over the unsafe consequences and dangers of decisions. As in any other policy arena, federalism presents a set of challenges distinct from those faced by unitary systems. In federal states that task is further complicated by the presence of multiple levels of government that enjoy autonomy within their realm of constitutional jurisdiction. Federal citizens continuously negotiate both the limits and powers of state intervention to ensure a free, safe, and prosperous society, and how these are to be assigned to different levels of government. How much independence is one to surrender to the state, and what protection does one want to gain in return that only a social existence can provide? The ensuing constitutional and legislative arrangements necessitate that governments coordinate among themselves, and with civil society and the private sector.

The case studies in this book represent different federal responses to security challenges of differing quality and quantity: the Naxalite rebellion in India, terrorist activities of Basque nationalists in Spain, seemingly ungovernable urban spaces in Brazil, skyrocketing crime rates in South Africa, violence by Mexican organized-crime syndicates, increasing criminal police competences of federal authorities in Switzerland, and local implementation of federal counterterrorism priorities in the United States, Canada, and Germany. Initially, however, this introduction will present the framework that guides this book. The first section will establish the research problem, explain the scope of the selection of country case studies, introduce methodological caveats about comparability as a result of endogenous historical and institutional effects, and explain the common structure that guides each of the case studies in order to facilitate comparison. The second section operationalizes the contentious concept of security for the purposes of this study. The third section situates the concept of security within federal theory in general, and comparative federalism in particular. Finally, the fourth section concludes with two different findings: after a survey of the highlights of each of the nine country case studies presented in chapters 2 through 10, that final section also gives the reader a preview of key comparative findings as analysed in chapter 11, which concludes this volume.

1. About the Book

This study compares public security across federal polities with the aim of identifying commonalities and differences, best practices, lessons learned and controlling for endogenous effects by distinguishing those aspects that are unique to any one federal system from those that may be transferrable to others. The nomenclature is quite deliberate, and meant to problematize the concept of "security," how it is exercised, and in whose interest. Thomas Hobbes famously writes that life without the state (i.e., in the State of Nature) is "nasty, brutish, and short." In this vein, security is commonly provided by a third party, which, in return for ceding certain rights, provides "freedom from" actual occurrence of danger, injury, fear, loss, anxiety, crime, attack, etc. By contrast, safety is the general condition that gives rise to feeling secure. Public safety, then, is the welfare of the general public. Public security, by contrast, refers to concrete measures of protection: policing activities aimed at protecting goods and people, which encompasses public and private actors with intent, and strategic capacity to fulfil policing functions with the objective of maintaining order, public safety over a defined territory, and the application of the rule of law.

As a heuristic device, this security function has two basic dimensions: preventive and repressive, and, as such, includes everything from the fight against delinquency and transnational crime, different police forces (federal, sub-state, local), borders and border guards, to private actors. To this end, Jean-Paul Brodeur (1983) famously distinguishes between "high" and "low" policing, while James Sheptycki (2011) surmises that the evolution of policing must be understood as a dialectic between top-down dynamics and internal bottom-up ones. National security is premised on high policing: centralized norms, interests, and priorities, along with a hierarchical arrangement in which some conceptions of security are eliminated or neutralized in favour of others by the coercive apparatus of the predatory (nation-)state that enforces, protects, and seeks to legitimate its monopoly over the management of (physical) violence (Tilly 1985). In the famous words of Arnold Wolfers, "National security, in an objective sense, measures the absence of threats to acquired values, in a subjective sense, the absence of fear that such values will be attacked" (Wolfers 1952, 485). Its quintessential symbol is the police protecting and enforcing state sovereignty across a territory delimited by state borders: the state whose agents are authorized to use physical force to guarantee order and public security (Althusser 1976; Bittner 1979; Bayley 1983). Through the surveillance and control of space and the spatial strategies put in place to this effect, space becomes an instrument in the service of the particular mission that has been devolved to police activity (Germes 2011). This mission and its accompanying spatial strategies differs among federations and their sub-state governments, and police activities are necessarily a function of territorial specificities. Federal territory and institutions thus constrain and enable police competencies and activities. Inherent in the idea of public security is the notion of low policing: the concept of public security is meant to signal an ongoing negotiation among competing norms, interests, and priorities. In this book, public security is thus conceptualized as reconciling competing norms and interests.

Federal states effectively institutionalize this tension. Although institutions, including those that envelop federal structure, can affect federal structure by converting incentives to behave opportunistically into a motivation to cooperate, federal process does not follow perforce from federal structure. Ergo, the underlying normative assumption that guides the study is that the process intrinsic to democratic constitutionalism is a necessary condition for a robust state to generate political order as a legitimate outcome, where democratic constitutionalism is understood in the form of two bedrock principles (Fukuyama 2012): (1) the rule of law to which the state is subordinate (in the form of the independence of the judiciary, the application of the law through the impartial administration of justice, and the legality, legitimacy, impartiality, and proportionality of police investigations); and (2) political accountability in the form of democratic oversight of the exercise of the power of the state to ensure that it is not corrupted. Federal political systems are both the result and the cause of differences over these principles and the way they are operationalized.

The delivery and administration of security to the satisfaction of *all* members of a federal community is predicated on an appropriate balance between shared rule and self-rule in governance arrangements.[2] Shared rule is a function of the institutional capacity to reconcile federal and local priorities, while self-rule is a function of the degree of flexibility afforded to constituent units to respond to local preferences. With respect to security, shared rule thus effectively amounts to sharing not only the state's monopoly of the legitimate use of physical force in the enforcement of its order, but also the constitutional framework and rule of law that govern its use, and the ability to hold security actors to account.

Realizing federalism as an institution and a process to generate security outcomes is thus fundamentally political: In balancing self-rule and shared rule, how are responsibilities and powers to be divided yet shared between the central government and constituent units? Since this research question is ultimately driven by a state's capacity to reconcile freedom and security, only federations that qualify as democratic are included. Still, space in insufficient to include them all. Some readers may take issue with the inclusion of some countries and the omission of others: Australia, Belgium, and Iraq, for instance, are omitted even though security features prominently in each. Whilst would-be federations such as Cyprus, Yemen, and possibly Libya where security is a first mover do not feature either among the case studies, the comparative findings in the conclusion are meant to advance the underlying body of knowledge that informs constitutional negotiations that envisage a federal endgame. All cases in this volume – Brazil, Canada, Germany, India, Mexico, South Africa, Spain, Switzerland, and the United States – have previously figured prominently across the Forum of Federation's aforementioned Global Dialogue series, are either member countries of or closely associated with the Forum of Federations, and share three quintessential features: de facto constitutionally enshrined (1) jurisdictions with (2) a combination of shared and self-rule (3) by at least two agents in the form of autonomous levels of government.

In each country case study, federalism and security have undergone quite particular and highly contingent developments. That limits

2 The epigram of federation as "regional self-rule plus shared rule" was introduced by Elazar (1987).

comparability. Perhaps that is precisely why no effort has thus far been made to compare public security across federal polities. Nonetheless, that caveat has not impeded systematic comparison in other policy areas, as exemplified by the Forum of Federation's Global Dialogue. Endogenous effects and each state's particular manifestations of security notwithstanding, they share federalism's basic structure within a democratic framework.

Brazil and Mexico exhibit the challenges of democratization in a federal polity confronted with large-scale violence as a result of organized crime, and the struggle central governments face when trying to resolve security issues that are ultimately local. These federations face a dilemma in administering and delivering security: central intervention is driven by insufficient security capacity at the local level, yet further calls into question the ability to bolster local capacity and reinforce local jurisdiction in the area, thus precipitating suboptimal outcomes for the federal arrangement as a whole. India faces similar administrative challenges as a result of local under-delivery and capacity, but these play themselves out differently because security issues are driven largely by local insurgency and various forms of terrorism. South Africa is particularly illustrative of the way the division of powers can exacerbate security problems; the case study is highly suggestive of the importance of institutional design. Canada and the United States contrast the symmetric with the asymmetric delivery and administration of security. The American case shows the perils of not finding an adequate equilibrium between shared rule and self-rule, and the disjuncture between federal and local security priorities. The Canadian case, by contrast, demonstrates that, contrary to widespread belief, not only can decentralized and asymmetric delivery and administration of security yield effective and efficient security outcomes, but they may in fact be a precondition of such outcomes in large, diverse societies. The German federation is witness to the creeping centralization of security in a country whose security structure was intentionally designed to curtail the central government's purview over security through decentralization. Similarly, security has also seen (limited) centralization in the Swiss federation. The Spanish case illustrates the problems of inefficiency to which overlap and coordination give rise in a decentralized polity where the division of powers and labour between the central and constituent governments with respect to security are at times unclear and competitive.

The case studies include two Anglo-Saxon systems of government along with a number of systems that are foreign to Anglo-Saxon liberal democracies. While some of these cases are also advanced democracies, and their ideas happen to be somewhat liberal and republican, akin to those that inform the United States, most are not modelled on Anglo-Saxon principles or institutions of government. The distinct legal histories of each country case study have a path-dependent impact on contemporary policy choices as mediated by current constitutional and legal frameworks. In Brazil, for instance, American legal and philosophical legacies influenced the way the Brazilian federation was designed and powers were divided among federal, state, and municipal levels. At the same time, these ideas were grafted onto primarily Portuguese conceptions of colonialism that necessarily affected how power was understood, divided, and operationalized organizationally. Similar provisos apply to Mexico with its Spanish colonial influence, India and its British colonial history, and South Africa with its Dutch and British legacies as well as the aftermath of the apartheid regime. These are all circumstances under which power, control, and security are quite particular and distinct from the book's other case studies. That is, they differ fundamentally from the liberal ideas and value systems that gave rise to Commonwealth and North American constitutionalism, which in turn are different from social-democratic principles in continental Europe. For example, liberal democracy in the Anglo-Saxon world is premised on limited state intervention and the state as an arbiter that adjudicates competing interests; by contrast, social democracy in continental Europe is much more comfortable with state intervention to direct society and the market and their development. In the same way that these nuances have enabled different varieties of capitalism to emerge in Europe, they have given rise to different and particular varieties of federalism on the one hand, and security on the other hand.

Concerns about the methodological nationalism that pervades comparative federalism notwithstanding, the nine country case studies in this book actually comprise over 200 Constituent Units. The precise number is difficult to ascertain, as it depends on whether entities such as Canada's three northern territories, India's seven union territories, or U.S. dependencies are counted towards the total. In Brazil and South Africa, municipalities have constitutional status as bodies politic distinct from provinces; in other federations they are mostly appendages of provinces, states, or cantons. Yet in the case of three German city states and Mexico's Federal District, some municipalities have the same standing as states, whereas in India the National Capital Territory of Delhi enjoys the status of a union territory rather than a state.

First, to ensure comparability, the chapters broadly follow a similar structure. However, some latitude is dictated by circumstance and leeway for flexibility and adaptation. Initially, each chapter surveys the country's principal public security challenges, its federal dimensions and related institutional structures and intergovernmental processes.

Second, the chapters map each country's constitutional and legal foundations for legislative competencies and the provision of public security in the federal polity, including the division of exclusive, concurrent, and paramount powers. This part surveys the principal security mechanisms of each level of government, the extent to which these mechanisms actually reinforce or undermine the constitutionally ordained division of power, and how well mechanisms are matched with oversight. It goes on to examine the extent to which these mechanisms are the result of explicit provisions in the constitution, as opposed to political practice in the form of conventions. In the process, the section situates the federal arrangement along the symmetry-asymmetry and centralization-decentralization continua. It closes out by examining the public trust and perception of different levels of government as a function of their contribution to public security.

With an eye to investigating the importance of a federal political system's adaptability and flexibility, the third section analyses the way each public security system actually works in practice, whether it is plagued by overlap and duplication, how well it actually works, the way the system has changed over time, and the explanations for change and inertia. To this end, this section also delves into the reasons for the system's institutional design, including whether security was a major driver in the establishment and evolution of the federal system. That is important if we are to learn about the conditions that enable public security in federal polities in the first place. It asks about the role of municipalities, especially in federal polities, the extent to which the federal government's role has waxed and waned over the years, and the causes for any oscillation observed. One of the goals is to measure the extent to which public security arrangements adhere to (or depart from) the principle of subsidiarity.

The fourth section seeks to gather fiscal data on public security. This is less a matter of ascertaining whether the system per se is funded adequately than it is to gauge the adequacy of financial resources within and among the different levels of government. Part of the issue here is to measure the degree of interdependence, the extent to which political autonomy is reflected in fiscal autonomy, and the proliferation of unfunded mandates where one level of government can obligate another to take certain action without (adequate) fiscal compensation.

To identify the dynamics that make intergovernmental collaboration successful, the fifth section surveys the available intergovernmental mechanisms, their effectiveness, and whether they set appropriate incentives for cooperation. It gauges how politicized these mechanisms are so as to understand whether it makes a difference if they are run by politicians or bureaucrats.

For illustrative purposes, one or two critical policy case studies follow in the sixth section, before rounding out each country study with an overall assessment of the adequacy and appropriateness of public security arrangements in that particular polity by assessing the federal polity's performance in delivering and administering security. It summarizes the drivers of change and unintended consequences to which they may have given rise. Since federalism and democracy are functionally dependent, this assessment is also meant to discern how well the federal system and its operation actually conform to basic liberal-democratic values – freedom, equality, and justice – and operating principles, including the rule of law and representative government as a manifestation of popular sovereignty.

2. The Comparative Study of Public Security

First, security is a function of the state's ability to constrain – and enable – human behaviour. The modern state is premised on a social contract to provide citizens with public goods in the form of security, law, public order, and basic services in return for taxation (Collier 2009, 220; Milliken and Krause 2002, 752; Holsti 1998). It does so by maintaining effective and legitimate institutions of government that preserve and enforce the monopoly over the use of violence within a given territory (Weber 1946, 1958; Tilly, Mann, Carment, Prest, and Samy 2010; Tikuisis and Carment 2017, 1; Patrick 2011, 8). States, then, are instrumental to social order; but only democratic states are equally instrumental to public welfare. Democracies distinguish themselves by factoring considerations of individual and collective freedom, equality, justice, well-being, and prosperity into the equation. To capture this more precise notion, for the purpose of this book the concept of security is qualified as public security. Public security comprises acts ranging from ordinary measures taken by law enforcement authorities within the framework of constitutional and relevant special laws to extraordinary measures to safeguard human rights and fundamental freedoms.

Second, security (and insecurity) comes in many forms: national, regional, international, global, collective, local, social, and so forth. This *problématique* is compounded by the way epistemic communities perceive in/security: security is ultimately in the eyes of the beholder. Even the vernacular is commonly problematic: does the term *national* security make much sense in a context where most states are actually multinational? Or does it implicitly acknowledge that security provided in the interests of one "nation" may not be in the interests of another? Or perhaps that the purpose of security is as much "national defence" as it is to build, construct, and unify diverse states – through coercion and the imposition of force if necessary. Charles Tilly (1985) famously likened the state to an organized crime syndicate that eliminates internal opponents and extracts resources to protect its supporters. Institutions, patterns, and processes that reinforce security for some groups thus inherently raise the prospect of making others – or making them feel – less secure.

Third, security, and how it is operationalized, is controversial and contingent. The way the United States and Canada commonly understand security is steeped in the prevailing approach of neorealism, where the role of state institutions places the armed forces in particular and security institutions in general – such as intelligence and law enforcement – at the core of security policy. They distinguish between security and safety: security is commonly understood as the actual services the state provides, such as law enforcement, whereas safety is commonly associated with the broader role and obligations that the institutions of the state have in fostering an environment where citizens, organizations, as well as private and non-governmental institutions can flourish and prosper.

In Europe, by contrast, security tends to be understood as more multifaceted and complex, and dependent on a much wider range of bureaucracies beyond the armed forces, law enforcement, and intelligence services, to include health, infrastructure, and social development. Perhaps the best-known academic manifestation of this Atlantic divide is the critical turn in security studies, especially the so-called Copenhagen school of security studies and its interest in the multiplicity of discourses concerning security, and the role that discourse by different security, public, and political actors plays in the construction of threats (Buzan, Wæver, and de Wilde 1998). Although not discussed explicitly, the different meanings denoted by the referent *security* emerge somewhat implicitly from the various chapters. So, while all chapters use the common referent of *security*, there are important nuances in what they understand by that referent, and what that referent signifies in a particular political, social, institutional, historical, and discursive context.

This raises a dilemma: broaden the scope of *security* beyond institutions and processes to include critical perspectives along with less traditional takes on security, and the chapters become unwieldy; cast the remit too narrow, and risk being criticized as a traditionalist for reducing security to state actors and institutions. The referent *public security* was chosen to bridge this divide: to signal on the one hand that the state has a broader role in security than simply fielding domestic security actors such as police while, on the other hand, reining in the temptation to stray too far from the conventional understanding of security. While the term *public security* may not be English vernacular – for precisely the aforementioned reasons – for the purpose of this book it strikes a balance, however inchoate, between competing conceptions while intimating an understanding of and respect for a phenomenon that is variegated and contingent.

In the panoply of the machinery of modern democratic government, no relationship is more fraught than that between government and the citizens, organizations and institutions – broadly referred to as society – it needs to protect from both external threat and internal disorder. The principles that govern it are universal to democratic government, but their application in the way security is administered to citizens is controversial because they authorize and legitimate the expectation and right of the use of coercive force in the assertion of the state's monopoly of violence. Security forces – police, paramilitary, or military units – maintain order, protect people and property, and/or uphold legitimate (or illegitimate) governments. One of the hallmarks of democratic federations is that they divide these. Authoritarian regimes, by contrast, centralize control over all security forces because they want to monopolize violence.

In democratic states, security external to the state largely is the purview of the armed forces, and such protection, according to Hamilton, Madison and Jay in *The Federalist Papers*, is a major benefit of federating. Central governments seek jurisdiction over security instruments where power is scaled up to avert collective-action problems and harness economies of scale, such as defence from external attack and preservation of territorial integrity: armed forces, national or federal enforcement agencies, such as customs and immigration, coast guard, federal police, security and intelligence services, and criminal investigation agencies. By contrast, internal security – security within the territorial confines of the state – is usually the task of police. Federated units are likely to have at their disposal their respective civilian police services, special police, or militia forces. In practice, though, assignment of responsibilities can be controversial. Overlapping mandates, mission creep, and different institutional cultures can give rise to inter-service competition and thwart cooperation. This in turn creates potential operational problems and hinders the effective provision of security. Other actors, state and non-state, have an expanded public security mandate: building inspectors, firefighters, rescue workers, emergency planners, and health-care workers. This expanded concept of security includes not just the maintenance of public order, but also the mitigation of risk and making communities resilient (Ferrier 2008).

In the provision of security, the state is thus complemented by other agents,[3] institutional[4] structures, and social and cultural norms. The state's role is to enforce and codify security by means of legislative and social boundaries.[5] Security, then, is the result (outcome) of a political process (input) that requires the support of a social collective that acknowledges a threat and the need for decisive action to deter, contain, or eliminate it (Buzan, Wæver, and de Wilde 1998). Security thus understood is a social construct: threats are identified, plans are made, and actions are taken. Underlying the identification of threats is a set of

---

3 *Agency* refers not only to individuals, but also to groups of individuals who act on behalf of others (Onuf 1998, 59–60). Agents are defined by their participation in society, to the extent that rules exist that allow for that participation. Thus, individuals, and groups of individuals, such as policymakers, participate as social actors within the bounds and limits set by rules. Scott (2001, 76) takes the definition one step further by arguing that agents have the capacity to effect some change on the social world around them either by altering the rules or the distribution of resources. In short, agents have the capacity to take action.

4 March and Olsen (1998, 948) define institutions as a "relatively stable collection of practices and rules defining appropriate behaviour for specific groups of actors in specific situations." Practices and rules are embedded in "structures of meaning and schemes of interpretation that explain and legitimize particular identities and the practices and rules associated with them." Moreover, they also assert that practices and rules are embedded in resources and their allocation that make it possible for individuals and collectivities to act in a certain way, and to penalize deviant behaviour.

5 Government in failed or failing states does not have the capacity to enforce legislative and social boundaries pertaining to the provision of public security.

norms and values. Those have traditionally been defined by the central state, but need not necessarily be so. Structure is dynamic and change occurs when actors, responding to a stimulus (broadly defined as the social collective) redefine their conceptualization of security (Wendt 1999). This dynamic process has three effects. First, security conditions are temporally bound, that is, they will change over time. Second, security agents are equally dynamic. Who defines security will vary by situation and social, cultural, and/or political context. Third, the issues that become securitized will change over time. As the result of variation across time and space, conceptions of security across any state are never monolithic. In unitary states, however, the government has the capacity to enforce a particular conception of security. Not so in federations where, by virtue of the constitutional division of sovereignty, variation in the conception of security as a referent object manifests itself in the application of self-rule of territorial entities as well as in controversies over shared rule. In sum, the fact that different actors prioritize security threats differently across a broad geographic spectrum necessitates a federal arrangement in the first instance but subsequently institutionalizes and, consequently, reifies competing conceptions of security.

Bounded by a set of cultural, political, economic, or social understandings that are particular to any given unit of a federal polity, security will vary horizontally and vertically. The extent of variation is a function of differences in these understandings. By virtue of their fundamentally different expressions of sovereignty, their instantiation differs in federal as opposed to unitary countries. As a result of this dialectic, security needs to be understood not only within the context of what is being securitized but also who is securitizing. Security, then, has a number of important attributes that are critical to understanding how it is provided, articulated, and becomes manifest within federal polities and their constituent units.

3. Comparing Public Security across Federal Polities

The purpose of this book, then, is to examine federalism not as an end, but as a means to the provision of public security. It is not the existence of the federal system per se that matters, but its performance, measured, in part, as a function of decentralized institutions. The study systematically compares the complementarity of functional capacity – rather than the mere existence of particular institutions per se. In the process, the book strives to identify ingredients and designs to address endogenous security contexts adequately and how to engineer just distributive effects of both safety and security, and individual and collective freedoms of all citizens. What makes security in federal systems robust so that citizens can live in security while enjoying the spoils of constitutional democracy? What aspects of the constitutional architecture of different models of federalism that are thought to be striking this balance effectively are (not) transferrable to federations that are struggling to provide security for their citizenry? And to what extent are federal security institutions, practices, and outcomes a function of federalism per se, as opposed to other general governance and societal factors?

The notion of federal polity is meant to capture a federation's institutional ecology as well as institutional variation. The high degree of structural variation among federations is also a function of any number of subsidiary dynamics: (1) federations are generally the result of compromises that arise in circumstances where a unitary system is simply not feasible; (2) there is a tension, inherent to the structure of federations, between the central governments' tendency to impose common values and standards, and efforts by federated entities to protect their own sphere of powers; (3) "big" (usually central) government in most federal states grows; and (4) there is a tension between different normative conceptions of federalism (Karmis 2009, 53). As a result, federations sustain themselves through a permanent state of optimization.

Optimizing freedom, equality, and justice on the one hand and security on the other hand is necessarily controversial: how to deliver both efficiently and administer both fairly. Federal polities premised on the principle of subsidiarity (a principle of vertical power-sharing that vests a political decision with the lowest level of government best able to deal with a particular issue) take a "bottom-up" approach where security is ultimately understood as local, as is the case in Switzerland where the cantons have to come up with the necessary security resources; or they may take a "top-down" approach, as is the case in India and Mexico where security resources are largely centralized, to the detriment of subsidiarity. The problem of delivery is one of contributing enough so that all governments have an incentive to partake and not monopolize divisible goods for themselves. The problem of administration, by contrast, concerns the distribution of divisible goods to the satisfaction of all members. Whether a federal structure offers an incentive to governments to free-ride on others' investments in delivery is a function of the possibilities that federal structure offers for democratic decision-making.

Since security is very expensive, governments may be tempted to shirk their responsibilities in delivering security by offloading costs of delivery to another level of government. If security is under-delivered, the performance of the federal government is likely to suffer and/or governments may simply attempt to skirt the division of powers and enact policy that exceeds their constitutional competence. An institutional structure that is unable to reduce the degree of shrinking may become, according to Riker's (1964) terminology, "overperipheralized." Under such conditions, constituent units will accrue an advantage over the central government, and the benefits of coordinated action will be impaired. The federal government will be tempted to compensate for under-provision by centralizing security but, in the process, risks encroaching on competencies that are beyond its constitutional jurisdiction. Yet the central government knows that moral hazard might encourage further under-investment by other levels of government. Moreover, it may precipitate a shift from coordination to zero-sum bargaining among governments (Scharpf 2001): pure-coordination problems can be resolved by any mode of governance, but zero-sum conflicts, such as those involving security, require a hierarchical authority. Although constitutional and supreme courts have the constitutional and legal duty to adjudicate intergovernmental disputes over the distribution of divisible goods, they are usually reticent to do so. Alternatively, the central government could just abrogate responsibility and shift the burden away from the centre.

How, then, to optimize the delivery and administration of security in a democratic federal polity? In *Federalist Paper 17*, Hamilton observes that federal arrangements attribute powers related to local interests to federated entities, while powers over general matters and matters that are more remote from the immediate interests of citizens belong to the central government. On the one hand, economies of scale stand to be harnessed through coordination and centralization. On the other hand, security is ultimately local, because local communities are best positioned to make credible commitments under conditions where efficient delivery has to reflect different values, interests, and preferences, and transaction costs for reconciling diversity grow exponentially the higher the order of government. Public security is thus premised on the principle of subsidiarity: ultimately, local communities are best positioned to ensure public security. They know their values, priorities, interests, and preferences. However, these may not necessarily be coincident with those of the central government.

In fact, in a federal polity, they are bound to differ: while local communities, for instance, are concerned about crime, the central government is preoccupied with terrorism. John C. Calhoun observes that the larger a country, the more likely it is that its population faces different circumstances that give rise to different characteristics and interests. Political community, Calhoun (1811, 23–4) suggests, is "made up of different and conflicting interests, as far as the action of the government is concerned." Since each level of government embodies a distinct set of values, interests, and preferences, we would expect it to affect the quantity and quality of delivery. Controversy over the efficient delivery and administration of security in federal polities gives rise to a set of hypotheses:

H1.1: The degree of competitiveness over security between a federal polity's central and constituent governments is a function of the extent to which values and preferences differ among governments and their constituencies. That is, the more heterogeneous a federal policy, the more difficult a centralized, top-down approach to security.

H1.2: Conversely, the more values and preferences differ by community, the greater the incentive for a decentralized, bottom-up approach if the gap is vertical between the federal and some or all other levels of government, and

H1.3: the greater the incentive for asymmetry if the gap is horizontal.

H2.1: In federal polities where values and preferences are fairly homogeneous, we would expect security to be less contentious to administer and thus be more likely to find security more centralized

H2.2: than in heterogeneous states, such as pluri-national federations where, depending on the variation in differences, we would expect a more bottom-up and asymmetric approach to security (if differences are distributed vertically) to be administered less centrally, asymmetric (if differences are distributed horizontally), or both.

H3: Although the administration of public security may be relatively uncontroversial as long as a federal polity is highly efficient in generating ample security, we might expect decentralized institutions to perform better – measured as a function of public satisfaction with security outcomes – than centralized ones.

H4: Heterogeneity may encourage opportunistic behaviour that instrumentalizes security, thereby reducing the efficiency with which a federal polity delivers security and exacerbating problems of administering security to the satisfaction of all members.

However, just because security is delivered efficiently does not necessarily mean that it is administrated effectively. Efficiency in delivery can be measured in terms of stability; effective administration, by contrast, can be measured in terms of the satisfaction of citizens a federation's constituent territories. Administrative and redistributive decisions are necessarily political and give rise to different federal outcomes: centralized or decentralized, symmetric or asymmetric.

Those who see opportunistic behaviour by member governments as a destructive but natural tendency created by the decentralized structure that is inherent to all federations are inclined to centralize security to protect the union. They reckon that opportunism runs counter to cooperation between governments that flows from the respect for the terms of the federal constitution, treating it like a covenant. As the result of a "natural" tendency towards particularism, fragmentation, factionalism, and disorder that gives rise to a propensity towards dismemberment or instability and the progressive weakening of central governments, universal federalists, including James Madison, Alexander Hamilton, John Jay, and Alexis de Tocqueville, insist on the virtues of central institutions and on the political and institutional necessity to subordinate, to various degrees, federated units to central institutions. Universal federalism regards demands for asymmetry as the manifestation of particularism, which contradicts the principle of equality between federated units, threatens minorities, and jeopardizes the unity of the country – which is why universal federalists are loath to decentralize security, let alone tolerate the asymmetric allocation of powers over security.

However, the way in which the state administers security to some citizens creates insecurity for others "Public" order provided by the state thus has the potential to be both discretionary and discriminatory. That explains why the genesis of many a federal polity is rooted in disagreements over the way security is administered, scepticism about letting the central government monopolize security, or both. Security, after all, always runs the risk of being instrumentalized as an expedient means of policing views that those in power deem politically deviant. Any government, Madison famously writes in *Federalist Papers 10*, can be taken over by the interests of a faction, and can thereby jeopardize individual liberty. To preserve the republican character of its constituent elements and protect and safeguard community interests, powers given to central institutions need always be limited and conditional; hence Tocqueville's (1990) idea of "divided sovereignty":

constitutionally, powers are divided between at least two levels of government precisely to forestall this eventuality. The fundamental interests of territorialized communities – whose populations necessarily find themselves in the minority – have a "right of self-protection" against central institutions that can become an instrument of tyranny by the majority. Such a theory of a compact of sovereign entities attributes a moral superiority to state institutions over the institutions of the central government and supports a political and constitutional subordination of central institutions.

4. Findings

Political unity of the federal polity is thus premised on the capacity to reconcile and overcome diverse conceptions of security. The study postulates the success or failure of the politics of public security in federal polities as the ability to be responsive to, incorporate, and reconcile variegated values and priorities among local communities. How "secure" the outcome is, then, is partially a function of how "public" it is, that is, it hinges the equilibrium between shared-rule and self-rule. That is because security and the dynamics of securitization are inherently political, especially in federal polities where the conceptions of multiple constituent entities are constitutionally entrenched, legitimated, and institutionalized within their respective geographic, institutional, and social constraints. To this effect, a brief summary of each chapter follow.

In Brazil, as chapter 2 points out, public security has long been understood almost exclusively as protection against armed violence. However, a recent shift in public security policies has gradually been replacing militarized approaches based on repression with policies based on citizens' rights to the provision of services. This shift has begun to alter the relations within the country's federal system of government. The past strict focus on centralized policing – often using force, and carried out by state-level governments – is slowly giving way to a more comprehensive understanding of security through education and health. Since these are under municipal jurisdiction, the realization of these integration programs has engendered invigorated intergovernmental relations.

Chapter 3 on Canada's asymmetric, decentralized approach to public security documents a system of local control that is flexible enough to meet diverse demands, yet centralized enough to benefit from federal support in times of need. An equilibrium of de/centralized service delivery makes possible a relatively standardized albeit asymmetric service delivery in day-to-day operations and during times of disaster or emergency relief. The functionality of the Canadian public security model is premised on local engagement and accountability. Apolitical federal bureaucratic coordination encourages and supports national standards and provides surge capacity in times of crisis. The chapter discusses challenges of intergovernmental affairs and coordination caused by the multilevel provision of public security in Canada, notably the difficulties of shared sovereignty in security governance. These are manifest in coordinating priorities and disconnects that arise when much of the first-response capacity resides with municipal and local governments whereas jurisdictional authority is vested with provincial and federal authorities.

Chapter 4 on Germany focuses on the constitutional configuration of public security within the federal system. Cooperation between the federation and the Länder is described in the example of the Interior Ministers' Conference. Recent years have seen greater functional integration, as well as integration of competencies and structures in the public security sector. The chapter discusses the evolution of the relationship between federation and Länder and concludes with the current debate on (re)structuring federal and intergovernmental security arrangements.

As Chapter 5 shows, public security in India is divided between the union government and the states, but with plenty of overlapping and conflicting responsibilities. Despite a clear division of power, the Constitution authorizes the central government to intervene in public security. Yet the centre has not always been able to perform its self-assigned role. Reform of the police that is managed by the twenty-nine states and seven union territories has been capricious. The police have organizational, personnel, and training deficits, while security challenges mount. The chapter finds synergies between the central and state governments deficient in streamlining public security.

Mexican federalism is confronted by pervasive violent crime associated with organized-crime syndicates. Chapter 6 decries corruption and insufficient capacity within law enforcement agencies at all levels of government in Mexico, but especially at the municipal level in regions with a strong presence of organized crime. Mexico's public safety crisis has given rise to tensions within the current intergovernmental arrangements of the security and public safety system, which has given rise to a re-centralization of authority and resources at the federal level. These major reforms seek to reshape the distribution of power and the governance of Mexico's security and public safety system. It is a volte-face from reforms in the 1990s that promoted decentralization and multilevel governance that had been triggered by a democratization process after decades of a federation characterized by a strong central government and dominated by a single hegemonic political party.

Chapter 7 depicts a major public safety crisis threatening constitutional democracy in South Africa: violent crime is among the highest in the world, the public service is rife with corruption, violent public protests about poor service delivery are frequent, xenophobic attacks are on the rise, and industrial strike action is common. In South Africa, institutions concerned with public safety and corruption are located mainly at the national level, but perform poorly to meet the challenge. The national government's response to crime has focused largely on law enforcement, while neglecting primary, secondary, and tertiary crime prevention of a socio-economic nature. The South African Police Service (SAPS) has been demoralized by corruption, it has been politicized, and its public order policing is ill-equipped and inadequately trained to deal with public disturbances. The National Prosecuting Authority, too, has been politicized, and its success rate is declining. The court system is backlogged, and the national Department of Correctional has been Services reduced to warehousing a large and growing prison population. Sentenced prisoners seldom receive the necessary services to reduce the risk of reoffending. Against this backdrop, the provinces play a very limited supervisory role over the SAPS, but metropolitan municipalities are increasingly complementing the SAPS's efforts through their own metropolitan police forces.

Chapter 8 starts with Spain's process of decentralization after the Franco dictatorship that accompanied the transition to democracy. The original objectives included the accommodation of Basque and Catalan nationalists, a reform of the concept of public order to public security, and a redefinition of the role of police. However, self-government enjoyed broad support, and practically all Spanish constituent units – autonomous communities (ACs) – sought it. Although the transition to democracy was characterized by a broad compromise among all political forces, ETA terrorists raised the spectre of public security in the new democratic state. While the impact of ETA terrorism on the initial debate about the distribution of responsibilities was limited, the 2004 Madrid train bombings had a bearing on reforming the model. The economic and institutional crisis has been decisive in spawning debate on reforms to decrease redundancy, overlap, and duplication.

Switzerland's pluralist cooperative federal system that reflects *diversity in unity* of languages, religions, cultures, and traditions is the focus of chapter 9. Swiss security policy is generally perceived as adequate but with significant weaknesses: law enforcement at the federal and cantonal level is understaffed to confront legal and illegal immigration and trafficking, crime, emergencies, and growing demands. At the same time, the competencies between federal and cantonal authorities are not always clear-cut and thus can occasion uncertainty and conflict between jurisdictions.

Chapter 10 concerns the United States of America with its precepts of separating and sharing governmental powers. The challenges the founders faced in the 1700s are not so different from today's: how to balance security threats and the preservation of national unity with respect for autonomy among individual states, and protection of civil liberties and civil rights, especially given how decentralization has enabled past and present abuses of human rights in some states. Historically, public security concerns have trended towards an increased role played by the federal government at the expense of local communities and states. Federalist arguments in the 1700s for a stronger central government to defend the collective interests of the thirteen individual states from outside aggression, fragmentation, and even internal rebellion have reverberated throughout subsequent centuries as a function of the nature and imminence of the threat.

Since each of the nine cases is historically and institutionally contingent, there is perforce no single "solution" to the multifaceted problem of public security. Nonetheless, the concluding chapter 11 identifies some distinct patterns that emerge from the limited sample of cases: a checklist of variables to consider, and their bearing.

First, the findings validate the hypothesis that federations are prone to centralize public security when confronted with looming internal or external security threats. Second, public security tends to be more centralized in heterogeneous countries than in homogeneous ones. This finding is indicative of the importance of endogenous effects: the extent to which contemporary security policy choices are contingent on particular legal histories that continue to influence current constitutional and legal frameworks. However, the effect appears to be not entirely path-dependent. Rather, centralization appears to oscillate with the nature and extent of security threats, since even homogeneous countries have seen a propensity towards centralization of public security in the aftermath of 9/11. However, the division of powers in the constitution may not reflect the potentially overbearing security capacity of the federal level. At the same time, their more limited constitutional competencies notwithstanding, sub-state and especially municipal levels seem to fill some of the void when federal will or capacity are found wanting. In homogeneous countries, the principle of subsidiarity seems to prevail: public security is fairly decentralized but scaled up selectively to overcome collective-action problems or resource constraints. In fact, the necessity to ensure that sub-state constitutional jurisdiction over public security is accompanied by a commensurate jurisdictional capability to raise resources, or at least benefit from a guaranteed transfer of resources by the federal government, is a recurring theme. In other words, public security and its decentralization go beyond mere division of powers and require a genuine commitment by all levels of government.

Third, whether a federation has a top-down or bottom-up approach to security seems to be driven both by whether they were once unitary states, and how homogeneous they are. Fourth, the decentralization of security and prospective inequitable distribution of resources gives rise to concerns about asymmetry in public-security outcomes across constituent units, including inequitable human-rights outcomes. The developing countries in our sample seemed particularly prone to asymmetry in the delivery of public security, which ends up being indicative of deficient federal commitment in this area. Conversely, equity in public-security outcomes emerges as a litmus test for the maturity of public security in a federal polity. However, equity does not necessarily imply symmetry. On the contrary, in deeply diverse asymmetric societies the delivery of public security may actually be a precondition to equitable outcomes because of extensive variation in values, interests, and priorities across sub-state units.

Fifth, the impact of the degree to which intergovernmental relations are politicized has a bearing on vertical and horizontal coordination only if there is not a concomitant level of maturity and trust among politicians and bureaucrats at various levels of government. Sixth, where institutional capacity and legitimacy are low, whom citizens tend to trust with matters of public security depends on the level of government more closely associated with their interests: while minorities may tend to mistrust the federal government when they reside in a sub-state unit where minorities comprise the majority, they may tend to place greater trust in the federal government when they reside in a sub-state unit where they, too, are in a minority. However, low levels of accountability and transparency need not necessarily occasion mistrust as long as public-security outcomes are adequate. Seventh, good intergovernmental relations, high levels of mutual trust, and robust institutional capacity give rise to more proactive policymaking and prevention; where the converse obtains, policy response tends to be reactive and the central government, preoccupied with enforcement, emerges as the sole guarantor of public security. In other words, proactive, preventive measures are difficult to operationalize, let alone sustain, in federations whose constituent units lack the necessary capacity, resources, or competencies and the concomitant intergovernmental relations and mechanisms.

Public security outcomes are as much a function of institutional design and operational differences as they are of the nature of the security threats as well as federal and democratic culture and commitments. In their absence, public security institutions, practices, and outcomes are more likely to be centralized, less responsive to local values, interests, and priorities, and less focused on proactive policymaking and prevention. The less optimal the performance of the federal system, the less likely it is that the federal system will optimize for public-security outcomes, and the more different levels of government are likely to compete rather than cooperate with one another. On the one hand, then, serious security threats and colonial legacies of power and security seem to diminish the ability of a federal system to optimize public security. On the other hand, the greater the consensus on collective conceptions of public security, the better aligned public security is likely to be with divergent values, priorities, and interests across the whole of the federation.

However, because variables such as de/centralization, a/symmetry, intergovernmental relations, and resource allocation can be constitutionalized and institutionalized differently, optimizing the federal machinery for security with democratic ends in mind is a differentiated process that is highly contingent. Still, the comparative findings from the country case studies in this book suggest that there are better and worse ways to achieve these ends; so identifying and breaking down the component variables, the range of options for their assemblage, and the advantages and disadvantages that are likely to accrue at least establishes as much a manual as it does a benchmark to provide and improve security in federations while safeguarding and enhancing democratic outcomes. Federal governance is never easy; but without effective institutions and processes to respond to diverse local values, interests, and priorities for freedom and security, neither federalism nor governance is likely to succeed.

References

Althusser, Louis. 1976. "Idéologie et appareils idéologiques d'État." In *Positions (1964–1975)*, ed. L. Althusser, 67–125. Paris: Éditions Sociales.

Bayley, David H. 1983. "Police: History." In *Encyclopedia of Crime and Justice*, ed. Sanford H. Kadish, 1124–5. New York: Free Press.

Bittner, Egon. 1979. *The Functions of the Police in Modern Society: A Review of Background Factors, Current Practices, and Possible Role Models*. Cambridge, MA: Oelgeschlager, Gunn, and Hain.

Brodeur, J-P. 1983. "High Policing and Low Policing: Remarks about the Policing of Political Activities." *Social Problems* 30:507–20.

Buzan, Barry, Ole Wæver, and Jan de Wilde. 1998. *Security: A New Framework for Analysis*. Boulder, CO: Lynne Rienner.

Calhoun, John C. 1811. "A Discourse on the Constitution and Government of the United States." In *Union and Liberty: The Political Philosophy of John C. Calhoun*, ed. Ross M. Lence. Indianapolis: Liberty Fund.

Carment, David, Stewart Prest, and Yiagadeesen Samy. 2010. *Security, Development, and the Fragile State: Bridging the Gap between Theory and Policy*. London: Routledge.

Collier, Paul. 2009. "The Political Economy of State Failure." *Oxford Review of Economic Policy* 25(2): 219–40.

Collins, Alan. 2016. *Contemporary Security Studies*. 4th ed. Oxford: Oxford University Press.

de Tocqueville, Alexis. 1990. *Democracy in America*. New York: Vintage Books.

Elazar, Daniel J. 1987. *Exploring Federalism*. Tuscaloosa, AL: University of Alabama Press.

Ferrier, Norm. 2008. *Fundamentals of Emergency Management: Preparedness*. Toronto: Emond Montgomery Publishers.

Fukuyama, Francis. 2012. *The Origins of Political Order*. London: Farrah, Straus, and Giroux.

Germes, Mélina. 2011. "Conflict and Territory Narratives: Sensitive Neighbourhoods in Police Discourses." https://www.jssj.org/wp-content/uploads/2012/10/JSSJ4-10-en.pdf.

Holsti, Kalevi J. 1998. *The State, War and the State of War*. Cambridge: Cambridge University Press.

Karmis, Dimitrios. 2009. "The Multiple Voices of the Federal Tradition and the Turmoil of Canadian Federalism." In *Contemporary Canadian Federalism:*

Foundations, Traditions, Institutions, ed. Alain-G. Gagnon, 53–75. Toronto: University of Toronto Press.

Madison, James. 1961. Federalist No. 10. In *The Federalist Papers*, ed. Clinton Rossiter. New York: New American Library.

Mann, Michael. 1984. "The Autonomous Power of the State." *European Journal of Sociology* 25(2), 185–213.

March, James G., and Johan P. Olsen. 1998. "The Institutional Dynamics of International Political Orders." *International Organization* 52 (4): 943–69. https://doi.org/10.1162/002081898550699.

Milliken, Jennifer, and Keith Krause. 2002. "State Collapse, State Failure and State Reconstruction: Concepts, Lessons, Strategies." *Development and Change* 33(5): 752–74.

Onuf, Nicholas. 1998. "Constructivism: A User's Manual." In *International Relations in a Constructed World*, ed. Vendulka Kubálková, Nicholas Greenwood Onuf, and Paul Kowert, 58–78. Armonk, NY: M.E. Sharpe.

Patrick, Stewart. 2011. *Weak Links: Fragile States, Global Threats and International Security*. New York: Oxford University Press.

Riker, William H. 1964. *Federalism: Origin, Operation, Significant*. Boston: Little, Brown.

Scharpf, Fritz W. 2001. *European Governance: Common Concerns vs the Challenge of Diversity*. Working Paper 1/6, September. Cologne: Max Planck Institute for the Study of Societies.

Scott, W. Richard. 2001. *Institutions and Organizations*. Thousand Oaks, CA: Sage.

Sheptycki, James. 2011. *Transnational Crime and Policing*. London: Ashgate.

Tikuisis, Peter, and David Carment. 2017. "Categorization of States beyond Strong and Weak." *Stability: International Journal of Security and Development* 6(1).

Tilly, Charles. 1985. "War Making and State Making as Organized Crime." In *Bringing the State Back In*, ed. Peter Evans, Dietrich Rueschemeyer, and Theda Skocpol, 169–91. Cambridge: Cambridge University Press. https://doi.org/10.1017/CBO9780511628283.008.

Watts, Ronald L. 2007. *Comparing Federal Systems*. Montreal and Kingston: McGill-Queen's University Press for the Institute of Intergovernmental Relations.

Weber, Max. 1946. "Politics as a Vocation." In *From Max Weber: Essays in Sociology*, eds. Hans Gerth and C. Wright Mills, 77–128. New York: Oxford University Press.

Weber, Max. 1958. "The Three Types of Legitimate Rule." Trans. Hans Gerth. *Berkeley Publications in Society and Institutions* 4(1): 1–11.

Wendt, Alexander. 1999. *Social Theory of International Politics*. Cambridge: Cambridge University Press. https://doi.org/10.1017/CBO9780511612183.

Wolfers, Arnold. 1952. "'National Security' as an Ambiguous Symbol." *Political Science Quarterly* 67 (4): 481–502. https://doi.org/10.2307/2145138.

2 Public Security and Federalism in Brazil

KAI MICHAEL KENKEL

Introduction

Public security in Brazil has long been understood almost exclusively as protection against armed violence. Recently this definition underwent significant, if temporary, changes, as a shift in public security policies gradually replaced militarized approaches based on repression with policies based on citizens' rights to the provision of services, at least at the level of public discourse. These changes accompanied preparations for the mega-events held in Brazil between 2014 and 2016 (Confederations Cup, FIFA World Cup, and Olympic Games). However, once these events came to an end there was a swift return to repressive policies and a quick deterioration of public security.[1] This shift has begun to alter the relations within the country's federal system of government. The past strict focus on policing – often using force, and carried out by state-level governments – is slowly giving way to integrated programs that include elements such as education and health, which are provided by municipalities.

Defined in this way, public security is consistently ranked among the most important issues affecting the daily lives of Brazilians. There are solid data for comparisons through 2016, which also denote a turning point for the worse in the effects of gun violence on the country. A study in 2012 revealed that 87.8 per cent of respondents nationwide feared

1 The present chapter deals exclusively with the period prior to those events, terminating – save for the overall data on this page – its analysis prior to major shifts that occurred in response to international scrutiny and visitor influxes beginning in 2014.

armed assault, and 85.4 per cent feared being killed (Brazil, Ministry of Justice 2012, 1). This fear is warranted: there were 61,283 violent deaths in Brazil in 2016 (FBSP 2017), and there were 1,091,125 homicides between 1980 and 2010. This compares to an estimated 70,000 direct conflict deaths per year globally (GDAV 2015); indeed the 310,049 homicides in Brazil over the period 2007–12 come close to equalling the 420,000 annual direct conflict-related deaths worldwide over the same period (Waiselfisz 2016, 20; GDAV 2015.). Public security policy has not been effective: numbers for the same period show an overall growth rate of 259 per cent, or 4.4 per cent a year (ibid.). Brazil's homicide rate (29.9/100,000) (FBSP 2017, 6) is almost four times the global average (7.4/100,000) (GDAV 2015), making it one of the least-secure countries in the world.

The root causes of the country's daunting public security challenges are complex; four main factors include persistent socioeconomic inequalities; a legacy of (selective) repression by the forces of order; the separation of the repression of violent crime from policies addressing its root causes; and policy inefficiency worsened by a significant gap between the formal structure and the actual implementation of the federal system of government.

At 8,514,877 km^2, Brazil is the world's fifth-largest state by area; its population encompasses approximately two-thirds of South America's total at 204,259,812 (United States CIA 2016). It is divided into twenty-six states and a Federal District, as well as 5,565 municipalities. Following twenty-one years of military rule and a three-year transition, a democratic Constitution took effect in 1988 that gave the country a strongly presidentialist form of government. Brazil is faced with profound socioeconomic inequalities: according to the most recent data from 2010, its least-developed municipality had a Human Development Index of 0.418 (comparable to Mali in 2014), while the most-developed enjoyed a rating of 0.862 (on par with Estonia, the world's thirtieth-highest, in 2014) (Atlas do Desenvolvimento Humano 2013; UNDP 2015). Tax receipts per capita vary among municipalities by a factor of up to forty-six; all of these factors complicate the creation of truly overlapping competencies among levels of government (Arretche 2004, 19).

Originally inspired by the model adopted in the United States of America, the Brazilian federal system formally contains horizontal checks and balances between the three branches of the federal government, though the political crisis following the impeachment of Dilma

Rousseff in 2016 has shown that these are susceptible to collusion at the highest levels. In horizontal terms, however, its genesis is quite different: rather than unifying independently pre-existing entities, the adoption of the federal form was intended to act as a counterweight to the highly centralized postcolonial form that preceded it. This both resulted from and exacerbated regional asymmetries that continue to shape the system today.

As a result of the evolution of the Brazilian system and an incremental, crisis-driven approach to reform, Brazilian federalism is characterized by the presence of actors with veto power over institutional cooperation and a strong bias towards constraining the will of the electorate in favour of the preferences of politicians and institutions – what Reames (2008) has termed "institutional duplicity" – and numerous measures at the federal level aimed at improving intergovernmental coordination. The brunt of public security tasks are delegated to the states, while the Union – as the federal level of government is known – is responsible for overall guidelines and crimes against federal property and institutions. The current Constitution is also significant in that it is the first to recognize formally and equally the municipal level of government, to which it accords the right to establish police forces with limited powers.

Brazilian federalism has oscillated between periods of centralization, associated with authoritarianism, and decentralization, associated with democratization. In the public security arena, changes in the federal balance have been driven by policy shocks, such as the hijacking of Bus 174 in Rio de Janeiro in June 2000, in which – broadcast live on national television – a hostage was killed by police and the suspect died in police custody. Recent mega-events such as the 2014 FIFA World Cup and the 2016 Olympic Games have also created circumstances in which greater involvement of the federal level was necessary in cities such as Rio de Janeiro and São Paulo.

These events led to the promulgation of a series of initiatives at the federal level aimed at coordinating and funding an overarching policy to combat armed violence, organized crime, and drug trafficking, and reforming police institutions mired in a philosophy of repression. The Bus 174 hijacking in particular consolidated pressure from civil society groups for police to abandon violent repression – a legacy of military governments' pursuit of "internal enemies" – and instead to provide public security as a service and a basic human right, integrated into comprehensive policies that address the socioeconomic root causes of violence.

One indicator of progress in this regard has been the establishment of "police pacification units" (UPPs) in the favelas of Rio de Janeiro in the run-up to recent mega-events. The UPPs were intended to combine an initial wave of increased repression by force (often applied by the Armed Forces) with a continued constructive police presence, as the first step in bringing the full provision of state services to disenfranchised populations housed in the favelas.

Constitutional and Legal Landscape

The current Brazilian Constitution of 1988 is unique in that it devotes an entire chapter entirely to questions of public security. Its Article 144 divides public security functions, which it defines as "the duty of the state and the right and responsibility of all," across the levels of the Brazilian federal system as indicated in table 2.1.

The 1988 Constitution is highly decentralizing in the Brazilian context; at a broader level, it realigns fiscal federalism to the detriment of the Union (Grossi 2011, 38–9); more specifically, public security is established as a duty of all levels of government. The document creates a

Table 2.1. Public Security Functions under Brazilian Constitution Article 144, 1988

Level of government	Public security forces	Public security functions
Union (federal)	Armed forces	Guarantee law and order, in exceptional circumstances, upon request (Art. 142)
	Federal police (PF)	Enforcement of federal crimes
		Interstate crimes
		Border, maritime, airport policing
		Combat drug trafficking
	Federal Highway Police (PRF)	Highway crimes
	Federal Railway Police (PFF)	Nearly inexistent
States (incl. DF)	Civil Police (PC)	Investigative and judicial police
	Military Police (PM)	Patrolling and maintenance of public order
		Fire brigades and lifeguards
Municipalities	Municipal Guard (e.g., GM)	Municipal infraction (property/traffic/minor)

Source: Brazil (2010, articles 142, 144).

three-tier system that significantly reduces the power of the states in certain areas of public policy. Though residual competence lies with the states, the detailed Constitution leaves little room for its exercise. This has led, in the words of one analyst, to "a compartmentalized federalism [featuring] predatory and non-cooperative intergovernmental relations" (Ballesteros 2012, 90).[2] In general, whereas direct attributions of powers have been devolved to lower levels, federal influence on public security policy has been maintained, if not increased, through funding, coordination, and creation of universal guidelines and standards.

State-level police forces are set up symmetrically. All twenty-six states and the Federal District possess civil (Polícia Civil – PC) and military (Polícia Militar – PM) police[3] forces. In part as a result of poor civilian control and lingering military prerogatives, often the relationship between these forces is one of competition; each is entirely isolated and independent in culture (Ballesteros 2012) and training; there is frequent duplication and overlapping of roles (Rocha 2009, 9). According to Reames (2008, 65), "The Constitution of 1988 requires each state to have these two functionally and organizationally different police forces, but the federal government does not require mechanisms for the PC and PM to share information, resources, planning, or jurisdictions. As a result, the dual police system has created divergent command systems, pay scales, and rules that regulate conduct. Infamous rivalries, competitiveness, and conflicting institutional cultures often further complicate the ability of the PM and PC to work together.

The municipal level is less symmetrical; the 1988 charter was the first to make municipal guards possible; by 2004 only 17.1 per cent of municipalities had done so. They are found mostly in the largest cities in the Southeast region (Miranda, Freire, and Paes 2008, 33). This is a function of funding capacities, and the correlation between crime and armed violence and urbanization. Many tasks of municipal guards are related to public security: school patrols, assistance to the Military Police, law-and-order patrolling, and registering "police occurrences" (32).

---

2 Unless otherwise noted, all translations from the Portuguese original are free and by the author.

3 Considered a military organization, organized in military terms and considered reserve units for the *Federal* Armed Forces (Army), under whose control they fall in wartime. The state Military Police are, however, not a military police in an anglophone sense: they carry out tasks aimed at the civilian population.

The municipalities also gained a larger role under the recently emerged holistic conception of public security (see case study on UPPs below), as implementers of most policies directed at combatting the root causes of insecurity, such as education, infrastructure, and poverty reduction (Marchiori 2009, 13). Here, the explicit constitutionalization of the policy area of public security is helpful per se in that it subordinates activities in the area not only specifically to article 144 but the ensemble of democratic rights-based provisions contained in the document (Neto 2008, 4).

Historical Development

Federalism was established in Brazil together with the republican form of government in 1889. The model chosen was that of the United States of America, in part as a result of the precedent of forming a union out of pre-existing colonial provinces. Together with the system of checks and balances, a further distinctive element of the Brazilian federal tradition is the adoption of the Lockean paradigm in which fundamental rights reside with the people, and not directly with the state (Souza 2005, 106). Most Brazilian Constitutions have included some form of the clause "all power emanates from the people."

Federalism was treated by the republican movement almost as a synonym of freedom; decentralization was seen as emancipation from the strongly centralizing imperial government. Further, it coincided with the interests of the country's strong regional elites; indeed the existence of strong regional centres of power, and vast geographical inequalities, continue to characterize Brazilian politics. Despite these inequalities, the federalist option in Brazil was not the result of the necessity to prevent the secession of minorities or to assuage other threats to the integrity of the state. Brazilian Constitutions have not provided means for secession, and the 1988 document establishes that no amendment may abolish the federal form.

The first republican Constitution of 1891 maintains the administrative autonomy granted the provinces under the empire, entrenching regional inequality and creating what Celina Souza (2005) has termed an "insulated federation": the Brazilian federation was born under the aegis of the concentration of resources in a few states, and weak relations existed between the constitutive units of the federation (107). This "oligarchic regionalism" has been aptly described as the "original sin" of Brazilian federalism (Camargo 2009, 218).

During this period, relations within the federation were dominated by the states of São Paulo and Minas Gerais, in an arrangement known as "coffee and milk" (*café com leite*), alluding to these states' main products. Fiscal arrangements during this period were highly unequal, with federal funds flowing predominantly to these two states. Another coup in 1930 brought Getúlio Vargas to the presidency. In the name of counterbalancing the inequalities plaguing the federal system, Vargas's centralizing government became increasingly authoritarian as it moved to push the country towards industrialization, trading efficiency for representativeness. Regionalized political cultures and often severe fiscal inequalities have strengthened state governors in public security issues and made coordination by the federal level both necessary and difficult.

Electoral reforms under Vargas created an overrepresentation of small states in the legislative branch that persists. The short-lived 1934 Constitution initiates a tradition of constitutionalizing socioeconomic policies, leading to a stronger role for the Union in coordination and financing (Souza 2005, 107; Abrúcio and Franzese 2007, 4). Under Vargas's leadership, the 1937 Constitution strongly curtailed states' fiscal rights, effectively abolished the Congress, and replaced elected state governors with federally appointed *interventores*. Vargas's rule saw the inception of a still-present association in Brazil between authoritarianism, centralization, and a focus on efficiency, versus democracy, decentralization, and representativeness (Abrúcio and Franzese 2007, 3; Costa and Grossi 2007, 9).

The 1946 Constitution was inspired by liberal thinking and sought to re-decentralize power. Thus for the first time it favoured the municipal level, establishing a transfer scheme that nonetheless fell short of a true equalization system as well as a tentative mechanism to assist economically underdeveloped regions (Souza 2005, 108).

This was deepened by the further centralizing Constitution of 1967 drafted under military rule. This document centralized fiscal relationships, implanting a stronger equalization scheme based on the federal–municipal relationship. The period of military rule further saw the centralization of public security policy, in the form of a strong role for the armed forces and police in the repression of leftist "internal enemies." This period left lasting nefarious legacies in Brazilian politics, including decades of public security policies based almost exclusively on repression by force. The adoption of a military mindset is seen as reinforcing centralizing pressures in the federal system.

In part for this reason, the current 1988 Constitution, drafted three years after the effective end of military rule, stands for (particularly fiscal) decentralization, seen as favouring civilian control (Abrúcio and Franzese 2007, 6). With it the devolution of power, federalism became associated with democracy, representativeness, and proximity to the citizen. Although it bears the marks of democracy and devolution, in areas touching upon their corporate interests – including public security – the lingering influence of the armed forces is clear.

The relationship between the levels of federal power is complex; while significant elements of decision-making authority are decentralized, by explicitly constitutionalizing (and declaring as shared competencies) a number of policy areas (Constitution, article 23; Abrúcio and Franzese 2007, 7), the Union increasingly coordinates policies for whose implementation it is not formally responsible. Similarly, while devolving power to lower levels of government, its simultaneous tendency is to regulate particularly state-level entities in constitutionalized policy areas through uniform guidelines (Souza 2005, 110).

The establishment of uniform institutional structures has tended to aggregate efforts around critical policy elements, despite significant difficulties due to entrenched regionalism and fiscal inequalities. The state level in particular saw a decrease in its power vis-à-vis the municipalities; for example, constitutional amendments no longer require the approval of states, whose interests are considered to be represented by their envoys in Parliament (Souza 2005, 111).

The area of public security, particularly policing, has reflected this historical oscillation between centralization and decentralization (Costa and Grossi 2007, 11). While essentially within the purview of normally autonomous state governors, during centralizing authoritarian periods (such as the Vargas and military governments) these areas came under federal control (see Arantes 2011, 190–5). Attempts at intergovernmental cooperation are rare, historically seen only as attempts at cooperation between the levels of government, due largely to federal reluctance, given the perceived high cost of failure of leadership by the Union in this policy area (Abrúcio and Franzese 2007, 16). This reticence is clearly based on experiences from the past (Cano 2006, 134).

However, in a system that depends heavily on policy shocks for effective change (Ballesteros 2012, 87), particularly in state-level public security policy (ibid.; Cano 2006, 136), this balance has experienced a shift in recent years. Worsening public security since the mid-1990s has increasingly led the federation to become more involved in coordinating and financing efforts of lower levels of government to deal with the problem. However, this action is of a qualitatively different nature from the oscillations of centralization described above; it refers not to formal transfers of competencies but to vertical (and horizontal) coordination within institutional arrangements. Freire argues that the current system makes this coordination role difficult and impedes policy efficiency (Freire 2009, 104–5).

Two tendencies are especially important in evaluating the current Brazilian federal system in the area of public security: Reames's concept of institutional duplicity, and the notable shift in approaches to public security in Brazil from repression by force to the provision of rights to citizens over the past two decades. Interestingly, rather than fomenting a return to "high policing" and repressive politics designed to further elite interests, increased federal involvement tends to cement the commitment of all levels to guaranteeing full rights to all citizens.

Overall, analytical assessments of the efficacy of Brazilian federal structures in producing policy solutions – particularly in the area of public security, are pessimistic both inside and outside Brazil. Reames has identified a culture of "institutional duplicity" as a main cause of this inefficiency (2008, 61):

> Institutional duplicity grows out of dichotomies embedded in the Brazilian justice system: written rules and regulations do not permit police to achieve the goals and expectations that are placed on them; police mandates outstretch their capacity; the political system is expressly egalitarian but overlays a socioeconomic system that is extremely hierarchical; and multiple agencies share responsibility for law enforcement, often leaving no single agency accountable. Often the prescribed means do not lead to the intended ends, so detours and shortcuts are invented to subvert the system; the shortcuts then stay in place and the two systems – one legitimate, the other illegitimate – operate side by side. The result is a confusing justice system, which serves different people differently, conceals commonplace corruption, and is inefficient and resistant to reform.

Reames couches the notion of duplicity in what he dramatically terms the "neofeudal" context of the Brazilian justice system, in which what Macaulay (2011) has termed "political-criminal networks" arise to both prevent the state from exercising its authority and thrive in that very absence. In addition, one team of Brazilian scholars sees certain elements of public security policy in the country as examples of "a minimalist notion of planning, based on a 'philosophy of satisficing,' which sets deliberately suboptimal objectives and develops a fragmented and antisystemic vision of planning" (Dellasoppa and Branco 2006). As a key civil society document on public security points out, "One of the greatest hindrances to attaining better result in public security policy resides in the culture of improvisation present in its management, which creates an ad hoc working style and short-term [planning] horizons. Rationality has never been the mark of policies in this field and the basic principles of management (the elaboration of diagnostics for the problems faced, strategic planning and the systematic monitoring of results) are foreign or uncustomary actions in this universe" (Brazil, Ministry of Justice 2009, 25).

The federal system itself, by increasing the relative clout of smaller states and failing to counterbalance the influence of regional elites, creates numerous veto players in the system (Arretche 2002, 432) and entrenches patrimonial and clientelist tendencies (see Camargo 2009). This places Brazil at the "extreme end" of what Stepan has termed "demos-constraining" federal systems, in which the popular will is easily stymied by coalitions of well-placed veto players at lower levels (Arretche 2002, 432–3; Reames 2008, 4; Stepan 2000).

Metrics and Fiscal Dimensions

Thoroughgoing public security statistics have recently become available in Brazil, based on publicly available data on government spending. This is in large part a result of the emergence of the Brazilian Forum on Public Security (Fórum Brasileiro de Segurança Pública), founded by civil society movements, academics, and members of the police forces in March 2006. Since 2009 the Forum has published a yearbook[4] of statistics and analyses of public security statistics such as homicides as well as government spending at all levels. Concomitantly, the various levels of government have improved the availability of their own numbers on which these analyses are based.

Sophisticated breakdowns of public security spending are provided, for example, in the 2015 edition:

- Total spending by the Union and the states rose 17.1 per cent from R$57,537,462,340.21 to R$67,362,640,705.05 between 2013 and 2014;

4 All editions available at Fórum Brasileiro de Segurança Pública, http://www.forumseguranca.org.br/atividades/anuario/.

over this period total Union spending dropped 2.6 per cent from R$8,270,903.209.92 to R$8,057,404,000.00. As a result of this increase, the Union's share of spending fell from 14.37 per cent in 2013 to 11.9 per cent in 2014 (FBSP 2015, 53). These numbers represent significantly higher absolute spending, and much lower federal participation, than, for example, five years prior in 2010 (FBSP 2011, 43).

- As a percentage of overall expenditures, public security accounted for 0.4–0.5 per cent of Union spending between 2010 and 2014, down from 0.8 per cent in 2010; among the states, in 2014 this varied from 0.8 per cent in Piauí to 13.8 per cent in Rondônia, and 5.2 per cent in Piauí and 13.4 per cent in Minas Gerais and Alagoas in 2010. Large states in the southeast such as Rio de Janeiro and São Paulo saw decreases from 12.3 to 8.0 per cent and 8.5 to 5.5 per cent, respectively (FBSP 2015, 54; FBSP 2011, 46).
- Average per capita yearly spending, combining the Union and the states, went from R$246.26 in 2010 to R$329.79 in 2014. The federal level itself decreased its expenditures from R$47.56 per citizen to R$39.44 (FBSP 2011, 46; FBSP 2015, 53).

Increased federal spending can be traced back to increasing involvement by the Union in nationwide public security programs beginning in the mid-2000s (see below), particularly conditional transfer payments from the National Public Security Fund (Fundo Nacional de Segurança Pública), established in 2001. Public spending in Brazil rose substantially under the Workers' Party government until 2016, with public security labelled a policy priority in the face of the mega-events held in 2014 and 2016. Subsequently, since 2016 there has been a draconian reduction in public policy spending in an effort to balance the budget and efface the social legacy of the Workers' Party. While public security spending remains the responsibility of state-level organs where events are held, there has been a significant federal contribution as well. Most notably, the Extraordinary Secretariat for Large Event Security was created within the Federal Ministry of Justice in August 2011 (Brazil, Presidency 2011). It plays a coordinating role, establishing clear competences between numerous federal ministries and state-level secretariats (Brazil, Ministry of Justice 2012, 52), backed by a dedicated budget of R$1.17 billion (then ca. US$600 million) (Brazil, Portal da Copa 2012). Beyond extraordinary spending for mega-events, the statistical relationship between per capita and overall spending on one hand, and homicide and crime rates on the other, diverge from region to region (Daher 2009, 40).

Notably, the Federal Government in June 2016 issued R$2.9 billion of emergency funding to the state government of Rio de Janeiro, destined entirely for the maintenance of security for the Olympic Games (Matoso 2016).

Municipalities and states, though in charge of implementing the brunt of public security policies, have little ability to raise funds to cover these expenses entirely. These cannot be considered unfunded mandates, though, since these entities do receive dedicated transfer payments from the Union. In 2009 federal funding made up 75.3 per cent of total public security spending, state expenditures 16.3 per cent, and municipal spending 2.6 per cent. The remaining 5.8 per cent were spent in the Federal District (Morais, Cario, and Nogueira 2011, 46). Between 1980 and 1995 the municipal share of federal funds for public security thus rose from 8.7 to 16.6 per cent (Abrúcio and Franzese 2007, 6). State receipts from federal coffers rose from 23.3 per cent in 1980 to 27.6 per cent in 1990 (ibid.). Increased federal involvement in funding and coordinating public security policy – spurred on by the crises of organized crime and drug trafficking – has been accompanied by greater transparency and oversight. The federal government has not only sought to spur the integration of law enforcement databases, but also their public availability, together with public health data related to homicides and crime.

Assessment of Intergovernmental Integration Mechanisms

In Brazil's disarticulated and crisis-driven policy system, plagued by duplication, competition, and huge inequalities, only a shocking event could spur federal-level activism in an area of state-level responsibility. After a series of critical focusing events, the last decade has seen greater federal coordination and financing of public security actions under state and municipal competence, without formal legal centralization. Notably this has consisted of the establishment of a national fund and an elite force of state military police placed under federal command.

The National Conference on Public Security (Conferência Nacional de Segurança Pública – CONASP) was established at the national level in 1989. It was slow to institutionalize (it did not receive formal internal rules until 2003), and had a purely technical mandate and no mandatory participation by civil society. A precursor agency to the current organs was created on 1 January 1995: the Planning Secretariat for National Action on Public Security (SEPLANSEG). This was transformed into the current National Secretariat on Public Security (SENASP) in 1997. Under the Ministry of Justice, SENASP's tasks include working towards the horizontal and vertical integration of government policy, and the deployment of the National Public Security Force created in 2004 (see below).[5]

The botched rescue of Bus 174 in June 2000 led President Fernando Henrique Cardoso to issue in haste an inchoate National Public Security Plan (PNSP) (Soares 2007, 83). The plan was introduced prematurely and was more a list of intentions and possibilities than a coordinated policy: it listed fifteen priorities grouping together 124 individual objectives. Nevertheless, some of its proposals were turned into significant policy advances (Macaulay 2012, 2).

The most significant of these was the National Public Security Fund, which provides funding for the implementation of program guidelines to states and municipalities. The fund's priorities were equipment modernization for state police forces, professional training, establishment of community policing programs, and integration of information systems across law enforcement (Costa and Grossi 2007, 12). As a result, federal government spending jumped from under R$2 billion a year before 1999 to R$4.2 billion in 2001. The fund also allowed for previously dispersed resources to be consolidated under two ministries, which improved the conditions for policy coordination (13–14). Most importantly, the fund required each requesting entity to sign an agreement committing it to establishing an integrated policy mirroring that at the federal level and based on concrete statistical indicators. However, given the crass disparities among federal entities, these indicators proved difficult to satisfy uniformly, and the initiative was gradually abandoned (16). Nevertheless, between 2000 and 2005, 820 such agreements were signed, worth more than R$1.2 billion, 86 per cent of which went towards purchasing new equipment (18).[6] This destination of funds reflected the primacy of a militarized public security mindset: "The Fund ended up limited to confirming old procedures, ancient obsessions, and traditional habits: the act of passing forward the resources, instead of serving as a political tool directed to the induction of structural reforms" (Soares 2007, 85).

---

5 Information available at Rede EaD-SENASP, portal.ead.senasp.gov.br.

6 See also the overall analysis on the PNSP in Dellasoppa and Branco (2006, 27–37).

As a presidential candidate in 2002, Lula da Silva presented an ambitious new public security plan, "intended as a comprehensive, non-partisan, technical blueprint of joined-up state policy. In particular, it would have tackled the vertical and horizontal fragmentation of policing and public security in Brazil" (Macaulay 2012, 2). More in line with a "citizen security" approach (see below), Lula's plan notably called for the creation of a Unified Public Security System (SUSP), echoing those established in the areas of health care and welfare. The proposed SUSP was to work along "six axes – training, information and data sharing, management, investigative technologies, external oversight and coordination with social policy providers – that would generate shared protocols, norms, practices and performance indicators" (3; see also Soares 2007, 86–90; Ferreira and Fontoura 2008). Upon Lula's re-election, flagging interest in the plan was revived, and it was reinitiated under a more integrative guise as the National Public Security and Citizenship Program (PRONASCI).[7] PRONASCI funds actions as diverse as the strengthening of social and community networks based on the inclusion of youth, victim support programs, and re-socialization measures as well as the strengthening and coordination of public security institutions. Symptomatic of the often piecemeal creation of institutional arrangement in Brazil, PRONASCI's relationship with the SUSP was initially unclear: in its founding legal measure, "the only reference to the regulation of the ... [SUSP] is very brief, superficial, not very clear, and suggests a limited understanding, reducing it to the operational dimension" (Soares 2007, 94). PRONASCI does not recognize SUSP's six target activities, instead reformulating a new proliferation of essentially similar measures (96).

PRONASCI's broad spectrum of measures calls for a significant increase in top-down federal coordination as well as adequate incentives for subnational entities to participate. For example, the plan calls for integration across nineteen federal ministries (Soares 2007, 92). Each subunit requesting funding – R$6.707 billion were committed to be spent by the end of 2012 – must create an Integrated Management Committee (GGI), together with concrete plans for institutional reform, civil society participation, and police training. The GGIs are intended to

7 For information see Observatório de Segurança Pública, http://www.observatoriodeseguranca.org/seguranca/pronasci.

serve as loci for the vertical and horizontal coordination of policy from all three levels of government without reducing the autonomy of the subnational units (Raposo e Lima 2010, 38–9).

PRONASCI increases the influence of municipalities by focusing on social policies beyond traditional public security, which are implemented municipally. In financial terms, increases in relative spending reflect this shift to the detriment of the state level: "Federal government spending in 2009 had risen 200 percent in relation to 2003 levels, while municipal contributions rose 168 percent, compared to increased investment by the state-level authorities of only 98 percent" (Macaulay 2012, 3).[8]

Finally, a crucial component of federal interaction in the area of public security is the creation of the National Public Security Force (Força Nacional de Segurança Pública). Characteristically, this key development once again took place largely independently of simultaneous institutional rearrangements. The Force was created by presidential executive decree – a form frequently criticized as insufficiently democratic – on 29 November 2004. Composed of officers from the Federal Police and state Military Police, it can act under emergency and exceptional circumstances following a formal request from a state governor. Its duties consist of patrolling, maintaining order, and protecting the safety of individuals and property.

Placed under the control of the head of SENASP in the Ministry of Justice, the financing of purchasing and per diems for the Force falls to the Ministry. Members of the force remain part of their original state units and receive several weeks' specialized training with an eye to internalizing norms on the use of force and the notion of integration into a larger, not exclusively military, policy effort. As of 30 August 2012, 7,676 officers had undergone training and were eligible to serve in the force's contingents; of these 582 are women.[9]

---

8 It is important to note that a large number of initiatives begun under the Workers' Party governments (2003–16) have been terminated or suspended, many with no attention to policy impact, by the current administration under Michel Temer.

9 See the legacy link at http://web.archive.org/web/20130615020236/http://portal.mj.gov.br/main.asp?View=7C55F195-1FBE-4FE2-9F13-14B250044A4A&BrowserType=NN&LangID=pt-br¶ms=itemID%3D%7B03426B26-7B9F-433C-AB4E-27A723369D83%7D%3B&UIPartUID=%7B2868BA3C-1C72-4347-BE11-A26F70F4CB26%7D.

Reaction to the Force has been mixed. On the positive side, it results in less recourse to the Armed Forces in emergencies. On the other hand, its constitutionality has been questioned, as it places troops executing a subnational-level mandate under federal control. One context in which the force has been deployed is the establishment of Police Pacification Units (UPPs) in the favelas of Rio de Janeiro, which are a further example of vertical and horizontal integration in the fight against armed organized crime and drug trafficking, Brazil's dominant public security issue.

Case Study: Police Pacification Units (UPPs)

Formed in 2008 under a project funded by PRONASCI's anti-drug-trafficking component, Rio de Janeiro's UPPs are the culmination of an ongoing shift from a mentality of repression to one of citizens' rights in public security in Brazil. The resulting effect on federal relations in public security has been considerable. It has gone hand-in-hand with improvements to democratic governance, as the adoption of a progressive approach had long been hampered by the lingering military predilection for repressive policies.

Changing Philosophies of Public Security Policy and Their Effects on Federalism

Bruno César Grossi de Souza (2011) emphasizes that public security in Brazil is based largely on the repression of crime, revealing strongly militarized origins. This has delayed the adoption of models that devolve services and rights to the municipal level, seen as the most democratic for its proximity to the population. There remains an adversarial aspect to this interaction; according to specialist academic Ignacio Cano, the transition from a police that protects elites to one protecting the populace is far from complete. This is reflected in a vocabulary replete with metaphors of warfare and the designation of enemies within the country's own populace, to be vanquished through superior firepower (Cano 2006, 137).

"In a more modern understanding," according to Grossi, "public security is conceived of as a public service to be offered to society, which comes to be seem as a beneficiary of state action – or, as it were, the enemy is substituted by the client" (2011, 37). Brazilian scholars point out that there has been considerable normative progress in public security policy since 1988, particularly as security was enshrined as a basic right in the current Constitution. Whereas the period immediately following the return to democracy was characterized by polarized debate between advocates of militarist approaches and those militating for human rights (Brazil 2009, 12), by the mid-1990s soaring crime rates had coalesced the notion of public security around a specific agenda. By the end of the 1990s, a more concrete policy agenda had crystallized, followed by pragmatic and specific debate in the late 2000s (Mizne 2011). Expressed in terms of paradigms, this meant that the national security paradigm was replaced by public security in 1988, which gave way to the notion of citizen security – prevalent in the region and developed in Colombia in the mid-1990s – by the mid-2000s (Freire 2009, 102).

This shift in thinking from repression to rights of citizens has had significant effects on the federal architecture in the area of public security in Brazil (Cunha 2009, 66). As the philosophy of public security in Brazil shifts from one of repression to one of the provision of rights and services (see Ballesteros 2012) – leading to greater attention to the root causes of violence and insecurity – the need to coordinate programs originating at the federal level with the municipalities, where basic services are provided, increases, as efforts in the areas of health, sewers, and now public security (see case study below) have shown (see Grossi 2011, 38).

The citizen security paradigm is particularly important to federal arrangements, in that it adopts a holistic view and calls for horizontally and vertically integrated action:

> The concept of citizen security takes as its base the multicausal nature of violence and, in this sense, calls for taking action both in the spectrum of control and in the sphere of prevention, by means of integrated public policies in the local ambit. In this way, a public policy for citizen security involves various dimensions, recognizing the multicausality of violence and the heterogeneity of its manifestations. An intervention based on citizen security necessarily requires involving various public institutions and civil society in the implementation of planning actions based on those problems identified as priorities for the reduction of indices of violence and delinquency in a territory, encompassing initiatives in diverse areas such as education, health, recreation, culture, citizenship, and others. (Freire 2009, 105–6)

Implementing a New Paradigm: UPPs in Rio de Janeiro

In keeping with this shift from state-level repressive policies to the provision of integrated and municipally centred comprehensive rights, the UPPs' objectives are: to regain state control of the communities currently under the influence of criminal groups; to bring peace and public security in the favelas; and to contribute to break the "logic of war" in Rio (Silva and Nougier 2010, 7).

The UPP process typically follows four phases, whose focus is on prevention and trust-building. A prerequisite is police reform to transform the mentality of war and repression still prevalent in police training. The first stage is the invasion of the territory in question. The Military Police Special Operations Battalion (the notorious BOPE) secures a given area, if necessary with the tactical assistance of the armed forces. As operations are often publicized in advance, many favelas have been reclaimed without a single shot fired. This phase is often celebrated as the re-establishment of Brazilian state sovereignty over its territory. The second phase, stabilization, sees BOPE remaining until the last vestiges of resistance are eliminated. Specialized police units known as UPPs then follow in the third stage, labelled occupation. Finally, in the post-occupation phase, the idea is for state institutions to return to the area and provide services such as health care and education to the disenfranchised denizens of the favelas.

Forty-two UPPs were implanted between 2008 and 2015; the first entered the Dona Marta favela on 28 November 2008. The entire process resembles peacebuilding efforts undertaken by the United Nations; indeed many of the federal Armed Forces personnel involved have served in the Brazilian-led UN operation Haiti, MINUSTAH. Feedback between the Armed Forces and the Rio State Military Police is extensive and bidirectional, with Brazilian soldiers also applying police tactics in areas of the Haitian capital, Port-au-Prince.[10]

From the standpoint of the federal system for public security policy, the UPPs have the potential to play a profoundly transformative role. Fiona Macaulay explains:

> These operations are distinguished firstly by the vertical integration of military, federal, state and municipal police, which are deployed in

10 For an excellent analysis of the UPP process, see Tierney (2012).

> a "wave" ... This is followed by specially trained state military police and municipal police with a more "community" orientation centred on rebuilding citizen-police relations, something already tried in several locations but often in a piecemeal manner by a single branch of the police ... Achieving collaboration rather than substitution or competition is no small thing. Such operations are also intended to change the institutional culture and operational culture, especially of the military police, many of whom are keen to embrace a more professional image and practice ...
>
> The second feature is multi-agency horizontal integration, with policing just one component in the provision of other state services. This approach has also been attempted before but this is the first time it has been initiated from the top down and has been accepted by lower level authorities. (Macaulay 2012, 10–11)

Rio State's Secretariat for Security has been relatively successful in bringing together vertical and horizontal elements of the pacification strategy; this achievement is due both to the motivation offered by the image that the city would project during mega-events such as the 2016 Olympics and the 2014 FIFA World Cup, and to the alignment of political forces in key posts, without which intergovernmental cooperation might have been significantly more challenging. This process was made easier by political affinities, an important factor overall in overcoming the inertia that the Brazilian federal system is prone to create. The dependence of policy change on external shocks is illustrated with chilling sharpness by the collapse and retrenchment of the UPPs after the end of the 2016 Olympic Games and their attendant international attention. A renewed public security crisis, and return to repressive policies, has ensued; federal involvement in Rio de Janeiro has increased somewhat following the States' declaration of bankruptcy and public servants' remuneration freeze in 2016.

Concluding Assessments

The Brazilian federal system is characterized by oscillation between moments of centralization and decentralization. Centralization has been associated with authoritarian rule, and decentralization with democracy and civilian control. Reform has been particularly difficult in the militarized area of public security. However, a profound crisis of public security has shifted policies away from repression towards human rights and service provision, leading to movement away from the state level and towards municipal action under federal coordination.

Several historical factors lower policy effectiveness in Brazil's federal system: socioeconomic inequality; "demos-constraining" institutions and numerous veto players; insular, reform-resistant. individualized bureaucracies; the sheer extent of corruption among the country's political and administrative officeholders; and a crisis-driven approach that flounders without triggering events. Public perception is that policy program delivery in Brazil is woefully inadequate and resistant to positive reform. When leadership from above does occur in Brazil, it is often undertaken through the creation of new institutional arrangements – often by decree – that are not placed in clear relation to their predecessors, discussed in a participative democratic fashion, or given clearly defined competences. This creates an intricate maze of institutions, further raising the risk of inertia. Significant progress has been made nonetheless in rendering policy spending transparent – scholars of policy now have extensive and accurate statistics at their disposal, and access to legal texts is excellent. Federalism remains understudied in the Brazilian context and devoid of public attention save for its association with civilian democracy.

As public security policy continues its tortured road towards a service-provision mentality, it may become a forerunner in advancing the potential for both horizontal and vertical integration in the Brazilian system. Concomitantly, as the delivery of new policies, such as Rio's UPPs, brings the forces of order (from various levels) in closer contact with the population outside the antiquated and nefarious context of militarized repression, this may cause the Brazilian citizenry to identify more closely with its state and its federal system.

References

Abrúcio, Fernando Luiz, and Cibele Franzese. 2007. "Federalismo e políticas públicas: o impacto das relações intergovernamentais no Brasil." In *Tópicos de Economia Paulista para Gestores Públicos*, vol. 1. ed. Maria Fátima Infante Araújo and Lígia Beira, 13–31. São Paulo: FUNDAP.

Arantes, Rogério B. 2011. "The Federal Police and the Ministério Público." In *Corruption and Democracy in Brazil: The Struggle for Accountability*, ed. Timothy J. Power and Matthew M. Taylor, 184–217. Notre Dame: University of Notre Dame Press.

Arretche, Marta. 2002. "Federalismo e Relações Intergovernamentais no Brasil: A Reforma de Programas Sociais." *Dados* 45 (3): 431–58. http://www.scielo.br/pdf/dados/v45n3/a04v45n3.pdf. https://doi.org/10.1590/S0011-52582002000300004.

– 2004. "Federalismo e políticas sociais no Brasil: problemas de coordenação e autonomia." *São Paulo em Perspectiva* 18 (2): 17–26. https://doi.org/10.1590/S0102-88392004000200003.

Ballesteros, Paula K. Rodriguez. 2012. "Governança democrática: por uma nova perspectiva de análise e construção das políticas de segurança pública no Brasil." MA thesis, School of Business Administration São Paulo, Getúlio Vargas Foundation (EAESP-FGV).

Brazil. 2010. *Constitution of the Federative Republic of Brazil. 3nd [sic] edition.* http://www.stf.jus.br/repositorio/cms/portalStfInternacional/portalStfSobreCorte_en_us/anexo/constituicao_ingles_3ed2010.pdf.

Brazil. Ministry of Justice. 2009. *1ª Conferência Nacional de Segurança Pública. Texto-Base.* Brasília: Ministério da Justiça. http://www.ipea.gov.br/participacao/images/pdfs/conferencias/Seguranca_Publica/texto_base_1_conferencia_seguranca_publica.pdf.

– 2012. Extraordinary Secretariat for Large Event Security. "Planejamento Estratégico de Segurança para a Copa do Mundo FIFA Brasil 2014." http://web.archive.org/web/20120907091929/http://blog.justica.gov.br/inicio/wp-content/uploads/2012/07/Planejamento-Estrat%C3%A9gico-Atualizado-.pdf.

Brazil. Portal da Copa. 2012. "Planejamento Estratégico de Segurança para a Copa do Mundo de 2014 é publicada no DOU." http://www.copa2014.gov.br/pt-br/noticia/planejamento-estrategico-de-seguranca-para-copa-do-mundo-de-2014-e-publicado-no-dou.

Brazil. Presidency. 2011. Decreto N° 7.538, de 1° de agosto de 2011. http://www.planalto.gov.br/ccivil_03/_Ato2011-2014/2011/Decreto/D7538.htm.

Camargo, Aspásia. 2009. "Federalism and National Identity." In *Brazil: A Century of Change*, ed. Ignacy Sachs, Jorge Wilheim, and Paulo Sérgio Pinheiro, 216–52. Chapel Hill: University of North Carolina Press.

Cano, Ignacio. 2006. "'Public Security Policies in Brazil: Attempts to Modernize and Democratize versus the War on Crime.' *Sur* –." *International Journal of Human Rights* 3 (5): 133–49.

Costa, Arthur, and Bruno C. Grossi. 2007. "Relações intergovernamentais e segurança pública: uma análise do Fundo Nacional de Segurança Pública." *Revista Brasileira de Segurança Pública* 1 (1): 6–20.

Cunha, Eduardo Pazinato da. 2009. "Os Sentidos da Participação para a Construção de Políticas de Segurança Municipais." LLM thesis, Federal

University of Santa Catarina. http://www.egov.ufsc.br/portal/sites/default/files/anexos/33919-44610-1-PB.pdf.

[Daher] Gonçalves, Lígia Maria. 2009. "Política de segurança pública no Brasil na pós-transição democrática: deslocamentos em um modelo resistente." MA thesis, University of São Paulo. http://www.teses.usp.br/teses/disponiveis/8/8131/tde-16082011-105157/publico/2009_LigiaMariaDaherGoncalves.pdf.

Dellasoppa, Emilio Enrique, and Zoraia Saint'Clair Branco. 2006. "Brazil's Public-Security Plans." In *Public Security and Police Reform in the Americas*, ed. John Bailey and Lucia Dammert, 24–43. Pittsburgh: University of Pittsburgh Press.

Ferreira, Helder, and Natália de Oliveira Fontoura. 2008. "Sistema de justiça criminal no Brasil: quadro institucional e um diagnóstico de sua atuação." Texto para discussão 1330. Brasília: IPEA. http://www.ipea.gov.br/portal/images/stories/PDFs/TDs/td_1330.pdf.

[Grossi] de Souza, Bruno César. 2011. "Governança em segurança pública: capacidade de coordenação das secretarias estaduais de segurança pública." MA thesis, Faculty of Economics, Administration, Accounting and Information and Documentation Sciences, University of Brasília. http://www.ppga.unb.br/publicacoes/teses-e-dissertacoes/category/158-2011?download=343:2011_brunnocesargrossidesouza.

Fórum Brasileiro de Segurança Pública (FBSP). 2011. *Anuário Brasileiro de Segurança Pública*. 5th ed. São Paulo: Fórum Brasileiro de Segurança Pública. http://www.forumseguranca.org.br/storage/5_anuario_2011.pdf.

– 2015. *Anuário Brasileiro de Segurança Pública*. 9th ed. São Paulo: Fórum Brasileiro de Segurança Pública. http://www.forumseguranca.org.br/storage/9_anuario_2015.retificado_.pdf.

– 2017. *Anuário Brasileiro de Segurança Pública*. 10th ed. São Paulo: Fórum Brasileiro de Segurança Pública. http://www.forumseguranca.org.br/wp-content/uploads/2017/12/ANUARIO_11_2017.pdf.

Freire, Moema Dutra. 2009. "Paradigmas de segurança no Brasil: da ditadura aos nossos dias." *Revista Brasileira de Segurança Pública* 3 (5): 100–14. http://revista.forumseguranca.org.br/index.php/rbsp/article/viewFile/54/52.

Geneva Declaration on Armed Violence and Development (GDAV). 2015. *Global Burden of Armed Violence: Every Body Counts*. http://www.genevadeclaration.org/measurability/global-burden-of-armed-violence/global-burden-of-armed-violence-2015.html.

Macaulay, Fiona. 2011. "Federalism and State Criminal Justice Systems." In *Corruption and Democracy in Brazil: The Struggle for Accountability*, ed.

Timothy J. Power and Matthew M. Taylor, 218–49. Notre Dame: University of Notre Dame Press.

– 2012. "Deepening the Federative Pact? The Dilma Government's Approach to Crime, Justice and Policing." *Critical Sociology*. Published online before print. http://crs.sagepub.com/content/early/2012/07/23/0896920512440583.full.pdf.

Marchiori, Thaise. 2009. "A governamentalidade e o debate sobre políticas locais e prevenção da violência: um breve relato." *Aurora* 3 (4): 12–20. http://www2.marilia.unesp.br/revistas/index.php/aurora/article/view/1203/1071.

Matoso, Filipe. 2016. "Planalto edita MP que dá socorro financeiro de R$ 2,9 bilhões ao Rio." *G1*, 21 June. http://g1.globo.com/rio-de-janeiro/noticia/2016/06/medida-provisoria-da-socorro-financeiro-de-r-29-bilhoes-ao-rio.html.

Miranda, Ana Paula Mendes de, Letícia de Luna Freire, and Vívian Ferreira Paes. 2008. "A gestão da segurança pública municipal no estado do Rio de Janeiro." *Revista Brasileira de Segurança Pública* 2 (3): 30–54. http://revista.forumseguranca.org.br/index.php/rbsp/article/download/25/23.

Mizne, Denis. 2011. "Fases e Tendências no Debate sobre Políticas Públicas de Segurança no Brasil." In *Brasil: A nova agenda social*, ed. Edmar Lisboa Bacha and Simon Schwartzman, 335–44. Rio de Janeiro: LTC. www.schwartzman.org.br/simon/agenda15.pdf.

[Morais] Filho, Osvaldo Martins de, Rebeca Dias Cario, and Ronaldo Alves Nogueira. 2011. "Análise dos investimentos em Segurança Pública no Brasil entre 2000 e 2009." *Revista Brasileira de Segurança Pública* 5 (8): 38–59. http://revista.forumseguranca.org.br/index.php/rbsp/article/view/82.

Neto, Cláudio Pereira de Souza. 2008. "A segurança pública na Constituição Federal de 1988: conceituação constitucionalmente adequada, competências federativas e órgãos de execução das políticas." *Atualidades Jurídicas* 1. http://www.oab.org.br/editora/revista/users/revista/1205505974174218181901.pdf.

Raposo e Lima, Ana Clara. 2010. "A segurança cidadã como política criminal alternativa na América Latina: um estudo sobre o Programa Nacional de Segurança Pública com Cidadania." BA thesis, Centro Universitário de Brasília. http://repositorio.uniceub.br/bitstream/123456789/217/3/20836927.pdf.

Reames, Benjamin Nelson. 2008. "Neofeudal Aspects of Brazil's Public Security." In *Comparative Policing: The Struggle for Democratization*, ed. Ibrahim Cerrah and M.R. Haberfeld, 61–95. Thousand Oaks, CA: Sage: Web.

https://www.sagepub.com/sites/default/files/upm-binaries/19303_Chapter_3.pdf; https://doi.org/10.4135/9781483328997.n3.

Rocha, Claudionor. 2009. "Considerações sobre a criação de novos órgãos policiais." Nota técnica. Brasília: Consultoria Legislativa, Camara dos Deputados. http://www2.camara.leg.br/documentos-e-pesquisa/publicacoes/estnottec/areas-da-conle/tema21/2009_1726.pdf.

Silva, Anderson Moraes de Castro e, and Marie Nougier. 2010. *Drug Control and Its Consequences in Rio de Janeiro*. International Drug Policy Consortium Briefing Paper. https://papers.ssrn.com/sol3/papers.cfm?abstract_id=1909916.

Soares, Luiz Eduardo. 2007. "The National Public Security Policy: Background, Dilemmas and Perspectives." *Estudos Avançados* 21 (61): 77–97. http://www.scielo.br/pdf/ea/v21n61/en_a06v2161.pdf.

Souza, Celina. 2005. "Federalismo, desenho constitucional e instituições federativas no Brasil pós-1988." *Revista de Sociologia e Política* 24:105–21. http://revistas.ufpr.br/rsp/article/view/3719/2967.

Stepan, Alfred. 2000. "Brazil's Decentralized Federalism: Bringing Government Closer to the Citizens?" *Daedalus* 129 (2): 145–69.

Tierney, Julia. 2012. "Peace through the Metaphor of War: From Police Pacification to Governance Transformation in Rio de Janeiro." MPP thesis, Massachusetts Institute of Technology. https://riorealblog.files.wordpress.com/2012/07/tierney-pacification-police-thesis.pdf.

United Nations Development Programme (UNDP). 2015. *Human Development Report 2015: Work for Human Development*. New York: UNDP. http://hdr.undp.org/sites/default/files/2015_human_development_report_1.pdf.

United States. Central Intelligence Agency (CIA). 2016. "Brazil." In *CIA World Factbook*. https://www.cia.gov/library/publications/the-world-factbook/geos/br.html.

Waiselfisz, Julio Jacobo. 2016. *Mapa da Violência 2016: homicídios por armas de fogo no Brasil*. Brasília: FLACSO Brasil. http://www.mapadaviolencia.org.br/pdf2016/Mapa2016_armas_web.pdf.

3 Canada

TODD HATALEY AND CHRISTIAN LEUPRECHT

Introduction

Canada's asymmetric, decentralized approach to public security is characterized by a system of local control that is flexible enough to meet diverse demands, yet centralized enough to benefit from federal support in times of need. An equilibrium of de/centralized service delivery makes possible a relatively standardized albeit asymmetric service delivery in day-to-day operations and during times of disaster or emergency relief. The functionality of the Canadian public security model is premised on local engagement and accountability. Apolitical federal bureaucratic coordination encourages and supports national standards and provides surge capacity in times of crisis. This chapter begins by mapping the historical and constitutional roots of public security in Canada and surveying the institutional structure of the system, with an emphasis on the distribution of power and responsibility across three levels of government. It turns out that the theme of this volume, public security, is only part of the French-Canadian but not the English-Canadian vernacular and, in English, serves as a heuristic device instead: Canadians refer to "public safety" in English but *sécurité publique* in French (as distinct from *sûreté*, which French Canadians associate with what in English is commonly known as community safety). Even though the use of the referent *public security* in the Canadian context may seem unfamiliar to the English-Canadian reader, since this volume deals with anthropogenic issues of public security as distinct from naturogenic ones of public safety, the French connotation of the same phenomenon is more apt. The dualist power-sharing arrangement that emerged following Confederation gave rise to federal (shared-rule) control of *public security*, and territorial integrity with autonomous (self-rule) over local matters of individual and *community safety* largely relegated to the provinces, often delivered by municipalities as unitary appendages of the provinces. This arrangement is problematic in a country whose five largest cities are more populous and of greater economic import each than four of the ten provinces. In this light, the final section discusses challenges of intergovernmental affairs and coordination posed by the multilevel provision of public security in Canada, notably the difficulties of shared sovereignty in security governance, as manifest in coordinating priorities, and of the disconnects that arise when much of the first-response capacity resides with municipal and local governments, whereas jurisdictional authority is vested with provincial and federal authorities.

Canada has the world's second-largest land mass, the world's longest maritime and land borders, four climate zones, and some of the largest temperature differentials in the world. Yet, at 3.71 people per square kilometre (and only about one actual taxpayer per square kilometre) Canada is among the least-populated countries in the world. It also happens to border the United States, so Canada and its borders are in a unique security context. Canada is also among the world's most culturally diverse countries. Canada, then, suffers from fiscal, human, and organizational resource constraints to confront a disproportionately broad spectrum of high-impact, high-probability public-safety challenges (such as earthquakes, forest fires, floods, and snow emergencies). Public security challenges, by contrast, are modest yet can garner a significant profile, as the Vancouver Olympics (2010), the Pan-Am Games in Toronto (2015), the G8/G20 meetings (2010), the SARS episode (2003), the Vancouver (2011, 1994), Montreal (2010, 2008, 1993, 1986, 1955) and Edmonton (2006) hockey riots, and the Montreal student protests (2012) demonstrate. Canada also confronts gang violence, organized crime and associated smuggling of illicit good and of human beings, grievances by some part of Canada's Aboriginal population that have at times resulted in violent protests and disregard for the rule of law by some subsections of the Aboriginal population, a full spectrum of terrorism threats, including financing and the attempted export of weapons to other parts or the world, as well as myriad cybersecurity threats. On the one hand, a country as large and disparate as Canada has little option but to decentralize public security. On the other hand, the federal government has to balance decentralization against the need to provide equitable security for citizens across this vast country, play a coordinating role, and to step up with surge capacity as needed. The result is a public security system whose costs are estimated to have increased substantially (Office of the Parliamentary Budget Officer 2013). According to a study conducted by the Fraser Institute, between 1986 and 2012 the costs of policing in Canada are estimated to have increased by 45.5 per cent (Di Matteo 2014). Some estimates place that cost even higher, doubling between 2001 and 2011 (Macdonald 2011). The functionality of the public security system – and greatest challenge – hinges on decentralization, asymmetry, considerable fiscal autonomy, intergovernmental coordination, and multi-level governance.

Asymmetry, in the context of federalism, is often associated with different degrees of legislative autonomy or independence among constituent units. In the case of public security in Canada, however, de jure powers are the same across provinces. Their exercise, implementation, and administration, however, differ among provinces. Concomitantly, decentralization denotes not just a constitutional division of powers, but specifically a set of inviolable powers that the Constitution assigns to the provinces and that constitutional practice honours as such. Constitutionally, then, the policy and administrative provision of public security is an area where sovereignty is genuinely shared between the provincial and federal governments. By contrast, the relationship between provinces and municipalities is strictly one of devolution, where local self-rule is at the whim of the province. And although Aboriginal government is not enumerated as a constitutionally distinct level, some Aboriginal communities nonetheless enjoy some privileges of self-rule in the administration of public security. Pluralistic federalism is one way to refer to special recognition that sets select Aboriginal communities apart from the municipal, provincial, and federal orders of government. The resulting amalgam of multi-level governance in the provision of public security is a unique way of ensuring comparable security outcomes across a range of communal priorities, interests, norms, and values.

Constitutional and Historical Roots

Constitutional Roots

The preamble of article 91 of the British North America Act (BNAA 1867) assigns the federal government with powers over peace, order, and good government. The article gives the federal government jurisdiction over criminal law, emergency management, national security, policy on violent crime, and the political executive's prerogative over foreign and defence policy. By contrast, article 92 explicitly assigns matters that are "local" to the jurisdiction of the provincial government:

detention facilities, civil matters, and natural disasters, as well as the enforcement of laws made by the province. This arrangement is meant to preserve local solutions to local security issues.

In theory, articles 91 and 92 delineate jurisdictional boundaries; in practice, "the fundamental problem with the current regime is the absence of a clear and shared understanding of the roles and responsibilities of the various orders of government" in matters of public security (Federation of Canadian Municipalities 2008, 5). Ambiguity means having to rely on intergovernmental mechanisms to resolve the resulting conundrum: who pays and who delivers? The central government, for instance, has the legislative capacity to standardize certain security practices at the local level. Under section 91, the Parliament of Canada has exclusive constitutional jurisdiction over criminal law, but the legislative assemblies of the provinces are responsible for the administration of justice. As a result, the federal government's ability to legislate in certain areas of public security is locally contested and controversial, especially in Quebec, which has a more encompassing and expansive view of the role of the state than the liberal Lockean view of limited government intervention that prevails in the rest of Canada. Firearms legislation, for instance, which has been part of the Criminal Code of Canada since 1892, has long been considered by many a local matter (especially in rural and northern areas) and not one to be legislated federally.

While the core principles of the Canadian Constitution have remained largely unchanged since 1867, federal legislation has had to adapt. Canada's Anti-Terrorism Act and the Emergency Management Act are contemporary examples of the federal/provincial arrangement for sharing security responsibilities. The federal structure of disaster management recognizes the authority and capability of the provinces to deal with disasters, unless the provincial government requests the assistance of the federal government, or if the federal government believes that the disaster has national implications. Federal intervention is a function of these two conditions.

Historical Roots

Following the terms of the Treaty of Washington in 1871, the withdrawal of British troops was imminent. In light of the need to take responsibility for its own defence, and new emerging threats to Canadian territorial integrity, Canada had a strong incentive to expedite unification between the regional colonial holdings. Instability in the United States, in large part due to the Civil War, threatened to spill over into Canada, and Canadians were confronted with the very real possibility of an invasion from the United States as part of America's manifest destiny doctrine. Raids by the radical Irish-American Fenian movement across the border into Canada caused a good deal of local concern and caused the ranks of the Canadian militia to swell, unifying and at the same time defining federal-local security cooperation (Haglund 2008). Similarly, the creation of the Northwest Mounted Police in 1873 was equally a response to violence incited by American whiskey traders in western Canada.

Lacking in a military tradition and the funds to pay for a military, and faced with the impossible task of trying to secure the border between Canada and the United States, the Canadian government resorted to a system of shared responsibilities for local security. A system of public security was already in place in the form of local constabulary and militia. This ensured that the cost of public security was effectively "downloaded" to the provinces, at the same time, however, maintaining a legislative control over the powers being executed at these lower levels. This was not only politically expedient, but also a way to mitigate provincial concerns about federal encroachment – which have their roots in Ontario but would soon be shared by Quebec.

The mere establishment of an independent militia was viewed by Canadian statesmen at the time as an exercise in unifying the diverse interests of English and French Canada (Morton 1999). The Canadian militia model, based loosely on the organization of the American militia, created localized military units sensitive to such issues as language, religion, class, and even traditional styles of uniform, while exercising centralized control. Having witnessed the deleterious effects of local militias under local control as assigned in the American Constitution, in contrast to the United States, Canada centralized control of militias under the federal government. To discourage provinces from setting up their own militias, provincial entities, including municipalities, were given relatively free rein to call upon their assistance in emergencies.[1] However, any response was always at the discretion of the federal executive power and the military. The unintended consequence is for provinces and/or municipalities to

1 This long-standing practice was recently constrained when the federal government unilaterally changed the law. Henceforth, requests for aid to the civil power must come from the premier of a province.

abdicate some responsibility, which the federal government tries to counteract by billing provinces when called upon to supplement emergency services.

Prior to Canadian Confederation in 1867, security, defined in large part by police and fire services that predated Confederation, was a community responsibility modelled after the English and French traditions brought to Canada from Europe. The federal government took its initial foray into federal policing only in 1868 with the creation of the Dominion Police Force. Initially it was composed of about a dozen men, whose primary responsibility was the protection of federal buildings in Ottawa. The mandate was later expanded to include the protection of other federal structures, such as naval shipyards. The Dominion Police was eventually absorbed into the Royal Canadian Mounted Police (RCMP) in 1920.

Canada's most notable federal police force, the RCMP, was established in 1873 in response to lawlessness and violence in Canada's western territories. Initially known as the Northwest Mounted Police, the force was to patrol the territory that includes the modern-day Canadian provinces of Manitoba, Saskatchewan, and Alberta. The entry of Manitoba into Confederation in 1870, however, meant that the federal government no longer had the right to police that area. Instead a Manitoba provincial police force was established with funds provided by the federal government. Similarly, when Saskatchewan and Alberta entered Confederation as provinces in 1905, the now Royal Northwest Mounted Police provided policing services to the new provinces on a contractual basis. This arrangement lasted until 1916, when both provinces established their own respective provincial police forces. By 1928, however, Saskatchewan had reverted back to the RCMP; Alberta followed suit in 1932 (Marquis 1993). To this day, all provinces contract the RCMP to enforce provincial law (although some larger municipalities in these provinces have their own municipal forces that, for all intents and purposes, enjoy the same mandate as their provincial counterpart), except for Ontario and Quebec, which have long had their own provincial police forces.[2]

2 By virtue of its name, the Royal Newfoundland Constabulary is often thought of as a provincial force. In practice, however, it is more akin to a supra-municipal force that polices Newfoundland's major urban communities: St John's, Mount Pearl and the surrounding communities of the northeast Avalon Peninsula, Corner Brook, Churchill Falls, and Labrador West, including Labrador City. The RCMP patrols the rest of the province.

That is possible because policing per se (in contrast to the administration of criminal and other laws) is not actually regulated in the BNAA. Within a few years of Confederation both Ontario and Quebec had set up rudimentary policing structures at the provincial level that would eventually become the Ontario Provincial Police (OPP) and the Sûreté du Québec (SQ).

Asymmetry is a hallmark of Canadian federalism, including the provision of policing: a federal police force (the RCMP) that also provides police services to some provinces and urban areas on a contractual basis. Municipalities in Ontario and Quebec can contract with the province to provide police services at the municipal level in lieu of setting up their own police force (which is often attractive for smaller towns, for reasons that are beyond the scope of this chapter). And although some Aboriginal reserves are policed by the RCMP, currently 168 service agreements underpin First Nations policing in 408 communities. This relationship with Aboriginal reserves is significant for our purposes, since Aboriginal communities' ability to enjoy autonomy over some aspects of service delivery is a form of non-territorial, pluralistic federalism (Bauböck 2001; Karmis 2009) that stands in stark contrast to both universal and communitarian federal norms (see Introduction to this volume). About 77 per cent of Canadians live in communities served by municipal stand-alone police departments, 15 per cent in communities served by RCMP-contract members, 6.5 per cent in communities served by provincial police forces, and 0.5 per cent in communities served by First Nations police.

Canada demonstrates that there is no prima facie reason for a symmetric approach to delivering policing and security. Canada's federal security arrangements are sufficiently flexible to allow for different approaches for different communities. That Ontario and Quebec have opted for their own provincial police forces is more than a historical artefact. They are the two largest provinces in the federation. Quebec, of course, also likes to think of itself as a distinct society and, as such, has a long history of trying to maximize its autonomy by means of services provided by the province. Yet the structures of Quebec's provincial police service predate the advent of modern Quebec nationalism. The original reason for a provincial police force in Quebec was instrumental: a linguistic minority group is difficult to police if the police force in question is unable to communicate in the minority's vernacular. At its origins, the RCMP was a largely anglophone force and thus ill-suited to policing francophones. To this day, some four million Quebec francophones speak little or no English; consequently, French-language policing remains a necessity.

The same rationale applies to Ontario. Numerically, Ontario has the largest francophone community outside of Quebec. Although immigration has diluted the proportion of Ontario's francophone community over the years, in the latter half of the nineteenth century, there were large pockets of Ontario, especially along Ontario's border with Quebec as well as in Northern Ontario, that were almost exclusively French-speaking. So Ontario needed a police service with the linguistic ability to police these communities. To this day, French remains a sought-after asset among applicants to the OPP, Ontario being the country's only province that maintains a Ministry of Francophone Affairs. In sum, a territory's population size and its linguistic particularity drive policing asymmetry in the Canadian federation. A common lingua franca reduces the need for asymmetry of this sort.

Cultural and linguistic particularity is also the reason why some Aboriginal reserves enjoy the right and have chosen to police themselves. However, not all do. Some are just too small and/or have insufficient resources to support their own police service: having a community of a couple of hundred people police itself risks undermining basic rule-of-law principles of the impartial administration of justice. Others are too fractured to agree on whether and how local policing should be provided. Others yet face security challenges on a scale that would overwhelm a police service provided by the community. In other words, there are good instrumental reasons for asymmetry, both for and against the decentralized, asymmetric delivery of police services.

Institutional Structure

Canadian Public Security Apparatus

At the federal level, the primary mechanism by which the federal government discharges its operational security responsibilities is Public Safety Canada (PSC) (but called Sécurité Publique Canada in French) – created out of the former Department of the Solicitor General in the aftermath of 9/11 to centralize and coordinate what had hitherto been disparate organizations across various departments. Its mandate is to "keep Canadians safe from a range of risks such as natural disasters, crime and terrorism." This mandate is achieved, according to PSC, by working and coordinating with other federal agencies, other levels

Table 3.1. Division of Powers in the Administration of Security in Canada

	Federal jurisdiction	Provincial jurisdiction
Ministry	Public Safety Canada, Department of National Defence	Ministry of Community Safety and Correctional Services (Ontario)
Agencies	Royal Canadian Mounted Police, Correctional Services of Canada, Canadian Security Intelligence Services, Canadian Border Security Agency, Parole Board of Canada	Correctional Services, Policing Services, Public Safety and Security, Fire Safety Commission, Ontario Parole Board
Mandates	crime, disaster assistance under certain conditions, border safety, national security, emergency management and mitigation	crime, provincial fire safety, disaster relief, hazard elimination, workplace safety, highway/transport safety

of government, first responders, community groups, the private sector, and other countries. In addition to a (relatively small) departmental staff of about a thousand civil servants, PSC is composed of five agencies: the Royal Canadian Mounted Police, the Canada Border Services Agency (CBSA), the Canadian Security and Intelligence Service (CSIS), the Correctional Service of Canada (CSC) and the Parole Board of Canada (PBC). Three review bodies also fall under the Public Safety portfolio: the Commission for Public Complaints against the RCMP, the Office of the Correctional Investigator, and the RCMP External Review Committee.

Table 3.1 illustrates the practical division of responsibilities imposed by the constitutional separation of federal and provincial powers. The subsequent section examines these divisions in greater detail to explain the roles of the federal and provincial governments in protecting Canada. Because these organizations are designed to be interoperable, some overlap is inevitable in highlighting how these agencies are structured.

Federal Public Security Agencies and Enforcement

PSC is the primary federal ministry tasked with coordinating emergency management programs and policy. Its mandate is to protect critical infrastructure against natural or anthropogenic disasters that have national implications. To achieve that mandate, PSC performs two primary functions: delivering programs and developing policy.

PSC delivers programs in five distinct areas: emergency management, national security, law enforcement, corrections, and crime prevention (Public Safety Canada 2013). Within each of these five core areas PSC has developed programs that are available for delivery at both the federal and the provincial levels, and in some cases to the general public and the private sector. For example, as part of the crime prevention priority, PSC has developed the National Crime Prevention Centre (NCPC), which supports targeted crime prevention initiatives and disseminates best practices knowledge. NCPC partners with federal, provincial, and municipal governments, as well as community groups and the private sectors as part of its mandate.

Policy developed by PSC reflects its focus on the five core priorities. For example, related to the crime prevention priority and the NCPC is the National Crime Prevention Strategy (NCPS). First implemented in 1998, the NCPS is administered by the National Crime Prevention Centre in collaboration with the provinces. The NCPS provides a framework for the reduction of criminal activity in Canada. PSC per se does not have the capacity to administer and deliver policy; for that, it relies on the five agencies that are housed within the department.

By virtue of spanning federal, provincial, and municipal jurisdictions, the RCMP is arguably Canada's pre-eminent federal security agency. However, there are also four other organizations of note. The Canadian Security and Intelligence Service (CSIS) is Canada's intelligence service, mandated with investigating and reporting on activities that may threaten the security of Canada. In addition, CSIS provides threat assessments to the government of Canada and to other federal agencies. CSIS operates in both a domestic and foreign capacity. Canada Border Services Agency (CBSA) is responsible for ports of entry into Canada, including land border crossings, as well as entry points at international air terminals and sea terminals. CBSA enforces entry requirements for individuals seeking to enter Canada, as well as trade regulations and agreements on goods entering the country. The Correctional Services of Canada (CSC) manages correctional facilities housing individuals with sentences of two or more years in a federal prison. As part of its mandate, CSC is responsible for programs designed to reduce recidivism, including a variety of retraining programs within prisons and communities. The Parole Board of Canada (PBC) is responsible for making decisions on the release of prisoners from federal detention. In provinces that do not have provincial prisons, the PBC also acts in a provincial capacity to release, deny, or revoke parole (see table 3.2).

Table 3.2. A Representative Sample of Division of Power and Labour in Canada in the Field of Public Security

Jurisdiction	Investigate, detect, apprehend	Public order	Competence	Oversight
• Federal	• RCMP • CSIS • CBSA • CSEC • FINTRAC • Fisheries and Oceans • Environment Canada • Public Prosecution Service of Canada • Parks Canada • Coast Guard • Citizenship and Immigration • Transport Canada • National Transportation Safety Board • Passport Office • Canadian Human Rights Tribunal • CSC • DND (with respect to the CAF and its members) • Canada Revenue Agency • Agri-food and Agriculture Canada • Public Health Agency of Canada	• RCMP • CAF	• Criminal code • Customs and Excise • Criminal code legislation and enforcement • Immigration and refugees • Revenue and taxation • Environment • National parks • Fisheries and Oceans • Transport • Incarceration (for criminal-code offences over 2 years) and probation • National defence • Emergency measures (in effect concurrent jurisdiction)	• Parliament of Canada • RCMP Public Complaints Commission • Security Intelligence Review Committee • Judiciary • Auditor General • Military Police Complaints Commission • Inspector General of Correctional Services • Information Commissioner • Privacy Commissioner • Public Sector Integrity Commissioner • Ombudsman for victims of crime
• Provincial	• Provincial police services (including the RCMP on matters of contract policing) • Ministries of transport • Security and exchange commissions • Children's aid • Provincial human rights commissions	• Provincial and First Nations police services • CAF	• Provincial criminal code legislation • Criminal code enforcement • Highway traffic acts • Alcohol and tobacco • Environment	• Provincial assemblies/ legislatures • Independent police special investigations units (Ontario, BC, Alberta) • Police services boards

(*Continued*)

Table 3.2. (Continued)

Jurisdiction	Investigate, detect, apprehend	Public order	Competence	Oversight
			• Family and children's services • Property and civil rights • Revenue and taxation • Provincial offences	• Provincial human rights commissions • Coroner's offices • Correctional services offices • Victims of crimes offices • Judiciary • Provincial auditors general
• Municipal	• Municipal police services (sometimes in the form of the RCMP or provincial police services)	• local, Aboriginal, and/or provincial police services	• Criminal code • By-law enforcement	• Municipal councils • Police services boards • Judiciary

At the federal level, the RCMP enforces federal statutes, such as the Customs Act, Excise Act, Radio and Telecommunications Act, and the Corruption of Foreign Public Officials Act. Other federal statutes are also enforced by provincial and municipal police, such as the Controlled Drugs and Substances Act and the Immigration and Refugee Protection Act. The RCMP also provides protective services to other federal departments as well as to domestic and foreign leaders. In addition, it provides specialized training, research, forensic, identification, and informatics services to other law enforcement agencies.

In eight of Canada's ten provinces and all three territories, the RCMP is the provincial and territorial police of jurisdiction. The arrangement whereby a province can outsource to the RCMP police work that is constitutionally within the provincial mandate is referred to as contract policing and, although performed by the same police service, is distinct from federal policing: the former is paid for by the province, the latter by the federal government. Police Service Agreements are negotiated and administered not with the RCMP directly, but through the Department of Public Works and Government Service Canada. Provinces have several incentives to relinquish police work to the federal sector. First, cost-sharing incentives have the provinces (and territories) pay 70 per cent of the RCMP budget in their boundaries while the federal government covers 30 per cent. Although there are no actual metrics to this effect, the share assumed by the federal government is meant to approximate the amount of time the RCMP spends on federal policing responsibilities while delivering provincial police services. Municipalities can also contract the RCMP; however, it is more expensive per capita for municipalities to contract the RCMP than for the provinces, because the federal share has declined steadily from 50 per cent in 1976 to zero for all municipal RCMP contracts signed after 1992, although the federal government continues to cost-share 10–30 per cent of costs for municipal contracts signed prior to 1992 (Federation of Canadian Municipalities 2008, 17). Over the same period, however, demand for police services has increased substantially (Malm et al. 2005), which means reductions in federal (and provincial) cost-sharing effectively amount to downloading.

Second, it is an efficient way for the RCMP (and indirectly the federal government) to establish a national presence (while offloading some of the cost to the provinces), to ensure considerable uniformity in service delivery without the federal government having to resort to complex intergovernmental negotiations, as is the case in other policy areas of quasi joint jurisdiction, such as health, and, confronted with the ever-mounting complexity of investigations and prosecutions, to reduce vertical and horizontal collective-action problems by tackling cross-jurisdictional issues within a single organization. The RCMP is the police of jurisdiction in eight of ten provinces, all three territories, 190 municipalities, 184 Aboriginal communities, and three international airports.

Third, in the spirit of section 94 of the BNA, the arrangement amounts to provinces "opting in" to a federal program. The federal government has an incentive to avoid potential defections by locking provinces into long-term contracts (often of twenty years). This is attractive to provinces looking for certainty in the cost structure of police service delivery that is much harder to obtain for provincial services it administers directly. The federal government also has an incentive to prevent defections by providing a high and consistent level of service. Consistent with data for police forces in other advanced industrialized liberal democracies, levels of trust and satisfaction with the service are high, with 84 per cent of Canadians reporting "trust and confidence" in the RCMP (Lunney 2012, 441). Nonetheless, in principle, provinces are free to "opt out" and set up their own service, as Ontario and Quebec, with other provinces, notably more populous ones, having, at times, contemplated following suit for either financial or ideological reasons.

The other federal department that has a significant role in security is the Department of National Defence (DND). Strictly speaking, the Canadian Armed Forces (CAF) has no jurisdiction over the day-to-day security of Canadian citizens and property. Its domestic role is to provide a surge capacity in the case of extreme emergencies when its role is restricted to aid to civil power. Provinces can call on the CF when provincial resources are overwhelmed. Almost all deployments with which Canadians are familiar fall under one of the three forms of aid-to-the-civil-power deployments that come in response to an explicit request from one or more provinces to the federal government and are legally distinct from civil-order emergencies that allow the federal government to deploy the CF domestically without provincial consent.

The Administration of Public Security across Select Provinces

Like the federal government security apparatus, provincial security is marked by horizontal asymmetry in response to differing demands in each province. Since, provincially, the geographic and demographic scope is more limited than for the federal government, each province has developed legislation to suit its needs. Provincial security agencies are too varied to examine comprehensively, but four representative cases illustrate the way decentralization in the administration of security affords provinces the autonomy to respond to localized issues while harnessing economies of scale through access to federal resources and knowledge.

Ontario

Ontario's security structure is not unlike that of the federal government in that it is marked by a division of labour across several agencies. Ontario's Ministry of Community Safety and Correctional Services (MCSCS) fulfils three core tasks: correctional services are responsible for maintaining provincial jails (for sentences of less than two years), probation, and the Ontario Parole Board; policing services coordinate the activities of the OPP and all municipal police forces in the province;

and public security is mandated with coordinating services between municipal fire and emergency services. In addition, public security provides programs and services to the public and private sectors.

The OPP designs and delivers training to First Nations police services in Ontario, conducts Aboriginal awareness training for OPP officers, administers Provincial Liaison teams – a full-time bridge-building organization to link with First Nations communities – and provides them with access to support services, such as identification, criminal investigation, and, in some cases, dispatch. The OPP also has an Aboriginal policing bureau that administers policing for about a dozen and a half Aboriginal communities who have not exercised a self-directed policing agreement pursuant to the Ontario First Nations Policing Agreement (OPP 2013). While Ontario's First Nations policing program is managed by the OPP (because under section 54 of Ontario's Police Services Act only the commissioner of the OPP can appoint First Nations constables), most Aboriginal communities never actually see an OPP officer, because they have their own police services, officers, uniforms, and equipment. Not only is this force representative of the communities it serves, but specialized training ensures that each officer is sensitive to Aboriginal issues. Ontario's decentralized and asymmetric policing has become key to mitigating and defusing the volatile, complicated, and tense security relationship between the provincial government and many local Aboriginal communities.

Although there appears to be a clear division of responsibility between the federal and provincial governments in the security realm, cooperation and coordination in day-to-day operations is the norm. In some cases, such as the unit that investigates violent crime in prisons, the arrangement is formalized by an agreement. In other instances, such as investigations of organized crime groups, the arrangement is ad hoc. In both instances, leadership and funding is determined case by case.

Quebec

Sécurité Publique Québec (SPQ), and its provincial police force, the Sûreté du Québec (SQ), is similar to Ontario's MCSCS in its focus on crime prevention, fire safety, emergency preparedness, and correctional services, but its language of service is French. The SPQ provides programs and policy guidance to other provincial agencies, municipalities, the public, and the private sector. Like Ontario, Quebec has formal and ad hoc financial and staffing arrangements among police agencies operating in the province. For example, police agencies from three levels of government formally cooperated on Project Colisée, a three-year investigation that eventually led to the downfall of the Rizzuto crime family in Montreal.

Manitoba

Unlike Ontario and Quebec, the province of Manitoba does not have a centralized ministry for public security and emergency management. Manitoba has a Department of Justice and a Department of Infrastructure. Manitoba also does not have a provincial police force per se. Instead, it contracts the RCMP to police smaller communities and in rural areas. Larger urban areas, such as Winnipeg and Brandon, and even some of the smaller rural communities, have opted for their own municipal police forces. This allows smaller communities to maintain local control over community policing.

In the past, Manitoba has had to draw disproportionately from federal emergency resources. However, this is not because Manitoba has addressed security challenges inadequately. Rather, Manitoba's demographic distribution makes emergency evacuation difficult. For example, in the summer of 2007 Manitoba registered eleven tornados, one of which reached F5 intensity. Manitoba's sparsely populated rural areas worked to its advantage in this instance, as these tornados did not touch down in densely populated areas. By contrast, Manitoba has long been plagued by seasonal flooding. The Red River flood of 1997 was among the most severe of Manitoba's flood emergencies. Seven thousand military personnel were deployed over the course of thirty-six days to relocate over 25,000 evacuees, and over 1,000 homes were lost (Province of Manitoba 2013). In response, Manitoba established comprehensive flood controls that during the 2009 flood prevented $10 billion in damage (ibid.; Henstra and McBean 2005). As the case of Manitoba suggests, even provinces with fewer resources enjoy the full protection of the federal government.

British Columbia

Security in the province of British Columbia is part of the portfolio held by the minister of justice. This portfolio includes traditional areas, such as policing, emergency management and prisons, as well as child protection services, industry licensing, court services, and motor vehicles.

British Columbia is an anomaly in policing. Most police services in British Columbia are contracted with the RCMP. In BC, the RCMP covers provincial policing, sixty-one urban areas, eleven municipalities, and administers one First Nations police force. In addition, as elsewhere in Canada, the RCMP also investigates federal crimes.

To reduce the public health risks associated with intravenous drug use, the province of BC has opened a needle-exchange program in Vancouver, which has become a destination of choice for many IV drug users. The program, which goes by the name Insite, provides safe, clean needles to reduce the spread of illness related to IV drug use. Insite has traditionally been unpopular with Canada's federal government, which has attempted on several occasions to close down the clinics. The current Liberal government, however, has taken a more positive approach to working with safe injection sites. The RCMP continues, regardless, to work with provincial organizations to achieve provincial goals.

The examples of Ontario, Quebec, Manitoba, and British Columbia demonstrate that the provision of security across Canada is asymmetric. This asymmetry extends beyond resources to differences in culture, climate, and language. Canada is not spared the archetypal security issues that confront other federal polities: drug use and income disparity, natural disaster and violent domestic terrorist attacks. Decentralization is an integral part of a federal strategy to approach to crime and disaster management in a way that is sensitive to local needs. This decentralization of responsibility is matched by a decentralization of resources, without which it would not be possible for provinces to realize their responsibilities and exercise their autonomy.

Intergovernmental Relations and Coordination

The principal challenge in the delivery of public security is a Canadian federal system marked by shared, not pooled, sovereignty. Under shared sovereignty, institutions coordinate but remain separate under their respective areas of jurisdiction. In contrast, pooling sovereignty would mean building common institutions that subsume different areas of jurisdiction. Although the RCMP appears to exude features of pooled sovereignty, even its attributes of shared sovereignty remain problematic.

While tactical and operational cooperation has improved substantially in the wake of a series of focusing events, including 9/11, the SARS epidemic, the Vancouver Olympics, and the G8/G20, the system is plagued by a lack of intergovernmental coordination on strategic priorities and goals (Lunney 2012, 438–9). The federal government's position is that a single arrangement is workable for all the constituent entities, despite different demands by the provinces (436). Across the ten provinces the respective ministers of public security (or its approximate functional equivalent in the form of public or community safety) are responsible for setting the objectives, priorities, and goals for the provincial police service. Federal priorities, by contrast, are reported by the federal minister for public safety (*sécurité publique*) to Parliament as part of the federal strategic priorities. The resulting disconnect between federal and provincial priorities has some provinces considering setting up their own provincial police forces (see Alberta Agenda 2013). In effect, provinces have little input into the operation and management of the RCMP (Lunney 2012, 442). Policing contracts between the RCMP and the provinces allow the provincial authorities to request and participate in program review. Recent examples of federal-provincial coordination in this field include the establishment of Alberta's Serious Incident Response Team (ASIRT) (Alberta Views 2013) and British Columbia's civilian-led Independent Investigations Office (IIO), which conducts criminal investigations into incidents that involve BC police officers and result in death or serious harm. That effort would have been nugatory had it not included the RCMP, since no other province has more sworn RCMP members in absolute and relative terms: with over 6,000 of the RCMP's 19,000 operational members posted to BC, the RCMP accounts for almost two-thirds of police officers in BC.

Disconnects are not limited to federal-provincial priorities; they are also prevalent in local-provincial and local-federal priorities, thereby drawing attention to the difficulty in operationalizing pluralist federalism, especially with regard to local Aboriginal communities. Repeated crises in Aboriginal communities have galvanized national attention, such as Oka (1993), Gustafsen Lake (1995), Ipperwash (1995), Kashechewan (2005–6), Caledonia (2006), and Attawapiskat (2011) and have drawn attention to the issues of democratic oversight. Bureaucracies can exacerbate these disconnects when they pursue their own interests, which may well be at odds with the governments they supposedly serve (Lindsay 2009). The RCMP's infamously rocky relationship with the ministerial portfolio of the former Department of the Solicitor General and its successor, Public Safety Canada, is an *exemple par excellence* (d'Ombrain 1999). The picture that emerges is one of a multilevel government system where different levels of government, their bureaucracies, and local communities have different values, interests, preferences, and priorities that cause them to pursue competing, contradictory, or irreconcilable strategies.

These multi-level governance tensions are particularly apparent in controversies over the allocation of resources. Provincial governments can be reticent to spend on security and emergency infrastructure, as it tends to be a low priority for voters, who often fail to recognize the importance of preventive measures. Multi-level governance tensions can thus undermine the timely implementation of crime and disaster management legislation. Conversely, federal expenditures may be mismatched with local values and priorities. Canada's hosting of the G20 Summit in 2010 at the cost of $1.2 billion exemplifies the distrust and legitimacy issues conjured by federal security spending that is misaligned with local expectations and priorities, and the implementation of security measures and mechanisms that run afoul of local preferences. The auditor general's report on the costs associated with the G-20 summit only served to confirm the preoccupation by citizens and opposition parties with wasteful spending in the security sector.

The case of the G20 is just one illustration of the problems created by a federal system that constitutionally excludes municipalities from the federal-provincial structure of disaster and security management by treating them as appendages of the provinces instead. As a result of Canada's discursive focus on the primacy of federal-provincial relations, first responders end up being deprived of voice and resources (Juillet and Koji 2014). While the first-response capacity is largely vested with local communities – in 2006, municipalities paid 56.6 per cent of Canada's total policing expenditures and provided 65.8 per cent of Canada's police officers (including contracted provincial or RCMP officers), provinces provided 24.5 per cent of officers (including provincial contract policing), and the federal government, by means of the RCMP, 9.7 per cent (Federation of Canadian Municipalities 2008, 4, 13) – the top-down flow of funds does not necessarily correspond to their needs and realities.

The marginalization of municipal governments from the federal-provincial nexus also has an impact on standardizing emergency management at the local and/or provincial levels. Local governments, especially smaller ones, often have to rely disproportionately on volunteer first responders as their first line of defence (Ferrier 2008). In addition, emergency management mandates are often fragmented among other ministries or agencies, such as transport, wildlife, and utilities.

The ensuing horizontal and vertical coordination issues can pose a problem, especially with volunteer first responders and private sector partners such as utilities and transportation companies, where training and compliance with standards is a function of money, cooperation, and volunteer time.

Further challenges for public security in the Canadian federation loom on the horizon. Many of these challenges will be asymmetric in origin, delivery, and impact (Leuprecht, Hataley and Nossal 2012), climate change first and foremost among them. Throughout sparsely populated Northern Canada, passageways are opening up in Arctic ice, thus raising the spectre of having to police Arctic sovereignty more effectively and providing security, defence, and emergency services across a large swathe of land that is scarcely populated, inhospitable, and far afield from military bases and the location of other security assets. Likewise, meteorological trends promise to become more severe and unpredictable as storms once reserved for tropical climates threaten Canadian coastal cities. Financial trends suggest that income disparities will continue to grow, potentially fuelling popular discontent and regional instability. Moreover, the prevailing terrorist threat can be met only by an intergovernmental crime and emergency management system capable of responding promptly and resiliently. The compound effect of these developments will require not only improved intergovernmental cooperation, but also the judicious application of lessons learned by federal allies. Yet neither provinces nor municipalities have the requisite financial, organizational, and leadership resources; these are vested with the federal government, which has proven reticent to get involved for fear of intruding into provincial jurisdiction. The result is a collective-action problem that municipalities and provinces cannot overcome by themselves but on which the federal government is reticent to lead.

Case Study: Cornwall Regional Task Force (CRTF)

The CRTF demonstrates the capacity of the Canadian federal system to respond to local/regional security concerns by partnering resources at three levels of government, while at the same time ensuring that all agencies involved continue to operate within the legislative restrictions under which they would normally operate. Contrary to ad hoc arrangements, the CRTF distinguishes itself by being formalized and long-term.

The CRTF is mandated to rein in the smuggling of contraband through the Cornwall area, which is known to be a high-density drug trafficking area and of particular significance to American law enforcement partners. Specifically, it is mandated to enforce the Customs and Excise Acts, Controlled Drugs and Substances Act, the Immigration and Refugee Protection Act, as well as Criminal Code offences in eastern Ontario, along the St Lawrence River to the Quebec border (the Akwesasne Mohawk territory and surrounding area).[3] These ends are achieved through extensive integration and coordination with a variety of federal and sub-national public security agencies including CBSA, OPP, New York State Police, and U.S. Immigration and Customs Enforcement and the RCMP. However, the task force itself works primarily with the CBSA, OPP, the Ontario Ministry of Revenue's special investigations branch, and the Cornwall Police. The CRTF has successfully created working public security partnerships across all levels of the Canadian law enforcement landscape, as well as with American law enforcement.

The CRTF is a joint task force formed in April 2010 and coordinated by the RCMP, comprising forty-six officers and six civilian staff members (RCMP 2011). The original intention behind the formation of this task force was to stem the spread of illegal tobacco sales/consumption in the region; however the current task force is far more multi-functional. The CRTF operates under a formal memorandum of understanding that clearly states the roles, responsibilities, and associated costs for all member agencies, and, therefore, levels of government, involved in the task force. Members share a common enforcement mandate, but are restricted in the operational abilities by their respective internal policies and directives. In other words, the CRTF is a working relationship; however, each member is responsible to the specific policies and rules under which its organization operates.

---

3 The Akwesasne territory is not only governed by federal and provincial laws, but it falls under Native American (Mohawk) jurisdiction as well. This creates regulatory challenges for law enforcement, primarily since several federal law enforcement agencies have insisted that this reserve, which straddles the border between Canada and the United States, is rife with contraband and black market. In 2011 there were 682 police officers per 100000 and a Crime Severity Index of 132.5 (almost twice the index of Canada's most populated city, Toronto).

Conclusion

The relationship between public security and the Canadian federal systems is best described as decentralized and asymmetric. Other than delegating the maintenance of law and order to the provinces, the Canadian Constitution says relatively little about security. This flexibility may well be both the greatest strength and the greatest weakness of the system, making it possible to adapt to hazards and corresponding needs, while leaving the federal and provincial governments considerable discretion. The result is a hierarchy that leaves municipalities little control over their first responders (Federation of Canadian Municipalities 2008; Mukherjee 2011).

Provinces enjoy substantial autonomy, since they have some clearly enumerated areas of jurisdiction, have autonomy over much of their tax revenue, have access to many of the same revenues as the federal government, and receive substantial equalization and other transfers that are mostly unconditional. The same is not true for the relationship between province and municipalities. The unitary dimension of that relationship makes is tempting for provinces to offload responsibility to the municipal level (or, for the federal government, to the province, which promptly proceeds to offload to municipalities) without necessarily providing the requisite funding to accompany new requirements: "This results in diversion of scarce resources away from core municipal roles … into areas of clear federal jurisdiction, such as maritime interdiction and enforcement, cyber crime, drug investigations, non-returnable warrants, border security, national security and counterterrorism" (Federation of Canadian Municipalities 2008, 5, 14–16). Moreover, specific requirements associated with unfunded mandates cause municipalities to concentrate their efforts on specific risks instead of an all-hazards approach, which is likely to yield greater security payoffs (Henstra 2003, 2010).

The shortcomings found in Canada are not unique, but are found in other federal countries as well. So why does the Canadian system work relatively well? Is it because the system is decentralized and asymmetric? Or is this more reflective of a federation whose constituent units have the constitutional autonomy, financial means, and consequent capacity to address public security issues adequately and the strength of a liberal democratic political culture that respects the rule of law and encourages compliance and volunteerism? Canadian security issues are as diverse as the country is large. The Canadian system works well because it empowers provinces and localities to respond to and meet local needs by means of an ad hoc arrangement of paid employees and volunteers, complemented by surge support from the federal level. The system works, as the result of a combination of confidence, capacity, and autonomy for local levels of government to reflect and respond to local values, preferences, interests, and priorities, and a strong political culture that balances shared rule in the form of a strong commitment to the rule of law with self-rule in the form of a concomitant engagement by Canadian "publics" to take ownership of "their" security.

References

Alberta Agenda. 2013. http://www.albertaagenda.ca/police.htm.

Bauböck, R. 2001. "Cultural Citizenship, Minority Rights and Self-Government." In *Citizenship Today: Global Perspectives and Practices*, ed. A. Aleinikoff and D. Klusmeyer, 319–48. Washington, DC: Carnegie Endowment for International Peace.

Di Matteo, Livio. 2014. "Police and Crime Rates in Canada: A Comparison of Resources and Outcomes." Fraser Institute. https://www.fraserinstitute.org/sites/default/files/police-and-crime-rates-in-canada.pdf.

d'Ombrain, Nicholas. 1999. "The Federal Government and the RCMP." *Canadian Public Administration* 42 (4): 452–75. https://doi.org/10.1111/j.1754-7121.1999.tb02036.x.

Federation of Canadian Municipalities. 2008. *Towards Equity and Efficiency in Policing: A Report on Policing, Roles, Responsibilities and Resources in Canada*. Ottawa: Federation of Canadian Municipalities.

Ferrier, N. 2008. *Fundamentals of Emergency Management: Preparedness*. Toronto: Emond Montgomery Publishers.

Haglund, David. 2008. "The Parizeau-Chretien Version: Ethnicity and Canadian Grand Strategy." In *The World and Canada: Diaspora, Demography and Domestic Politics*, ed. D. Carment and D. Bercuson, 92–108. Montreal and Kingston: McGill-Queen's University Press.

Henstra, Daniel. 2003. "Federal Emergency Management in Canada and the United States after 11 September 2001." *Canadian Public Administration* 46 (1): 103–16. https://doi.org/10.1111/j.1754-7121.2003.tb01581.x.

– 2010. "Explaining Local Policy Choices: A Multiple Stream Analysis of Municipal Emergency Management." *Canadian Public Administration* 53 (2): 241–58. https://doi.org/10.1111/j.1754-7121.2010.00128.x.

Henstra, Daniel, and Gordon McBean. 2005. "Canadian Disaster Management Policy: Moving toward a Paradigm Shift?" *Canadian Public Policy* 31 (3): 303–18. https://doi.org/10.2307/3552443.

Juillet, Luc, and Junichiro Koji. 2014. "Reforming the Multilevel Governance of Emergencies: Municipalities and Discursive Politics of Canada's Emergency Management Policy." In *Canada in Cities: The Politics and Policy of Federal-Local Governance*, ed. Katherine A.H. Graham and Caroline Andrew. Montreal and Kingston: McGill-Queen's University Press.

Karmis, Dimitrios. 2009. "The Multiple Voices of the Federal Tradition and the Turmoil of Canadian Federalism." In *Contemporary Canadian Federalism: Foundations, Traditions, Institutions*, ed. Alain Gagnon, 53–75. Toronto: University of Toronto Press.

Leuprecht, Christian, Todd Hataley, and Kim Richard Nossal. 2012. *Evolving Transnational Threats and Border Security*. Kingston: Queen's Centre for International and Defence Policy; http://www.queensu.ca/cidp/events/conferences-and-workshops/transnational-threats-2011.

Lindsay, John. 2009. "Emergency Management in Canada: Near Misses and Moving Targets." In *Comparative Emergency Management Book Project*. Emmitsburg, MD: United States Federal Emergency Management Institute. https://training.fema.gov/hiedu/aemrc/booksdownload/compemmgmtbookproject/.

Lunney, Robert F. 2012. "Galloping Off in All Directions: An Analysis of the New Federal-Provincial Agreement for RCMP Contract Police Services and Some Implications for the Future of Canadian Policing." *Canadian Public Administration* 55 (3): 433–50. https://doi.org/10.1111/j.1754-7121.2012.00232.x.

Macdonald, David. 2011. *The Costs of 9/11 and the Creation of a National Security Establishment*. Ottawa: Rideau Institute.

Malm, Aili, Nahanni Pollard, Paul Brantingham, Paul Tinsley, Darryl Plecas, Patricia Brantingham, Irwin Cohen, and Bryan Kenney. 2005. *A 30-Year Analysis of Police Service Delivery and Costing: "E" Division*. Abbotsford, BC: Centre for Criminal Justice Research, University College of the Fraser Valley, and International Centre for Urban Research Studies, Simon Fraser University.

Marquis, Greg. 1993. *Policing Canada's Century: A History of the Canadian Association of Chiefs of Police*. Toronto: University of Toronto Press.

Morton, Desmond. 1999. *Canada: A Millennium Portrait*. Toronto: Dundurn.

Mukherjee, Alok. 2011. "Avoid Crisis, an Opportunity: Transforming the Toronto Police Service. A Discussion Paper." Toronto: Toronto Police Services Board.

Office of the Parliamentary Budget Officer. 20 March 2013. *Expenditure Analysis of Criminal Justice in Canada*. http://www.pbo-dpb.gc.ca/web/default/files/files/files/Crime_Cost_EN.pdf.

Ontario Provincial Police. 2013. "What We Do." https://www.opp.ca/index.php?id=121.
Public Safety Canada. 2013. "What We Do." http://www.publicsafety.gc.ca/abt/wwd/index-eng.aspx.

4 Germany

KLAUS STÜWE

Introduction

The public security system in the Federal Republic of Germany is shaped by two basic principles: (1) the federal government (the federation) and the Länder possess their own security services and carry out their respective duties; and (2) the functions of the police and the functions of the intelligence services are exercised through distinct administrative bodies that are organizationally separate from each other. As a result, the federal government and each Land has its own police and intelligence services.

The architecture of public security in Germany is thus vertically and horizontally divided: vertically through the separation of the security services belonging to the federation and the individual Länder, horizontally through the separation of the police and the intelligence services. This system has a decisive advantage over unitary security systems: certain aspects of security measures taken by the Länder with the potential to jeopardize freedom can be reduced through the structural and functional distribution of responsibilities. It also comes at a cost: efficiency.

According to constitutional law, public security lies primarily in the jurisdiction of the Länder. In political praxis, however, a complicated system for the separation of duties, cooperation, and integration developed. New threats in particular, such as terrorism in the 1970s, the globalization of crime, and most of all the terrorist attacks on 11 September 2001, have led to a profound transformation of Germany's security structure. Four key trends can be observed: (1) an increase of federal activity in the public security field (centralization);

(2) the construction of joint institutions for federal and state security actors; (3) more cooperation of police and intelligence services in the European Union (Europeanization); and (4) the transfer of certain security services from the public sector to the private sector (privatization).

Public Security Risks and Concerns

Germany is regarded as a relatively secure country. The number of registered criminal offences in Germany has been on the wane for years (see figure 4.1). In 2015 the Federal Criminal Police Office (Bundeskriminalamt, or BKA) reported approximately 6.33 million criminal offences. In the same year, the offence rate (criminal offences committed per 100,000 inhabitants) stood at 7,797. Roughly 40 per cent of police-recorded criminal offences are offences against property. More serious crimes – those that affect the physical integrity of individual citizens – are quantitatively infrequent events.

At 56.3 per cent in 2015, the proportion of solved criminal investigations undertaken by the police is high, compared to the rate in other countries, despite a comparatively low density of police officers. For the 81 million inhabitants, there are 221,000 Länder police officers, in addition to the 40,000 federal police officers, and 5,500 people employed by the Federal Criminal Police Office.

Figure 4.1. Registered Crimes in Germany 1997–2015 (in millions)

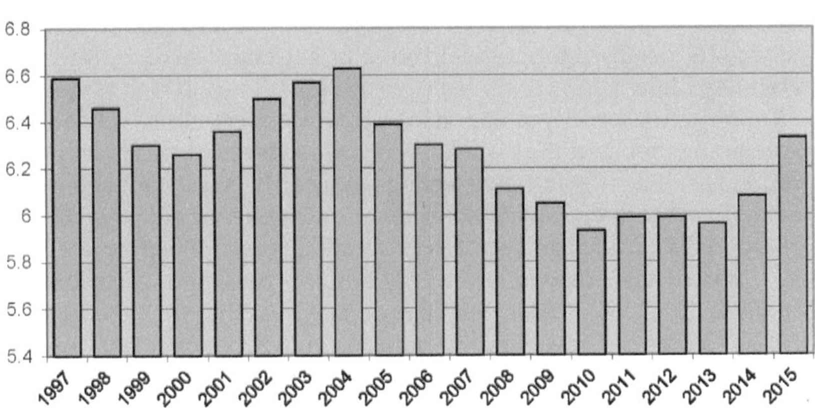

Source: Federal Criminal Police Office (BKA)

In Germany, politically motivated crime is prosecuted in the relatively unique context of *wehrhafte Demokratie* (defensive democracy). Coined by the Federal Constitutional Court, this term denotes the resolve of the state to approach enemies of free and democratic order not simply neutrally, but rather with stark opposition. The painful experiences that accompanied the end of the Weimar Republic led to the firm establishment of the principle of defensive democracy in Germany's Basic Law. Quantitatively, politically motivated crime is insignificant. The BKA reported 38,981 politically motivated criminal offences in 2015 (2014: 32,700). Out of these cases, 35.1 per cent were propaganda crimes, while 4,452 offences (11.4 per cent) were politically motivated violent crime (Bundeskriminalamt 2016).

Three forms of political crime can be said to have the biggest threat potential. In recent years, the number of right-wing extremist criminal offences has grown (2014: 17,020; 2015: 22,960). In 2011, the German public was shocked to find out that a right-wing extremist terrorist group had committed nine race-based murders between 2000 and 2006. Within the segment of left-wing extremists who are willing to resort to violence, the number of potentially violent actors seems to be increasing, too (2014: 8,113 violent crimes; 2015: 9,605). Islamic terrorism is also found in Germany. The spectrum of Islamic terrorist structures in Germany ranges from violent Islamic extremists who have close relationships with jihadi organizations abroad via extensive, independently operated micro-groups to lone perpetrators, who – to some extent over the Internet – become radical and plan autonomously. In 2016, three radical Islamic terrorist attacks were committed on German soil – in Ansbach, Würzburg, and Hannover. The general public still deems the potential threat of extremist Islamic terrorism relatively high.

The objective security situation in Germany objectively, which in comparison to other countries is relatively stable, does not necessarily correspond to citizens' subjective feelings of security. A substantial portion (44 per cent) of the population has the impression that today we live in an especially unsafe age in which everything is even more incalculable und unpredictable than it was twenty or thirty years ago (Allensbacher Archiv 2016, 11050). Older people especially fear that they themselves will be victims of crime. Since the attacks on 11 September 2001 as well as the Islamic acts of terror in 2015 and 2016 caught the public's attention, many citizens have become increasingly concerned about threats to the state by terrorism.

The Constitutional and Legal Framework concerning Security Issues

In German, there is no distinction between security and safety. *Sicherheit* means both "security" (the state of being free from intentional damages) and "safety" (the state of being free from accidental events). Neither the term *public safety* nor the term *public security* is found in the Basic Law of the Federal Republic of Germany. Yet the Federal Constitutional Court has identified public security as an objective of the state on multiple occasions. In the process, the constitutional judges emphasized two "indispensable constitutional values from which the state derives its authentic and ultimate justification": on the one hand, the "security of the state as a constituted force of peace and order"; on the other hand, "the guarantee of security for the citizens by the state" (BVerfGE 49, 56).

Public security is primarily the responsibility of the Länder. This basic constitutional premise flows from the Principal of Federalism rooted in article 20 I in the Basic Law, which is best known for the decentralization of other areas such as the school system. During the process of creating the Basic Law, however, representatives of the Western Allies – contrary to the centralistic plans of some German politicians – wanted the Länder to take responsibility for law enforcement (Kutscha 2006, 79).

The Länder are thus bestowed with extensive competencies in the field of public security. This policy area is shaped not only by a complicated system of task separation, but also by coordination and cooperation. At the same time, a multi-level federal governance system informs the relationship between the federation and the Länder in matters of public security. This dynamic is enhanced by the increasing Europeanization of public security policy. As in other areas of policy, three federal levels of agency are at work: (1) the unconnected, coexisting member Länder, (2) the federation, and (3) intergovernmental coordination and cooperation.

Public Security as a State Power

Public security is commonly understood as a fundamental responsibility assumed by the Länder pursuant to article 30 of the Basic Law: "Except as otherwise provided or permitted by this Basic Law, the exercise of state powers and the discharge of state functions is a matter for the Länder." In terms of legislative jurisdiction, article 70 I of the Basic Law stipulates: "The Länder shall have the right to legislate insofar as this Basic Law does not confer legislative power on the Federation." Aside from culture and administrative sovereignty, the police and regulatory law presents one of the core justifications of the state-like quality of the Länder.

As is the case for the federation, the Länder are also subject to the Polizeibrief (police letters) of 14 April 1949 from the allied military governors to the president of the Parliamentary Council, West Germany's constituent assembly that drafted the Basic Law in 1948/9. The Polizeibrief prohibits the affiliation of police and intelligence services. Consequently, all German Länder passed separate police laws that regulate the organization, duties, and authorization of the Länder police. The legislative basis of the Länder Offices for the Protection of the Constitution (Verfassungsschutz) are Länder laws for the protection of the constitution.

Under the framework of concurrent legislation as per article 74 of the Basic Law, the Länder have further responsibilities in the realm of civil law as well as criminal law and criminal procedure. Here, according to article 72 I of the Basic Law, the Länder have legislative authority as long and insofar as the federation does not supersede their jurisdiction by exercising its legislative jurisdiction through law. It can already be seen here, however, that the federation has effectively ceded hardly any leeway to the Länder.

Even more clearly discernible is the federation's growth of powers in article 23 of the Basic Law, which regulates the involvement of the Länder in EU affairs. Current collaboration between EU countries on issues of justice and internal affairs is increasingly affecting the responsibility of the Länder in the field of public security. Article 23 V of the Basic Law allows for the Bundesrat (the legislative body representing the Länder) to "be given the greatest possible respect" should "the legislative powers of the Länder, the structure of Land authorities or Land administrative procedures" be primarily affected. The particulars are regulated by the Act on the Cooperation of Federation and Länder in Affairs of the European Union (EUZBLG). This means that the legislative authority of the Länder can effectively be narrowed through EU law. The "significant involvement" of the Bundesrat does not sufficiently compensate for this less of autonomy. Such is the case not only the jurisdiction of the Länder in the area of public security, but also in other policy fields.

Public Security as a Federal Power

According to the Constitution, the fundamental jurisdiction of the Länder over public security is rarely breached. The origin of the federation's authority is found in the Polizeibrief. These letters prescribe precise standards as to which duties involving policing of particular federal bodies should be permitted to vary from the fundamental jurisdiction of the Länder, including

- the surveillance of civilian traffic and freight traffic that crosses the German border,
- the collection and dissemination of police information and statistics,
- the coordination of investigations of violations of federal law and the fulfilment of international obligations concerning drug surveillance, international travel, and treaties regarding criminal persecution.

Federal police authorities should furthermore not have the power to direct the Länder police. Yet the establishment of a position for the collection and dissemination of information regarding subversive activities against the federal government was permitted. However, this position was not to have any police authority (BVerfGE 97, 198).

The Parliamentary Council subsequently incorporated corresponding authorization in the form of article 73 subsections 5 and 10, as well as article 87 I 2 of the Basic Law. According to article 73 number 5, the federation now has exclusive legislative authority over tariff protection and border patrol. The inception of the federal border guard (now called the federal police) occurred in 1951 on the basis of this proviso.

Article 73 I number 10 of the Basic Law also concedes exclusive legislative power to the federation for "cooperation between the federation and the Länder" on criminal investigations, in the "protection of the free democratic basic order, existence, and security of the federation or of a Land (protection of the constitution), and protection against activities within the federal territory that, by the use of force or preparations for the use of force, endanger the external interests of the Federal Republic of Germany, as well as the establishment of a Federal Criminal Police Office and international action to combat crime."

In its substance, the regulation outlined in article 73 no. 10 of the Basic Law has far-reaching consequences, which leads to an immense increase of powers for the federation with regard to public security. For example, the provision legitimizes the federation's adoption of the "Anti-Terror Packet" of December 2001, which, in reaction to the 11 September attacks of the same year, among other things, strengthened the Federal Office's competence over the intelligence services and the Federal Criminal Police Office.

Still, in these areas the Basic Law grants the federation exclusive legislative competence over the collaboration with the Länder. However, vertical federal arrangements do not constitute the only path towards cooperation between the federation and the Länder on public security. Yet that does not delegitimize the contractual regulation in the framework of existing laws.

The provision requires that state and federal authorities be involved in criminal investigations and the intelligence services. Such federal authority is found in article 87 I of the Basic Law. Through federal law, this article enables the establishment of certain security services such as the federal police, "central offices for police information and communications, for the criminal police, and for the compilation of data for purposes of protection of the constitution." In 1950, the federation met this requirement through the Law for the Collaboration of the Federation and the Länder in All Matters Regarding Intelligence Services and for the Federal Office for Intelligence Services, and later in 1951 though the Border Patrol Law, as well as the Law for the Establishment of a German Federal Criminal Police Agency.

In the course of the federalism reform of 2006, article 73 I number 9a was included in the Basic Law, according to which the protection from international terrorism by the Federal Criminal Police Office is also allocated to the exclusive legislative competence of the federation in the following cases: if the threat is nationwide, if the jurisdiction of the state police department is not discernible, or if the highest state police agency makes a request to that effect. This provision limits the legislative action of the federation expressly to the dangers ensuing from international terrorism; nevertheless, this is bound to limit the competence of the Länder competence in matters of public security.

In the end, all constitutional provisions of the Basic Law recognize the fundamental jurisdiction of the Länder on public security. Formulations such as "cooperation of the federation and the Länder" as well as "Länder-overarching danger" show that the Basic Law assumes subsidiarity by virtue of the existence of state institutions for the protection of public security (Pütter 2000, 276).

Public Security as Concurrent Power

The type of federalism practised in the Federal Republic of Germany is generally defined as "cooperative." "Cooperative federalism" is a convention between the federation and member states (Länder) of the federal state who aid one another in their respective duties to reach agreements and customarily to reach decisions by consensus. On the one hand, this cooperation is the consequence of the development of political practice. The quid pro quo seems for the Länder to trade autonomy for a say at the federal level. On the other hand, however, the cooperation between the federation and the Länder is already laid out in constitutional law (as exemplified in matters of finance as well as public security).

The Basic Law contains various clauses which expressly refer to the cooperation between the security services of the federation and of the Länder, such as article 73 number 10 of the Basic Law with "cooperation between the federation and Länder." Article 35 requires all administrative bodies of the federation and the Länder to provide one another with administrative and legal assistance. In principle, administrative cooperation on public security falls under this provision. In the course of the adoption of emergency laws, two sections in article 35 were amended in 1968 to articulate this aspect of security: according to section 2a, Land "in particularly serious cases may call upon personnel and facilities of the federal border patrol to assist its police when without such assistance the police could not fulfil their responsibilities, or could do so only with great difficulty in order to maintain or restore public security or order." According to this paragraph, a Land can solicit the help of police forces from other Länder, forces and equipment of other administrations, as well as the federal police and armed forces, should the Land face a natural disaster or a severe accident. Should said natural disaster or severe accident jeopardize an area encompassing more than one Land, according to paragraph 3 the federal government can issue a directive to the institutions of the Land for support from police forces from other Länder. The federal government can deploy units of the federal police and armed forces in support of local police.

Article 91 of the Basic Law, which regulates the deployment of police forces during a national emergency, was also modified in the emergency legislation of 1968. Originally, the provision in section 1 made it possible for a Land to solicit the police forces of other Länder "in order to avert an imminent danger to the existence or free democratic basic order of the federation or of a Land." With this, the Basic Law initially granted exclusive vertical federal cooperation to the Länder in a national emergency. Since 1968 the "forces and equipment of other administrations and of the German border patrol" can also be called upon. The clause is thus augmented by an auxiliary horizontal dimension that included the federation in the form of, for example, the federal police.

Article 91 section 2 of the Basic Law involves not federal cooperation per se but rather a decisional authority of the federal government in a national emergency. If the Land being threatened is itself not "able or willing" to combat said danger, "the federal government may place the police in that Land and the police forces of other Länder under its own orders." Thus the federal government has to rescind its directive once the danger has passed as well as anytime the Federal Council of Germany so desires. In this way, the Bundesrat – at least in constitutional theory – can, in cases of national emergency, safeguard the Länder's security competence.

The Financial Dimension of Public Security

In 2015 Germany spent 38.0 billion euros on public security, about 3.6 per cent of all public expenditures, or 1.56 per cent of the GDP (Eurostat 2016). In 2014, the federation accounted for 4.8 billion (8.6 per cent), the Länder for 23.34 billion euros (72.3 per cent) and municipalities for 6.3 billion euros (19.5 per cent).

Public security is consequently first and foremost a duty of the Länder, both constitutionally and financially. Bavaria, for example, spends about 20 per cent of its budget on public security. Public authorities' expenditure on public security – police, *Ordnungsverwaltung*, courts, and law enforcement authorities – has risen steadily from 23 billion euros in 1992 to roughly 38 billion euros in 2015 according to the data from the Federal Statistical Office. Although current data are not yet available, one can proceed on the assumption that this increase seen in the past several years has only continued.

Municipal expenditure on public security and public order concentrates on traffic control, automobile registration offices, fire control, disaster management, and rescue services.

Intergovernmental Arrangements: The Conference of State Ministers of the Interior

One of the most significant and unique dimensions of the German federal system is that it aims to achieve equivalent living conditions throughout the federal territory. This is not only one of the postulates of the federal constitution (article 72) but also part of Germany's tradition of cooperative federalism. However, despite the multifaceted constitutional ties between federation and Länder regarding public security, the Basic Law says nothing about the concrete administrative and political forms that cooperation and coordination is supposed to take. They arise instead out of convention. This is also true for the most important council on federal cooperation in Germany: the Conference of State Ministers and Senators of the Interior – abbreviated as the Interior Ministers' Conference.

The Interior Ministers' Conference was established in 1954 by the heads of the Interior Ministry to secure collaboration at the political level; until then, it had been essentially performed by civil servants. The federal minister of the interior participates in the sessions of the Interior Ministers' Conference ex officio. In spite of this formal discrimination, the position of the minister in practice is not restrained.

The Interior Ministers' Conference is an informal council. There exist neither a statutory framework of operation nor rules of procedure. According to a resolution from November 1960, the conference meets in camera twice a year, provided that no special sessions are required on account of new political developments or dangerous situations related to public security.

Decision-making at the Interior Ministers' Conference is by unanimity. Such a "consensus form of organization" (Pütter 2000, 279) among sixteen Länder is possible only because the conference has a series of conflict-avoidance or conflict-minimalizing mechanisms at its disposal.

The nature of consensus found in the Interior Ministers' Conference is decisively shaped by the fact that its resolutions routinely result from negotiations at lower levels of the departmental bureaucracies. Most of the issues that the ministers and the state secretaries discuss are prepared by the six permanent working groups. The working groups fall under the auspices to the department heads of the interior ministries of the Länder and of the federation.

Ergo, federal cooperation in the field of public security takes place primarily on administrative levels. The political level – in the form of the Interior Ministers' Conference – amounts mostly to the "grand finale" of the communication between the Länder, as well as between the federation and the Länder. In sum, the Interior Ministers' Conference closes the constitutional "gap" of federal cooperation in the field of public security. It constitutes, however, only the tip of the of a cooperative bureaucracy that prepares the resolutions of the Interior Ministers' Conference and, in some cases, also depoliticizes and carries out consensually. "If one considers the history of the Interior Ministers' Conference," writes Pütter, "the day-to-day political controversies and the partisan controversies have remained until today isolated episodes" (Pütter 2000, 283).

As a result, the Interior Ministers' Conference can play a pivotal role as federal council in the field of public security: It is not only an institution of vertical federal cooperation among the Länder, but also an instrument of the federation for security policy cooperation with the Länder and a way for the Länder's interests to be represented vis-à-vis the federation.

The Interior Ministers' Conference performs this function at the expense of other actors in the federal system. Like other institutions of federal cooperation – such as the Bundesrat or the Cultural Ministers' Conference or the Minister Presidents' Conference – the Interior Ministers' Conference is an executive institution. Neither the Bundestag (federal parliament) nor the sixteen Land parliaments can influence the Interior Ministers' Conference. It depends on the government whether and to what extent they inform the parliaments about the work of the Interior Ministers' Conference. In other words, through the Interior Ministers' Conference, the parliaments have lost a good deal of power to shape and control public security.

Trends towards Integration and Centralization

Integration between the federal and state levels, then, is constitutionally enshrined. For example, law enforcement is fundamentally a matter of the Länder; however, as soon as the police prosecute, they are subject to the code of criminal procedure and thereby to the federal law.

While the particular authorities for the protection against threats to public security are laid down in the police laws of each Land, the code of criminal procedure as federal law also authorizes police to intervene within the framework of criminal procedure. The police of the Länder, therefore, act on the basis of both state and federal law. The system of public security system is thus said to be tightly interwoven, if not entangled.

In political practice, however, even more tendencies of integration have arisen – most heavily influenced by extreme factors such as focalizing events (9/11), supra-national developments (EU), or financial scarcity (privatization).

Centralization

The tasks and competencies of the federal security services have expanded considerably in recent years. As early as 1992 the authority of the federal border patrol was becoming more expansive. With the end of the division of Germany and following the Schengen Agreement, which phased out internal border patrols by creating of EU-international borders, the tasks of the federal border patrol changed fundamentally. A decrease in the tasks of border police was offset by greater responsibilities of the railway police and airport security. In 1992, a law formally transferred the responsibilities of the railway police and the protection from attacks to air traffic security to the BGS. In 1994, a revision to the federal border patrol laws formalized responsibilities that had already been assumed over time: for example, protection of German diplomatic missions, international police operations in the framework of the UN, EU, and WEU, etc. (Lange 1999, 207).

Upon application from the Land North Rheine–Westphalia in 1998, the Federal Constitutional Court reviewed the constitutionality of this kind of broadening of authority, but judged the new regulation to be constitutional. The Federal Constitutional Court ascertained, "The federal border patrol may not be enlarged into a federal police that would compete with the Länder police and with that lose its character as police with limited responsibilities." At the same time however, the judges in Karlsruhe used the terms *special police, police with limited responsibilities,* and *police of the federation* to describe the responsibilities of the BGS (BVerfGE 97, 198.). This ruling made clear that the federation's absorption of special police responsibilities does not infringe on the principle of police sovereignty of the Länder. Renaming the BGS the "federal police" in 2005 was a logical outcome.

The terrorist attacks of 11 September 2001 caused the federal security services to be strengthened further. Multiple counterterrorism laws came into effect, including the law to combat international terrorism (*Terrorismusbekämpfungsgesetz*) on 9 January 2002 and the Air

Traffic Act on 11 January 2005. Most notably, the Federal Office for the Protection of the Constitution and the Federal Criminal Police Office (BKA) was bestowed with greater authority. The BKA can now access flight information and telephone connections more readily, while the intelligence services received permission to retrieve information from banks, postal service operators, and air carriers. The supplementary law to fight against terrorism, passed by the grand coalition at the end of 2006, even further expanded the jurisdiction of the secret service.

A further development, is the effort to involve the Bundeswehr (federal armed forces) in the fight against terrorism and thus void the separation between internal and external security. The Basic Law stipulates in article 87a, section 2, "Apart from defence, the armed forces may be employed only to the extent expressly permitted by this Basic Law." Derogations for a deployment of the armed forces in internal security, according to articles 35, section 2, and 87a, sections 3 and 4 of the Basic Law, include "natural disasters," "a grave accident," or "to avert an imminent danger to the existence of free democratic basic order of the federation or of a Land." However, as early as 2001 Federal Interior Minister Otto Schily raised doubts about the sustainability of such sharp separation between internal and external security. The air safety law of 2005 allowed an "instantaneous action with the armed forces" against an airplane as an external measurement if the circumstances are such that the aircraft shall be employed against human life and the measurement is the only means of defence against the imminent danger (§ 14 section 3, air safety law). The Bundeswehr shall thus retain a kind of "authorization to shoot down the plane" in case of an extreme emergency involving a plane hijacked by terrorists.

Multiple people filed constitutional complaints against the air safety law before the Federal Constitutional Court. In a ruling of 15 February 2006, the first senate declared the provision to be unconstitutional and therefore invalid.

Six years later, in August 2012, the Federal Constitutional Court ruled in a rare plenary decision, that the Bundeswehr would be allowed to carry out domestic operations in major emergencies. The court decreed that it would be justifiable for the Bundeswehr to take military action on German soil, but the use of force would be restricted for clearly a delimited safety concern in "exceptional circumstances and catastrophic disasters." In any case, the deployment of the armed forces as well as the specific use of military means would be permitted only as a last resort, the ruling said. It stipulated that the final decision on the use of force by the Bundeswehr must be made by the federal government rather than the ministry of defence alone. However, the political debate over an expansion of potential domestic deployments of the armed forces is unlikely to rest with this ruling.

Establishing Joint Structures

The centralization of public-safety powers increasingly compromised Länder rights of sovereignty in the sphere of security policy, but another way to respond to the threat of terrorism included the construction of joint institutions for security actors. The joint institutions of the federation, Länder, police, and secret services maintain the checks and balances in the security landscape and improve the efficiency of security policies through coordination and collaboration.

This culminated in 2004 in the establishment of the Joint Terrorism Prevention Centre (GTAZ), which constituted a joint coordination centre of the security services of the Länder and of the federation to improve operational activity in the fight against international terrorism. It is devoted exclusively to combatting Islamist terrorism through improved communication, the exchange of information, better analytical competencies, early warning of possible threats, and coordination of operative measures against Islamist-motivated terrorism. The functions and objectives of GTAZ are similar to those of fusion centres in the United States.

Another joint federal-state organization is the Joint Internet Surveillance Centre (GIZ) – founded in 2007 – which analyses Islamist propaganda on the Internet. It is staffed by federal security service representatives; however, the Länder may participate as well. A National Cyberdefence Centre was established in 2011 to respond to attacks on government computers in Germany.

The most disputed of all joint institutions is the counterterrorism database, established in 2007 by thirty-eight different German security services. The database serves as an information network for affiliated intelligence and police services. It is run by the Federal Police Office (BKA), but many other federal and state security services have online access and can feed in new data. Data include terror suspects' names, addresses, date of birth, city of birth, email accounts, telecommunications, and bank accounts. In six years the database collected information on about 16,000 suspects. In September 2012, a separate database on right-wing extremists was set up.

As it became apparent at the end of 2011 that right-wing extremist terrorists could commit murderous attacks for years without the racist background of the attacks being recognized by the security services of the federation or of the Länder, the debate about centralizing the security services further was rekindled. Ten people died because security services in the federation and the Länder underestimated the danger of right-wing extremism and failed to cooperate. As a result of that debate, in November 2012 another Joint Counter-Extremism and Counterterrorism Centre (GETZ) was established to deal with right-wing and left-wing extremism, crimes committed by foreigners, sabotage, espionage and cyber defence.

Europeanization

The sovereignty of the Länder in the field of public security is increasingly being compromised in the process of Europeanization. The Europeanization of police cooperation had already begun in the 1970s, initially on the basis of an international treaty system and of the agreements to intergovernmental cooperation, which was typical for the European community (Knelangen 2001). With the third pillar of justice and domestic affairs, erected in the Treaty of Maastricht, along with the subsequent agreements, a distinct public security political field gradually developed at Community level, which transcended the originally strictly intergovernmental cooperation. Above all, the extension of the Schengen Agreement (1990) in the EU through the Treaty of Amsterdam (1999), as well as the terrorist attacks of 11 September 2001 led to significant acceleration of cooperation in the public security political field. The Treaty of Amsterdam stated that the EU must "maintain and develop the Union as an area of freedom, security and justice, in which the free movement of persons is assured in conjunction with appropriate measures with respect to external border controls, asylum, immigration and the prevention and combating of crime." The first work program putting this provision into effect was agreed at Tampere, Finland, in October 1999. After the Hague Program of 2004, the Stockholm Program of 2009 was the third five-year plan with guidelines for justice and home affairs of the member states. The program contained plans for a European security architecture through the extension of cooperation in police, military, and secret services, and measures in border-crossing data exchange between state authorities and surveillance of the Internet.

With time, structures of European public security emerged that are characterized by increasing institutionalization. To that end, count Europol (founded in 1998) as a law enforcement agency, its counterpart Eurojust (founded in 2002) in judicial criminal prosecution, and the Schengen cooperation and inclusive Schengen information system as a central instrument for police search and migration control. The European Police Academy (EPA), which was founded in 2005, provides collective police training. Already in the 1970s, joint terrorism–work groups consisting of police and secret services were developing, such as the TREVI-Group, among others (Aden 2015). After 2001, these structures were expanded to some extent. For example, a Counterterrorism Task Force was established at Europol. In 2004, following the terrorist attacks in Madrid, a new bureau called the European Union's Council to Ban Terrorism was created. The European Agency for the Management of Operational Cooperation at the External Borders of the Member States of the European Union (Frontex), founded in 2005, is the European Union agency for external border security. The EU Intelligence Analysis Centre (EU INTCEN) serves as an EU intelligence body. These European public security institutions possess no actual control – or at least no decisional authority vis-à-vis the national authorities. Rather, they have more cooperation and coordination functions or were designed as merely clearing offices.

Individual member countries stretched their cooperation in public security even beyond the EU structures. For example, in 2005 the interior and justice ministers of Belgium, Germany, France, Luxemburg, the Netherlands, Austria, and Spain arranged mutual access to national DNA databanks, fingerprint files, and vehicle registers in the Treaty of Prüm. What is more, the treaty's provisions contain the information exchange on crime prevention and general protection against threats to public security, deployment of air marshals, and the prevention of illegal migration.

Today's institutional characteristic seen in the public security systems of the EU is based on the regulations that stem from the Treaty of Nizza (2003). Article 29 of this treaty allows for a narrower coordination between member states' police and customs authorities, which includes the Europol cooperation, a narrower coordination of judicial authorities under the engagement of Eurojust, as well as a convergence of penal provisions.

EU integration of public security is in its infancy. Still, German federalism is being influenced by an EU public security system that has become increasingly dynamic. In the field of trans-border crime, European rules and norms have emerged that are shaping the work of police and justice on a national level. The federation has resisted interference in its areas of jurisdiction. Even the Länder were successful in constitutionally securing their involvement in relevant decisions made on the European level through the 1992 amendment to article 23 of the Basic Law.

The Länder have additionally tried to secure as much influence as possible over public security policymaking within the EU. Nonetheless, a series of shortcomings and problems interfere with the Länder's competencies in public security. First, the point should not be overlooked that the central course setting in European public security is intergovernmental. That means the national governments of member states, or rather the administrative bodies, comprise the negotiating and deciding actors. As a result, sub-national parliaments and governments are confronted with completed treaties, which they can affirm only.

Second, initiatives of the EU commission are forwarded to the Länder by the Bundesrat, whereupon coordination among the Länder can take place. By contrast, in intergovernmental cooperation on domestic politics and justice, the point of engagement of the Bundesrat and the involvement of the Länder remains unclear. Third, because of the inertia of the Bundesrat's process, it follows in practice that Länder make decisions predominantly on the level of the Interior and Justice Minister's Conference. Such an informal council lacks transparency.

Fourth, the Länder were successful in constitutionally securing their involvement in European public security politics via the Basic Law's article 23. In effect, however, when it comes to cooperation between national police departments and European security institutions, the federal authorities take on the role of gatekeeper, and then the federation, "like the BKA in the Europol Convention or the implementation of the Schengen Agreement, monopolizes external relations as the national central office" (Funk 2000, 307). Considering these problems, the German Länder are well advised to ensure that their sovereignty in the field of public security is not compromised further in the process of Europeanization.

Privatization

Another trend that increasingly influences Germany's public security structure is the fast growth of private security services. Financial scarcity and New Public Management have left their mark on public security (Kutscha 2006, 88). Today in Germany, aside from conventional police officers, there are several voluntary services under state supervision and based on police or security services: from the Sicherheitspartnern (security partners) in Brandenburg to the Sicherheitswacht (security guard) in Saxony and Bavaria (Elsbergen 2004). These services maintain public security and order through patrol duty in assigned territories. In this respect, they handle the domain of protection against threats to public security.

Most importantly, however, today the numerous private surveillance and security companies carry out operations that earlier were tasks of the police. The number of employed persons in those companies has multiplied since the 1980s; in more than 60,000 security companies in Germany, 2.2 million men and women are employed. In 2016, the revenue of surveillance and security companies accounted for approximately 35 billion euros (Bundesverband der Sicherheitswirtschaft 2016, 5). The attacks of 11 September have, moreover, initiated new markets in the security industry: for example in flight safety, maritime safety, and port security.

About 25 per cent of the assignments obtained by the firms come from the public sector. As a result, private facilities (such as firms' property) are not the only ones protected by private security services. Even publicly accessible buildings (warehouses, shopping malls, universities, hospitals, etc.) and public spaces (underground rail stations, stadiums, etc.) are watched and secured. According to article 33, section 4 of the Basic Law, unlike law enforcement, employees of private security services are not allowed to exercise sovereign coercion. However, in practice, a clear separation between sovereign functions and private business is in some sectors no longer recognizable as the contours of the spheres of action blur.

Notwithstanding the tremendously fast growth of private security services that will be controversially discussed for constitutional reasons, the further increased importance of the field is well anticipated. In fact, the actors who are actually responsible for guaranteeing public security – the Länder and the federation – can look not only for financial savings via the outsourcing. Efficiency is another reason that the cooperation between actors of the state and commercial actors is alluring to politicians involved in issues of security. Thus, well-trained Länder and federal police could attend to specialized security tasks while less-qualified operations could be overtaken by private security personnel.

The question of where the boundaries of this increasingly privatized public security lie – and then to what extent the state is allowed to delegate its monopoly on violence – has so far not been clearly answered. The constitutional arguments will not be decisive here, but rather it is the citizens' approval that is more important.

Case Study: Counterterrorism

Whereas in the 1970s and 1980s the domestic Rote Armee Fraktion (Red Army Faction, RAF) was perceived to pose the greatest terrorist threat to Germany, nowadays there is growing concern about global terrorist structures. A series of murders carried out by right-wing extremists showed that danger also emanates from domestic terrorist cells.

From the outset two trends have accompanied Germany's fight against terrorism: a gradual strengthening of federal security services and the effort to connect various security actors (federation/Länder and police/secret services) through joint structures.

Similarly, terrorism in the 1970s led to a strengthening of the Federal Criminal Police Office. Because of the RAF's activities, a special counterterrorism department was established in 1975. The BKA thereby effectively became a national coordination centre for the fight against politically motivated acts of violence. The BKA also experienced a vast expansion in personnel and materiel. The number of employees, which in 1965 was still 818, reached 3,339 by 1980. Similar developments followed the attacks of 11 September. In the context of the federalism reform of 2006, the responsibility for defence against international terrorism was transferred to the BKA for cases in which the danger transcends any one Land, the jurisdiction of a Land is not recognizable, or a Land requests assistance (article 73, section 1, number 9a of the Basic Law). For this purpose, numerous new competencies were conceded by the BKA as well as the federal police. The recent neo-Nazi murder series and Islamistic attacks have reinvigorated discussion about strengthening the federation's security authorities.

As the result of resistance from the Länder, who watched as this centralization increasingly compromised their rights of sovereignty in security policy, another answer to the threat of terrorism has been found: the construction of joint institutions for security actors. The purpose of joint institutions of the federation, Länder, police, and secret services are meant to maintain checks and balances in the security landscape and improve the efficiency of security policies through coordination and collaboration.

Debating Reforms of Public Security Arrangements in Germany

As a result of their complex security organization, federal systems face particular challenges in designing and successfully implementing appropriate and effective security measures. The situation in Germany is especially complicated. Germany's security system has as its antithesis the repression of the Nazi era. Experts have long warned that the integration structure typical of German federalism could lead to fatal consequences in the public security domain. Different organizations are sometimes unaware of information uncovered by others.

In 2011, the failure to identify a neo-Nazi terror cell, despite nearly seven years of assassinations, served as a wake-up call to improve cooperation between Germany's entangled federal and state security organizations. Collective-action problems between Germany's thirty-two Land police and intelligence agencies has been highlighted as a key shortcoming. Crisis meetings, information clearinghouses, and at least three investigative committees have been formed at the state or national level. Some experts requested that public security be overhauled completely.

A similar discussion took place seven years earlier. In 2004, Federal Minister of the Interior Otto Schily had proposed to redesignate the Land Offices of Criminal Investigation as branches of the Federal Criminal Police Office (BKA). In an interview, he sketched out his view of the ideal structure: "If I had a wish list, then it would be sensible to have a Federal Criminal Police Office which the 16 Land Offices of Criminal Investigation are assigned to as branch offices. Something similar would be conceivable for the intelligence services. Therein, to see a violation against federalism is simply false" (Süddeutsche Zeitung 2010). However, Schily did not count on the visceral reaction of the interior ministers of the Länder, with the result that his plans rapidly petered out. Still, public security has changed significantly in recent years. Shifting competencies, an increase in federal police activity, the Europeanization, and an increasing privatization of public security have all undermined the autonomy of the Länder in this area. However, this development runs up against constitutional limitations: to give up the Länder's sovereignty over policing would mean doing away with federalism in one of its core areas. This constitutional viewpoint has a theoretical complement. In modern democracies' quest to balance the state's objectives of security and freedom, federal systems have one decisive advantage: through the dichotomy of sovereignty, the authority of the state is limited. Particularly in times when, in response to threats and security risks, more and more people are quick to call for a strong government, the federal division of powers in the field of public security is a means to tame the leviathan.

To develop Germany's federal security structure further, the focus should, in principle, be on how improved coordination and cooperation can be realized without establishing new central authorities. Joint structures, which include both federal and Länder authorities in the field of public security (like the Joint Terrorism Prevention Centre), are a promising solution.

References

Aden, Hartmut, ed. 2015: *Police Cooperation in the European Union under the Treaty of Lisbon. Opportunities and Limitations*. Baden-Baden.

Allensbacher Archiv. 2016. IfD-Umfrage 11050 (January).

Bundeskriminalamt, ed. 2016. "Polizeiliche Kriminalstatistik Bundesrepublik Deutschland." Jahrbuch 2015. Wiesbaden.

Bundesverband der Sicherheitswirtschaft. 2016. *Ein Verband stellt sich vor.* Bad Homburg. https://www.bdsw.de/der-bdsw/downloads/3-pr-broschuere-des-bdsw-ein-verband-stellt-sich-vor/file.

Elsbergen, Gisbert van. 2004. *Wachen, kontrollieren, patrouillieren*. Wiesbaden: Kustodialisierung der Inneren Sicherheit. https://doi.org/10.1007/978-3-322-81012-0.

Eurostat. 2016. "Government Expenditure by Function." http://ec.europa.eu/eurostat/statistics-explained/index.php/Government_expenditure_by_function_%E2%80%93_COFOG.

Funk, Albrecht. 2000. "Das deutsche System der inneren Sicherheit im Zeitalter der Europäisierung." In *Staat, Demokratie und Innere Sicherheit in Deutschland*. Ed. Hans-Jürgen Lange. Opladen, S. 291–309.

Knelangen, Wilhelm. 2001. *Das Politikfeld innere Sicherheit im Integrationsprozess. Die Entstehung einer europäischen Politik der inneren Sicherheit*. Opladen: Springer. https://doi.org/10.1007/978-3-663-09548-4.

Kutscha, Martin. 2006. "Innere Sicherheit und Verfassung. In *Handbuch zum Recht der Inneren Sicherheit*, ed. Fredrik Roggan and Martin Kutscha. Berlin.

Lange, Hans-Jürgen. 1999. *Innere Sicherheit im politischen System der Bundesrepublik Deutschland*. Opladen: Springer. https://doi.org/10.1007/978-3-663-10355-4.

Pütter, Norbert. 2000. "Föderalismus und Innere Sicherheit." In *Staat, Demokratie und Innere Sicherheit in Deutschland*. Ed. Hans-Jürgen Lange. Opladen, S. 275–89.

Süddeutsche Zeitung. 2010. "Eigensinn der Länder lähmt Terrorbekämpfung." http://www.sueddeutsche.de/politik/sz-interview-mit-otto-schily-eigensinn-der-laender-laehmt-terrorbekaempfung-1.424894.

Further Readings

Beckman, James. 2007. *Comparative Legal Approaches to Homeland Security and Anti-Terrorism*, 89–112. Aldershot: Routledge.

Burgess, Michael, and G. Alan Tarr, eds. 2012. *Constitutional Dynamics in Federal Systems*. Montreal: Sub-national Perspectives.

Gunlicks, Arthur B. 2003. *The Länder and German Federalism*. Manchester: Manchester University Press. https://doi.org/10.7228/manchester/9780719065323.001.0001.

Hueglin, Thomas O., and Alan Fenna. 2006. *Comparative Federalism: A Systematic Inquiry*. Peterborough, ON: Broadview.

Jeffery, Charlie, ed. 1999. *Recasting German Federalism: The Legacies of Unification*. London: Pinter.

Leopold, Nils. 2002. "Eine Analyse der Anti-Terrorgesetzgebung." *Vorgänge* 3 (2002), S. 32.

Lioe, Kim Eduard. 2011. *Armed Forces in Law Enforcement Operations?* Heidelberg: Springer. https://doi.org/10.1007/978-3-642-15434-8.

Schönbohm, Arne. 2012. *Germany's Security. Cyber Crime and Cyber War*. Münster: Edition Octopus.

Terrill, Richard J. 2015. *World Criminal Justice Systems: A Comparative Survey*. 9th ed. New York: Routledge.

Wade, Marianne Wade, and Almir Maljevic, eds. 2010. *A War on Terror?: The European Stance on a New Threat: Changing Laws and Human Rights Implications*. New York: Springer. https://doi.org/10.1007/978-0-387-89291-7.

5 Public Security in the Indian "Union"

AJAY K. MEHRA

Introduction

Public security, which goes beyond the limited connotation of law and order as traditionally perceived, is meant to guarantee the protection of citizens, organizations, and institutions against threats to their well-being in order to ensure the prosperity of their communities. Clearly, there are qualitative, perceptional, and policy changes in the use of the police powers of the state that must focus on public good and get much more democratized. Significantly, the discussion on public security in a postcolonial society such as India needs to focus on transformation of the public security structures, police in particular, from traditions that made it an arm of the state to the new role to take on the emerging challenges of a democratic society and polity. Thus, on independence from British colonial rule on 15 August 1947 India retained many of the institutions and the culture of governance under its new constitution enacted in 1950. They also retained the police structure and the criminal justice system designed by the British under the framework of the Indian Police Act 1861 that came into existence following, and as a result of, the revolt of 1857.[1]

1 That followed enactment of the Criminal Procedure Code (CrPC) in 1861, the Indian Penal Code in 1862 (IPC), the Indian Evidence Act (1872), and the Indian (Imperial) Police (IP) in 1893. The three Acts codified and standardized a criminal justice system for the first time in India. Of these, the CrPC evolved from two different sets of criminal procedure laws existing in colonial India – one for the presidency towns and the other for the British provinces. In 1882, the CrPC was first enacted as a uniform law for the entire country, by consolidating the two. It was subsequently replaced by the CrPC of 1898. After Independence, the CrPC was first amended in 1955, then in 1969 and 1973. A significant amendment was with regard to the separation of Judiciary from the Executive. Law Commission of India (1969).

However, the postcolonial polity based on the Indian Constitution enacted on 26 January 1950 put the police and public security structure under its federal design that described the country as a "Union of States." As chairman of the drafting committee Dr B.R. Ambedkar explained the use of "Union" for "federation": "The [Indian] federation was not the result of an agreement by the states to join in a federation and that the federation not being the result of an agreement, no state has the right to secede from it. The federation is a union because it is indestructible" (*Constituent Assembly Debates* 1999, 43). This brought in a "unitary" bias in the federal framework of the Indian Constitution, which affects the police powers of the state too and hence the public security architecture as it has emerged. The strong-centre federal design of India nonetheless devolved the police to the states, but the structure operating under the British rule was retained. Some changes have been proposed in the past decade, and some have been adopted in some states, but the system remains largely the same. However, that the colonial police organization needed reforms was felt at the outset and, in keeping with the federal system, most states appointed police commissions beginning 1961, but they did not result in significant change. The first National Police Commission was appointed in 1979, but its eight-volume report was largely ignored by both the Union Government and the states, mainly as the result of political expediency.

Constitutional and Legal Landscape

Constitutionally, the framework of public security in India is enshrined in the principles of "justice, liberty, equality, and dignity" stated at the very outset in the Preamble as well as in Part III of the Constitution that details fundamental rights and elaborates upon the scope of the principles enshrined above. Within the overall framework of fundamental rights, physical safety is stressed in Article 21: "No person shall be deprived of his life and personal liberty except according to procedure established by law." However, a detailed discussion on "procedure established by law" vs "due process of law" in the Constituent Assembly (CA) in the context of life and liberty led to inclusion of Article 22 in the Constitution to ensure physical security of every individual within the territory of India by safeguarding against misuse of the laws by the police, either on their own or at the behest of their political masters (Mehra 2006, 116–17).

Physical security is entrenched as a federal power under Article 246 of the Constitution and the three lists created under it in the Seventh

Schedule – Union List (List I), State List (List II), and Concurrent List (III). For a discussion on structural aspects, the first two lists are important, and "security" is mentioned at the very beginning. List III has a bearing on public security because of provisions relating to procedural aspects of law.

List I begins with "Defence of India." The first ten entries deal with defence and/or security issues assigned to the Union Government (except entry 2A, which was added in 1976). List II begins with "public order" and entry 2 allocates "Police," therefore the function of policing, to the states. While the Constitution clearly distinguishes between national security/defence and public order (police)/internal security, India's "strong-centre" federalism was asserted in 1976 with entry 2A in List I. Items 1 to 4 in List III relating to criminal law, criminal procedure, preventive detention, and transfer prisoners from one state to another, support the public security framework.

Despite its strong-centre mindset, the Constituent Assembly unanimously delegated the public-order responsibilities to the states. Deployment of "armed forces of the Union" was neither considered nor proposed. Before the 42nd constitutional amendment (1976) brought in entry 2A, entries 1 to 9 in List I exclusively dealt with, and still do, responsibilities relating to the "defence of India." Entry 8 assigns the Intelligence Bureau and the Central Bureau of Investigation to the Union Government, and entry 9 empowers it with the use of preventive detention laws where necessary, but for defence, foreign affairs, or the security of India. List II was originally unambiguous in making the states responsible for "public order" and "Police."

Coalition politics in seven states following the fourth general elections in 1967 for the first time raised issues of federal imbalances, including in the field of public order. The Centre's right to deploy the central paramilitary forces, even to protect its own establishments, were questioned and tested in Kerala in September 1968 during the strike of the Union Government employees that threatened the government's properties, and twice in West Bengal in 1969, for the protection of Farakka Barrage and during clashes between workers of the Durgapur steel plant and the Provincial Armed Constabulary of Uttar Pradesh deployed by the Union Government. In each of these cases the Union Government made *suo motu* deployment (India 1988, 198). There has been no case of *suo motu* deployment of central forces since.

The 42nd Amendment of the Constitution of India, adopted in 1976 during the emergency, inserted Entry 2A in List I asserting the Union Government's right to intervene in internal security:

> 2A. Deployment of any armed forces of the Union or any other force subject to the control of the Union or any contingent or unit thereof in any State in aid of the civil power; powers jurisdiction, privileges and liabilities of the members of such forces while on such deployment.

Entries 1 and 2 of the List II were altered by the same amendment by making additions to "public order" in entry I and "Police" in entry 2, making the Central role unambiguous:

> 1. Public order *(but not including [the use of any naval, military or air force or any other armed force of the Union or of any other force subject to the control of the Union or of any contingent or unit thereof] in aid of the civil power).* (italics added)
>
> 2. [Police (including railway and village police) *subject to the provisions of entry 2A of List I.*][2] (italics added)

Significantly, the 44th Amendment (1978) of the Constitution, brought about by the Janata Party Government (1977–9) to undo the wrongs of the emergency era, retained these changes, reflecting a consensus across the political class on "federal supremacy," though the Congress government under Indira Gandhi was always criticized for its centralist attitude (see Mehra 2015). Article 355 of the Constitution, buttressed further by Article 365, which stresses the states' compliance with federal directives (a failure to comply could invite dismissal of an elected state government under Article 356), emphasizes federal supremacy. But no federal directive has been issued so far – the Union Government has issued only advisories on certain issues with no binding on compliance.

The Emergency Provisions

Part XVIII of the Constitution tilts the balance in favour of the Centre, even on issues relating to public order when the nation faces a national emergency. The much misused and criticized Article 356 empowers the

---

2 The texts in parentheses in both entries were inserted by the 42nd Amendment.

president of India to dismiss an elected state government, dissolve or put into suspended animation an elected state legislative assembly, bring a state under direct Central rule on the recommendation of the governor of the state, a Union Government appointee who has a five-year term, but enjoys office at the pleasure of the president of India (Articles 153 to 156 of the Constitution of India). However, dismissal of state governments on grounds of public order has been rare, except in Punjab, the Northeast, and Jammu and Kashmir, where public order deterioration due to terrorism and insurgency prompted the central rule. Since an imposition of Article 356 is not on grounds of good governance, public order cannot be used as an argument for its imposition. However, terrorism and insurgency are extraordinary situations involving special techniques of security agencies, state or Central. Hence, a use of this provision if public order disintegrates cannot be politically faulted. The provision thus provides extra advantage through a constitutional instrument to the Centre to take over governance, including law and order, in a state.[3]

National emergency under Article 352 has been in operation thrice, first in the wake of the Chinese war in 1962, which also saw the country through the 1965 Pakistan war, during the 1971 Bangladesh liberation war, and in that was first on the grounds of internal disturbance. The 1960s witnessed no controversy, and in 1971 the Bangladesh war brought in a rare political consensus. The use of an "internal disturbance" clause to declare national emergency in 1975–7 led to misuse of the provisions by the Union Government against political opponents;[4] i.e., misuse of the police and its powers for partisan politics. Consequently, the Janata Government substituted "armed rebellion" for "internal disturbance" through the 44th Amendment in 1978.

Article 355 stressing "the duty of the Union to protect every State against external aggression and internal disturbance and to ensure that the Government of every State is carried on in accordance with the provisions of this Constitution" empowers the Union Government to

3 While reversing the dismissal of the Arunachal Pradesh government on 15 December 2015 on the advice of the governor, the Supreme Court of India ruled on 13 July 2016 that the dismissal was ultra vires of the Constitution and that the governor's discretionary powers did not include advising the president to impose Article 356 without a floor test in the legislative assembly, thus limiting discretionary powers of the governor and the scope of Article 356. http://supremecourtofindia.nic.in/jonew/judis/43784.pdf.

4 See "Police during the Emergency," in Joshi (n.d., 4–5).

deploy the central paramilitary forces in a state where the state police is failing to maintain public order. Giving a paternalistic responsibility to the Union Government to protect the states, it reinforces federal supremacy. Similarly, Article 365 too gives greater responsibility to the Union Government to use Article 356 in case a state does not comply with its directives. However, Articles 355 and 365 have never been used together, neither has the Centre imposed Article 356 via 365 claiming non-compliance of a directive by a state. The Union Government has used Article 356 in disturbed areas, such as Punjab during the 1980s and Jammu and Kashmir (J&K) during the 1990s, but has never sent a directive to any state government, even under the worst circumstances of breakdown of public order. Instead it has issued advisories to concerned state governments, which were ignored.

Intergovernmental Assessment

Review of the Union-State relations in India has been undertaken twice – 1983 (Justice R.S. Sarkaria Commission) and 2008 (Justice M.M. Punchhi Commission). The Sarkaria Commission opined that supremacy rule is the cornerstone of federal power (India 1988, 28). Looking at the "federal supremacy" in comparative perspective, it maintained, "The rule of Federal Supremacy is a technique to avoid such absurdity, resolve conflicts and ensure harmony between the Union and State laws" (28). The commission maintained that "in case of conflict, the valid exercise of Union executive power must take priority over the valid exercise of State executive power. Indeed, it is an 'executive' facet of the principle of Union Supremacy."

The Sarkaria Commission, thus, in principle, justified the letter and spirit of Articles 355 and 365. In fact, responding to the commission, most states accepted the deployment of the armed forces of the Union as constitutional, if done "with the consent of the State Government concerned." Protecting their domain, some states qualified: "It is only when national security or integrity is threatened and the State Government adopts an intransigent attitude, that the Union Government should deploy its armed forces *suo motu*." There was also acceptance of the fact that the states needed the Union armed forces, because they lacked resources to build their police forces to respond to all contingencies (India 1988, 195). A few states disagreed about the extent of the Centre's power and constitutional responsibility under these provisions to deploy its forces "in aid of civil administration in States," while two state governments referred to the encroachments on the state rights made by the 42nd Amendment by altering Entry 2A in List I, and Entries 1 and 2 in List II. Another state government asserted its rights to requisition the CRPF on its requirement and convenience, and not at the Centre's discretion (195).

Even while accepting the doctrine of federal supremacy, the commission's overview of the internal security scenario was cautious. Aside from state police and the central paramilitary forces, the army, too, has had to step in a few times to tackle insurgency and terrorism. In fact, according to some reports, the Union Government considered using the air force to locate the hideouts of the Maoists in thick forests of Andhra Pradesh and Chhattisgarh when their ferocity increased during 2008–10. Had that happened, this would have been the first instance of the use of a defence force other than the army in tackling internal disturbance or armed rebellion. During a breakdown of public order, the normal legal criminal justice framework is insufficient; the Disturbed Areas Act is applied. But the application of this Act and its impact due to the sweeping powers it gives the security forces has met with severe resistance from the local population (e.g., in the northeastern states) and the civil rights movement in the country.

Observing that the state governments and their police organizations are often found wanting in training and professionalism when dealing with these extreme and abnormal situations, it also identified political partisanship as a bane of the state police. Without recommending a change in the relationship between the Union armed forces and state civil authorities, the commission advised that "before the Union Government deploys its armed and other forces in a State in aid of the civil power otherwise than on a request from the State Government, or declares an area within a State as 'disturbed,' it is desirable that the State Government should be consulted, wherever feasible, and its cooperation sought, even though prior consultation with the State Government is not obligatory." It also advised the states to strengthen their police forces (India 1988, 204).

Justice M.M. Punchhi Commission (2008–10)

The second Centre-State Relations Commission, headed by Justice M.M. Punchhi, applied itself to three issues with major import for the federal relations commission: "*suo motu* deployment of central forces in a state afflicted with violence and public order break-down," "creation of a national investigating agency (NIA)," and a "National Counter Terrorism Centre (NCTC)."

The Punchhi Commission was more cautious in considering the options of *suo motu* deployment of the central forces in the states. While admitting the use of Article 355, which has not been used by the Union Government, even where it could have been used, "depending upon the circumstances, the nature and gravity of the national disturbance." It even justified the possibility of using Article 356 in a limited area of a state. However, agreeing in principle with the states suggesting greater support by the Union in improving the lot of their police forces and other inter-security infrastructure, the commission also added a detailed cautionary note, insisting that India's federal character meant that the central intervention under Article 355 should happen "on rarest of the rare occasions and only after *suo motu* Deployment of Central Forces in the States all other remedial measures and interventions have failed to normalize the situation and that too for a shortest required period of time" (India 2010a, 56–7).

A major difference between the security scenario in the 1980s, when the Sarkaria Commission prepared its report, and end of the first decade of the twenty-first century, when the Punchhi Commission met, was that several major challenges confronting security of the country overlapping the domains of national and internal security had emerged: international terrorism, expanding terrain of Naxalism, cybercrime, and so on. The deficit of police reform that could have equipped the police to take on many of them on their own has been admitted, but the role of the Union Government both as a stakeholder in this task and as responsible for supporting the efforts of the states, too, has been acknowledged. The setting up of the NIA in 2008 in the wake of the 26/11 Mumbai terrorist attack has been highlighted and the need for a NCTC has also been recommended.

The review of the federal powers and views of the states indicate that though federal supremacy has been upheld, the states have accepted federal powers in public security with reservations. These reviews, however, have not led to many fundamental changes, though some of them are warranted.

Special Policing Powers

A significant and controversial dimension of federal policing powers is the Armed Forces Special Powers Act (AFSPA). Enacted in 1958 to deal with the insurgency in Nagaland, in India's northeast, it seeks to give special powers to the members of the armed forces in disturbed areas. It was further amended, as India's northeastern region was reorganized in the 1970s and subsequently in the 1980s, to create seven states, in 1960, 1970, 1972, and 1986.[5] In the 1990s, when J&K, simmering since partition of the subcontinent with rival claims from India and Pakistan, slipped into the politics of militancy, the Act was promulgated there (Mehra 2011b).

The two do not differ either in content or application to give the governor of the concerned state the power to declare the state, or part of it, disturbed. The Acts raise a statutory warning by underlining that the declaration cannot be arbitrary, meaning that the reasons have to be substantive and clearly stated. It also cannot be applied indefinitely and must be reviewed periodically. The Act is meant "to enable certain special powers to be conferred upon members of the armed forces in disturbed areas." Yet it has caused tension in the relationship between the Union and the states. Pronouncements by the Supreme Court of India have stressed that the armed forces must act in cooperation with the "district administration," which is under the concerned state government, and that the power or arrest must be with a responsible senior officer.

The AFSPA is clearly an extraordinary law for unusual situations. Since its origin and operations are in the realm of the state, the state perspective dominates. The state's perception is reactive to an atypical state of affairs for which it may or may not be responsible. In the Indian case, for example, several problems of insurgency and terrorism in the northeast region, such as the Naga, Mizo, and others, have been circumstantial, either inherited in the process of decolonization or developed as the result of geopolitics of the region. The problems in Assam, Manipur, Tripura, and Meghalaya on the other hand are political and rooted in the society and politics of these states developed since Independence. The J&K issue is more complex as the result of the legacies of the decolonization.

The AFSPA is rooted in paradoxes and dilemmas of a democratic state. While theoretically people take precedence, operationally the

5 See https://indiacode.nic.in/bitstream/123456789/1527/1/195828.pdf (accessed 13 May 2018).

state must protect itself before protecting its people. Hence *raison d'état* (reason of state) prevails over reason of the people. Yet the state, too, has to take into account that the laws are made for the people by people's representatives. If its execution hurts the people it is supposed to protect, both transparency (in the security scenario it becomes an ex post facto necessity) and accountability structures are not in place. In such a case, instead of offering a stout defence, the state must introspect and put such mechanisms in place to the satisfaction of people and communities. The defence of the armed forces in complex situations is obligatory, but protection and satisfaction of the people is paramount. This also means that the politics of compliance arising out of the current political culture and the politics of defiance arising out of electoral populism are both detrimental to people as well as the national interest. The northeast and J&K theatres are witnessing this, and an introspective national consensus is required. Since the party in power and political actors may change in New Delhi, the theatres need to be handled with people-centric deftness.

This was underlined on 8 July 2016 with precision by the Supreme Court of India. Delivering the judgment on the plea of Extra Judicial Execution Victim Families Association from the northeastern state of Manipur, a two-judge bench questioned continued promulgation of the AFSPA and ordered the Union Government, the state government, and the army to hold a judicial inquiry into the reported cases of extrajudicial killings. The judgment would have implications for the application of the AFSPA in the concerned states as well as federal responsibility and relations on public security.[6]

Metrics and the Fiscal Dimension

As per the constitutional division of power, the quotidian public security and policing functions in India are entrusted to thirty-six (twenty-nine states and seven union territories) organizationally similar police organizations situated in police stations and are unarmed, except certain higher-echelon officers in a rigidly hierarchical organizational structure. District Armed Police is a reserve at the headquarters that is deployed as needed. All states also have a special armed reserve paramilitary police, variously nomenclatured and with strength commensurate to

6 https://indiankanoon.org/doc/83144198/.

the state's needs. These are backed by specialized support agencies such as the Criminal Investigation Department, forensic laboratory, Special Branch,[7] the Home Guard,[8] and commando battalions for VIP security duties.

Between 1953 and 2013, total cognizable crime[9] under the Indian Penal Code (IPC) registered a 339.8 per cent growth (National Crime Records Bureau (2016). India's population of 370 million in 1953 grew to 1.27 billion in the next six decades. Obviously, crime has risen at a faster rate than the population, albeit at a different rate for different categories, in different states. A more recent perspective shows that total cognizable crime under the IPC and SLL was 6,028,781 in 2004, which increased to 7,229,193 by 2014 at the rate of 19.9 per cent. The IPC crimes were 39 per cent of the total cognizable crimes (ibid.).

The National Crime Records Bureau data on murder over a decade (2004–13) do not indicate an increasing trend (table 5.1). Organized, violent (such as terrorism), and technology-assisted crimes (such as cybercrime)[10] have added new dimensions to security threats and new challenges for the public security structure in the country. Terrorism and insurgency in the northeastern region, J&K and Maoist insurgency (referred as left-wing extremism or LWE) in over 106 districts in ten

---

7 Special Branch is a unit designed by the British colonial government responsible for matters of national security. A Special Branch unit acquires and develops intelligence of a political nature and conducts investigations to protect the state from perceived threats of subversion – particularly terrorism and other extremist activity.

8 An organization auxiliary to the Indian police, raised voluntarily and locally, the Home Guard rural and urban are recruited from a cross section of the society, for a tenure of three to five years. The selected ones are trained by the police further in law-and-order functions. The Union Ministry of Home Affairs (MHA) frames policies and shares resources for their raising, training, and maintenance.

9 The Criminal Procedure Code (CrPC) classifies all crimes into two categories: (1) cognizable crime, where the investigating officer does not require the order of a magistrate and can effect arrest without warrant; and (2) non-cognizable crime, which cannot be investigated by police without the order of a competent magistrate. http://mospi.nic.in/Mospi_New/upload/SYB2014/CH-37-CRIME%20STATISTICS/Crime-write%20up.pdf.

10 The cases of cybercrime under different categories of IPC increased from 49.1 per cent (1,115 cases) in 2013, to 69.9 per cent (2,272 cases) in 2014. Most were under the categories of forgery and cheating. This indicates how this category of crime poses new challenges to the security establishment in India. National Crime Records Bureau (2016, chapter 18, 168).

Table 5.1. Decadal and Quinquennial Percentage Changes in Homicide

Crime Head	Year					
	2004	2009	2010	2011	2012	2013
Murder	33529	33981	33335	34305	34434	33201
Percentage Change	(3.1)	(2.8)	(2.8)	(2.8)	(2.8)	(2.7)
Attempt to Murder	27890	29038	29421	31385	35138	35417
Percentage Change	(2.6)	(2.5)	(2.5)	(2.6)	(2.9)	(2.9)
Culpable Homicide not amounting to Murder	3935	3930	3782	3707	3620	3380
Percentage Change	(0.4)	(0.3)	(0.3)	(0.3)	(0.3)	(0.3)

Source: http://ncrb.gov.in/ (accessed 17 July 2016).

states (35 districts in seven states are declared by the Government of India as the worst affected) of the 707 districts[11] in twenty-nine states and seven union territories pose enormous challenges to India's public security. The Ministry of Home Affairs, *Government of India's Annual Report* (2015–16), mentions 1,088 incidents of LWE violence in 2015, resulting in 226 deaths, as compared to 1091 incidents with 310 resultant deaths in 2014.[12]

11 A district is the key administrative division below state level in India for general and public security administration. Known as *zilla* under the Mughal administration, the nomenclature that continues in north India, the British called them districts and reorganized them according to their convenience. The number of districts keep increasing from time to time, as the states are free to create new districts for administrative convenience. The number given is for 2017 and added up from the official website of each state (twenty-nine) and union territory (seven).

12 Precise data on the LWE are not available. The figures quoted here have been taken from the government sources (Ministry of Home Affairs 2013) and the South Asia Terrorism Portal (2001). Communist insurgency began in India in a few districts of Hyderabad state in 1946 but was withdrawn after Independence in 1951 after Stalin's advice to the Indian communists. It resurfaced in West Bengal in 1967 and was crushed in 1972. It has sustained since resurfacing in the southern part of the country since the late 1970s, going through several phases (Mehra 2008). The LWE affected districts are directly monitored by the federal government through a special division in the MHA. https://mha.gov.in/division_of_mha/left-wing-extremism-division (accessed 13 May 2018). For the MHA data, see Ministry of Home Affairs (2016).

Table 5.2. Sanctioned and Actual Strength of Police, 2015

Sr. No.	Items	Sanctioned	Actual
(i)	Population-per-policeperson	540	720
(ii)	Area in Sq. Km. per policeperson	1.4	1.84
(iii)	Transport Facility per 100 policepersons	7.24	9.53

Source: Bureau of Police Research & Development (2015).

Though still below international standards, the availability of policepersons in ratio to the population has improved over the years. While 712 people were being cared for by each policeperson in 2004, in 2014 the figure was reduced to 547. Still the government of India's own figures show that 24 per cent of the sanctioned vacancies are lying vacant. Calculated in terms of per 100,000 population, India had 147.10 civil policepersons in 2014, which came to 182.68 if the armed police were added. Obviously, each policeperson in India also serves a relatively larger area with limitations of transport and accessibility in rural areas (table 5.1). In comparison, Australia has 212, Canada has 202, France has 356, United Kingdom has 307, United States has 251, and Germany has 296 policepersons per 100,000 population. The Union Government has no powers to ensure that states fill the sanctioned strength.

An eleven-year perspective (2004–14) on police in table 5.3 is only indicative, as strength and facilities vary according to size and population of each state. The figures nonetheless indicate that the sanctioned strength of civil police has been four times that of population growth, yet policepersons per 100,000 population has been lower than international standards. That the states have not maintained the sanctioned strength only makes things worse. The resulting discrepancies have also been attributed to politico-administrative indifference to financial profligacy of the state governments, which are responsible for and autonomous in maintaining their public security agencies.[13] There are 215 training centres for police personnel in

13 The commissioned "performance audit" reviews covering select general category and special category states in 2010 by the controller and auditor general of India showed that in most cases, the actual release of funds fell significantly short of this outlay – in some cases the Centre did not contribute its share, in others the states lagged behind. PRS Legislative Research (2010).

Table 5.3. National Basic Police Data, 2004–2014

S. No	Particulars	2004	2006	2008	2010	2012	2014	% age change over last 11 years
1	Projected Population (1st October–Each year) in thousands	1,089,915	1,123,993	1,157,245	1,189,793	1,217,327	1,238,885	
			3.13	2.96	2.81	2.31	1.77	13.67
2	Sanctioned Strength of Civil Police including Distt. Armed Reserve Police	1,170,722	1,210,742	1,619,163	1,640,342	1,765,404	1,822,358	
			3.42	33.73	1.31	7.62	3.23	55.66
3	Sanctioned Strength of State Armed Police	359,667	421,909	436,878	424,028	443,623	440,864	
			17.31	3.55	–2.94	4.62	–0.62	22.58
4	Sanctioned Strength of Total State Police Force	1,530,389	1,632,651	2,056,041	2,064,370	2,209,027	2,263,222	
			6.68	25.93	0.41	7.01	9.63	47.89
5	Population per Policeman	712.18	688.45	562.85	576.00	551.07	547.00	
			–3.33	–18.24	2.34	–4.33	–0.74	–23.19

S. No	Particulars	2004	2006	2008	2010	2012	2014	% age change over last 11 years
6	Policemen hundred thousand of population							
	(i) Civil Police	107.41	107.72	139.92	137.87	145.02	147.10	
	(ii) Total Police	140.41	145.25	177.67	173.51	181.47	182.68	
			3.45	22.32	–2.34	4.59	0.67	30.10
7	Policemen per hundred square kms area							
	(i) Civil Police	36.97	38.24	51.14	51.80	55.75	57.55	
			3.44	33.73	1.29	7.63	3.23	55.67
	(ii) Total Police	48.33	51.56	64.93	65.20	69.76	71.48	
			6.68	25.93	0.42	6.99	2.47	47.90
8	Number of Police Stations	12,548	12,833	13,421	13,948	14,360	15,090	
			2.27	4.58	4.19	2.69	5.08	20.26

Source: Bureau of Police Research & Development (2015).

different states, but their statewise list (available from the Bureau of Police Research and Development) does not give a clear picture of their capacity to train personnel. Further, some new states created during the past two decades do not have proper training facilities for different ranks.

Police and public security organizations under the Union Government can broadly be divided into six categories: (1) police organizations of the union territories, which are directly under the Union Government and are like the police in any other state; (2) the IPS, which is recruited, allocated, trained, and managed by the Union Government, but once allocated to the states, the cadre is managed by the respective states; (3) training institutes such as the Sardar Vallabhbhai Patel National Police Academy (Hyderabad); (4) police organizations devoted to research and record-keeping, namely, the Bureau of Police Research and Development, National Crime Records Bureau (NCRB), National Investigation Agency (established 2008), and Crime and Criminal Tracking Network and Systems, a project started in 2009 within NCRB under the Common Integrated Police Application scheme); and (5) six armed police organizations – Border Security Force (BSF), Central Industrial Security Force, Central Reserve Police Force (CRPF), Indo-Tibetan Border Police (ITBP), Sashastra Seema Bal (SSB); and National Security Guards (NSG) – and one paramilitary organization – Assam Rifles (AR). Each one of these is under the MHA.

Their functions are as follows:

AR, BSF, ITBP and SSB are the "Border Guarding Forces" while CRPF assists the State Governments/UT Administrations in matters related to maintenance of Public Order and is also trained and equipped for assisting them in internal security/counter insurgency duties. The Rapid Action Force (RAF) and Commando Battalion for Resolute Action (CoBRA) are specialized wings of the CRPF to deal with riots and LWE respectively. CISF provides security and protection to vital installations, Public Sector Undertakings (PSUs), airports, industrial buildings, museums, Government buildings, etc. NSG is a specialized force for counterterrorism and anti-hijacking operations. It is also entrusted with the task of securing high-risk VIPs.[14] The CRPF (along with its wings RAF and CoBRA) is akin to armed police in States and is mandated to be deployed for internal security duties such as violent protests, communal riots, collective violence and armed uprising, such as Maoist Extremism.

14 MHA, *Annual Report* (2011–12).

Naturally, in the context of federal relations it has been the most controversial. The controversy is whether it can ever be deployed *suo motu*, as its mandate is to aid the civil administration of the concerned state, and the convention is that the deployment would be at the request of a state government.

Though the state governments fund their respective police organizations, the Union Government gives special grants to states from time to time to modernize their police forces and deal with any arising special problem.[15] The central assistance for modernization has two components: to upgrade their capabilities and acquire the latest equipment to modernize the police, and the to confront special challenges such as insurgency, terrorism, and Naxalism. The schemes of special grants are aimed at reducing "the dependence of the State Governments on the Army and Central Police Forces for internal security and law and order by equipping the State Police Forces adequately and imparting the required training."[16] The Union Government has been giving special assistance to some states to augment the drug law-enforcement capabilities of their police organizations and to procure necessary infrastructure and equipment. In fact, in cases of special challenges, such as the insurgency in the northeast, extremism in J&K, and Maoist challenges in a number of states, the Union Government has been underwriting almost the entire security expenditure in the affected states.

Police Expenditure

Given the federal division outlined above, the budgets are separately drawn up by the Union Government, which budgets for the Central Police Organizations and the seven union territories, and the twenty-nine states. In 2014–15, the Union Government expenditure on its eight police organizations was ₹ 385.87 billion in 2014–15, which was an

---

15 *Modernization of Police Force Scheme Book* of the MHA says, "'Police' and 'law and order' is a State subject … and it is primarily the responsibility of the State Governments to modernize and adequately equip their police forces for meeting the challenges to law and order and internal security. However, due to financial and other constraints, their efforts have often not been up to the desired level, hence, the Ministry of Home Affairs (MHA) has been supplementing their efforts and resources from time to time." https://mha.gov.in/division_of_mha/modernisation-of-state-police-forces-mpf-scheme (accessed 13 May 2018).

16 Op. cit., 268.

Table 5.4. Central, State, and UT Police Budgets (₹ billion)

	2013–14	2014–15	Change (%)
Total police	631.46	742.57	17.59
Police training	11.18	10.86	–2.87
Police housing	372.82	351.44	–5.74

Source: Bureau of Police Research & Development (2017).

increase of 40.55 per cent over ₹ 274.53 billion in 2010–11. This also indicates the increasing role of the CPOs in the public security role across the country, including on the borders, as three of the CPOs are border police (Bureau of Police Research & Development 2017).

The annual expenditure on police by the Indian states is 2.95 per cent of their budget, but varies from state to state, and the Union Government has little say in this except providing occasional additional funds (Bureau of Police Research & Development 2015, 72. However, the Union Government provides modernization funds to the states from time to time and also meets the expenditure of special policing needs arising from insurgency and terrorism.

The budget for each CPO as well as state and union territory separately, broken out by item, would be a subject for an independent analysis. The data put out by the Bureau of Police Research and Organization under the Union Ministry of Home Affairs indicates that while the total police expenditure increased in 2014–15 over the previous year by 17.59 per cent, expenditure on training and housing decreased by 2.87 and 5.74 per cent respectively (table 5.4). Obviously, policing consumes a greater part of the budget than training and infrastructure for personnel welfare.

Public Security Experiences and Federal Debate

Debates and disputes on public security from a federal perspective have come into the open since 1967 when the Indian National Congress weakened and opposition parties shared power in several states, intensifying political competition. The disputes over deployment of the central forces in this context, discussed earlier, are now essentially resolved.

A second dispute is over the AFSPA in the northeast and J&K. Protests by the states on its operation and demands for the repeal of the

Act are loud, shrill, and clear. However, since the armed forces and the Union Government consider it necessary for special security situation, the Supreme Court of India has advised oversight mechanisms against the complaints of abuse, on the basis of reports by a special commission headed by retired Supreme Court Judge Santosh Hegde, appointed to probe extrajudicial killings in Manipur.[17] This nonetheless continues to be a thorn in relations between the Union Government and the concerned states, while also being criticized by human rights groups. The Committee on Amendments to Criminal Law (2013), headed by retired Chief Justice of India Jagdish Sharan Verma to review laws against sexual assault, said that the AFSPA legitimized impunity for sexual violence, and recommended immediate review of the continuance of the AFSPA in internal areas of conflict (Amnesty International India 2013; Mehra 2011b).

One of the most discussed and disputed issues in the past twenty-five years is the demolition of Babari Masjid, a mosque purported to have been built in the name of the first Mughal emperor, Babar, by his general Mir Baqi in the pilgrimage town of Ayodhya in Uttar Pradesh (UP). Significant issues disputed and debated in the case were federal supremacy and state's responsibilities.

Ayodhya

Ayodhya is a town of 60,000 people, covering twenty-five square kilometres in central Uttar Pradesh. According to mythology, it was the capital of Awadh, ruled by a virtuous King Dashrath, whose eldest son, Rama, is worshipped as a prominent Hindu deity. Obviously, popular belief is that Lord Rama was born in the city.

On 6 December 2012, Babari Masjid (built 1529 CE) was demolished by a frenzied religious gathering prepared and armed with axes, hammers, and crowbars. The destruction was rooted in a dispute dating back to the mid-nineteenth century. Certain Hindu leaders and organizations claimed that the mosque was built upon the site of a Hindu temple commemorating the birthplace of Lord Rama. In the 1980s Hindu

17 The commission found that the killing of six persons in Manipur were not genuine encounters and the victims did not have criminal records. The report said that the guidelines on encounters laid down by the Supreme Court in the Naga People's Movement case was not followed. Human Rights Law Network (n.d.).

organization Vishwa Hindu Parishad (VHP) began a movement to reclaim the holy spot from the Muslims, and the group was politically adopted by the Hindu rightist party BJP. The party, its cultural patron Rashtriya Swayamsewak Sangh (RSS), along with the VHP, organized camps of militant Hindu volunteers in Ayodhya in a show of strength. When the demolition took place, UP was ruled by a BJP-led government and the Centre was being ruled by P.V. Narashimha Rao–led Congress government. BJP had assured the prime minister that there would be no violence when the devotees assembled.

However, at the instigation of VHP and its associate organizations the Hindu volunteers had come prepared to demolish the mosque. UP's Chief Minister Kalyan Singh (BJP), had instructed the police not to use force on the volunteers. It was later revealed that only a few kilometres away a CRPF reinforcement was camping for deployment and was ready to move in case of a trouble. The state government avoided requisitioning them; obviously, partisanship had better of the constitutional role of the state government. The Union Government was well within its constitutional rights using Article 355 and 365 of the Constitution of India to send in reinforcements of CRPF to prevent demolition under the federal supremacy clause. The prime minister and his home minister were taken by surprise and took no action (see Jha and Jha 2012; and Sitapati 2016). The case continues to be a major part of the debate on federalism, federal supremacy, and state autonomy in India.

Conclusion

A review of the public security framework in India brings to light a paradox. First, public security in India functions within the strong-centre framework of the Constitution. Second, within such a framework, states in India have a statutorily defined role. They have full autonomy to develop and augment their capacities to meet most public security challenges. However, all the states, without exception, have faltered in doing so since Independence for reasons of political expediency. That is also a factor for federal inaction in the matter (Mehra 2011a). Indeed, the states have had their security structures as well as resources, and over the years the Union Government too has developed special schemes to help the states to enhance their capacities. But a common complaint of the Union Government agencies has been that most states have squandered federal financial assistance on non-essential purchases. Although they have their own resources, states have missed the opportunity to develop people-centric public safety structures. As a result, their agencies face a growing deficit in funds, personnel, efficacy, and public trust.

Why have the states faltered? There are no ready answers. One needs to delve deep into fiscal management by states, the status of their perspective planning, their vision of significance of public security beyond a limited view built around traditional public order, partisanship of the Union Government during a twenty-five year era of coalition politics from 1989 to 2014 in both at the Centre and in states and a continuing political situation of weak-organization parties running the country's political show, and so on. The states have seldom displayed vision, if ever, in broadening their perspective to contextualize public order issues with public security; public safety as a larger concept has not yet entered the policy domain in states in India. Profligacy by the states notwithstanding, a larger issue that hinders good governance is the lack of security sector reform. Factors such as populism and partisanship have weakened their fiscal management further. Even funds for modernization of the police received as grant-in-aid from the Union Government have allegedly been diverted to other heads. Many new states do not have proper training facilities for police because in the process of their bifurcation, training institutes have remained with one part, while the other has not been able to create new facilities the required new facilities immediately. The paradox of autonomy under a federal setup that discourages states from enacting security sector reform is difficult to explain rationally.

These developments have naturally strengthened the hand of the Union Government during times of crisis. Federal balance in India on fiscal matters tilts towards the Centre; naturally it is so in public security as well. However, on balance, that has not necessarily given the Union Government the initiative to *suo motu* intervene in the states. The deployment of the central forces in critical times has faltered; the Ayodhya case 1992 discussed above clearly indicates that. Article 355 of the Constitution has never been used to give directives to any state; at the most, the Union Government has issued advisories. Article 365, too, has never been used. The use of Article 356, except in the 1980s at the height of terrorism in Punjab, has not even been considered.

Performance and efficacy of the central interventions on public security has been mixed. Whenever the central forces or the army has been deployed in riots or other kinds of violence, the situation has been brought under control quickly. However, wherever the central forces have been deployed for a prolonged period, such as in the northeast region (Das 2013) or in J&K (Ghosh 2010), even in the LWE areas (Mehra 2008), complaints of human rights violations have surfaced.

Following the 21 February 2013 terrorist-orchestrated twin blasts in Hyderabad, capital of Telangana state, demands for setting up a NCTC, which has been discussed since the 26 November terror attack in Mumbai in 2008, have resurfaced. However, despite having failed to prevent terrorist attacks or to investigate the cases efficiently, several states decry the violation of their autonomy. The Union Government wanted powers for the NCTC to move *suo motu* to take up a case of a terror attack and the powers of cordon, search, seizure, and arrest; the states have insisted that the NCTC operations should be initiated only if, on being informed, the concerned state has given its approval. Eventually the Centre relented: on 26 February 2013 it conceded that the NCTC operations would begin only after informing the states. Such cases of partisanship are real in India and get in the way of dealing with federal crimes efficaciously. The only way out is for the Union Government to take up the initiative to convene an all-party meeting to resolve the issue of partisanship and with the help of experts prepare an agenda for a bipartisan approach to federal crimes and use of federal agencies. It is also worthwhile for the Union Government to energize the Inter-State Council, the statutory intergovernmental body for federal policy planning and dispute resolution, which is set up under Article 263 of the Constitution as an agency to coordinate policies between the Centre and the states as well as among the states, more particularly identifying and coordinating common interests for a better federal relation. This institution, however, remains grossly underutilized.

Most reports of commissions and scholarly studies have, therefore, emphasized police and criminal justice reforms, strengthening the civil police in the states, and the creation of a strong accountability and oversight mechanisms (Sen 2010). The cited case study emphasizes that public security, like most areas of union-state cooperation, is increasingly emerging through cooperative federalism. Constitutional provisions and mechanisms exist where the two levels of government can take the cooperation forward and iron out any differences. The growing political mosaic of India's governing structure would have to recognize this and strengthen the available structures for public good.

References

Amnesty International India. 2013. "Briefing: The Armed Forces Special Powers Act: A Renewed Debate in India on Human Rights and National Security." https://www.amnestyusa.org/files/asa200422013en.pdf.

Bureau of Police Research & Development. 2015. *Data on Police Organisations.* New Delhi: BPRD. http://bprd.nic.in/WriteReadData/userfiles/file/201607121235174125303FinalDATABOOKSMALL2015.pdf.

– 2017. *Data on Police Organisation.* New Delhi. BPRD. http://www.bprd.nic.in/WriteReadData/userfiles/file/databook2017.pdf (accessed 13 May 2017).

Constituent Assembly Debates, Official Report. 1999. New Delhi: Lok Sabha Secretariat.

Das, Samir Kumar. 2013. *Governing India's Northeast: Essays on Insurgency, Development and the Culture of Peace, Springerbriefs in Political Science*, vol. 13. New Delhi: Springer India. https://doi.org/10.1007/978-81-322-1146-4.

Ghosh, Partha S. 2010. "Kashmir Revisited: Factoring Governance, Terrorism and Pakistan, as Usual." Working Paper No. 54. Heidelberg Papers in South Asian and Comparative Politics. Heidelberg: South Asia Institute, University of Heidelberg, Germany.

Human Rights Law Network. n.d. *Santosh Hegde Commission Submits Report on Manipur Extra Judicial Killings.* http://www.hrln.org/hrln/criminal-justice/reports/1501-santosh-hegde-commission-submits-report-on-manipur-extra-judicial-killings.html.

India, Government of. 1988. *Report of the Commission on Centre-State Relations*, Part I (Chair: R.S. Sarkaria). New Delhi: Ministry of Home Affairs.

India, Government of. 2010a. *Commission on Centre-State Relations Report, Volume-V: Internal Security, Criminal Justice and Centre State Cooperation* (Chair: M.M. Punchhi). New Delhi: Inter-State Council Secretariat, Ministry of Home Affairs. http://interstatecouncil.nic.in/wp-content/uploads/2015/06/volume5.pdf.

Jha, Krishna, and Dhirendra K. Jha. 2012. *Ayodhya: The Dark Night.* New Delhi: HarperCollins India.

Joshi, G.P. n.d. "Police Accountability in India." Commonwealth Human Rights Initiative. http://www.humanrightsinitiative.org/programs/aj/police/papers/gpj/police_accountability_in_india.pdf.

Law Commission of India. 1969. Forty-First Report (The Code of Criminal Procedure, 1898. http://lawcommissionofindia.nic.in/1-50/Report41.pdf.

Mehra, Ajay K. 2006. "'Due Process or 'Procedure Established by Law.'" In *Supreme Court vs Constitution: A Challenge to Federalism.* Edited by Pran Chopra, 115–30. New Delhi: Sage.

– 2008. "India's Experiment with Revolution." Working Paper No. 40. Heidelberg: Heidelberg Papers in South Asian and Comparative Politics, South Asia Institute, University of Heidelberg, Germany.

– 2011a. "Police Reforms in India: Imperatives, Discourse and Reality." In *The Police, State and Society: Perspectives from India and France*, ed. Ajay K. Mehra and Rene Levy, 263–86. New Delhi: Pearson India.

– 2011b. "When the Armed Forces Police." *Geopolitics* 2, no. 7 (December): 60–2.

– 2015. "The Emergency Needs Larger Reflections." *Mainstream Weekly*, 15 August.

Ministry of Home Affairs. 2013. "Lok Sabha, Unstarred Question No. 1374." http://mha1.nic.in/par2013/par2013-pdfs/ls-050313/LSQ.1374.Eng.pdf.

– 2016. *Annual Report: 2015–16*. https://mha.gov.in/sites/default/files/AR%28E%291516.pdf (accessed 13 May 2018).

National Crime Records Bureau. 2016. *Crime in India*. http://ncrb.gov.in.

PRS Legislative Research. 2010. "Modernization of Police Forces in Indian States." http://www.prsindia.org/theprsblog/?p=163.

Report of Committee on Amendment of Criminal Law (Chair: Justice Jadgish Sharan Verma). http://www.thehindu.com/migration_catalog/article12284683.ece/BINARY/Justice%20Verma%20Committee%20Report%20on%20Amendments%20to%20Criminal%20Law (accessed 13 May 2018).

Sen, Sankar. 2010. *Enforcing Police Accountability through Civilian Oversight*. New Delhi: Sage. https://doi.org/10.4135/9788132106005.

Sitapati, Vinay. 2016. *Half Lion: How P.V. Narasimha Rao Transformed India*. New Delhi: Penguin.

South Asia Terrorism Portal. 2001. "Worst Affected Districts." http://www.satp.org/satporgtp/countries/india/maoist/data_sheets/affecteddistrict.htm.

6 Mexico

EDGAR MOHAR

Introduction

Mexico faces persistent challenges in security and public safety. Foremost among these is violent crime associated with organized-crime groups (OCG) – mostly drug-trafficking organizations – that is responsible for a death toll in excess of 47,000[1] between 2006 and 2012. Although the crisis has multiple causes, it is fuelled by corruption and insufficient capacity within law enforcement agencies at all levels of government. This is particularly true at the municipal level in regions with a strong presence of OCGs. This public safety crisis has given rise to tensions within the current arrangements of the security and public safety system, with important actors calling for a re-centralization of authority and resources at the federal level. A new wave of reforms in this direction was initiated during the Calderon presidency (2006–12), and major reforms have been initiated by the Peña Nieto's presidency since 2012. This will be the second time in short succession that major reforms seek to reshape the distribution of power and the governance of Mexico's security and public safety system. The first one promoted decentralization and multilevel governance, and took place in the mid-1990s, triggered by a democratization process that ended decades of a federation characterized by a strong central government and dominated by a single hegemonic political party.

This chapter examines the relationship between security and public safety in the Mexican federation. It shows that little attention has been

1 Figures vary from 47,000 to 70,000, depending on the source (Crisis Group 2013).

paid to improving the effectiveness of current arrangements by focusing on processes, outcomes, and results, instead of just making changes in the institutional design, which has proven to be ineffective to address Mexico's public safety problems.

The first part of the chapter describes the constitutional and legal framework of the security and public safety system, as well as its historical development. A comparison of the different outcomes of two case studies follows. Finally, the chapter presents an overall assessment of the adequacy of the current arrangements of the system.

The Constitutional and Legal Framework

The Mexican Constitution refers to "public security"[2] (*seguridad pública*) as a concurrent function that includes the prevention, investigation, and prosecution of crimes. This definition does not include "civil protection" (*protección civil*), which is implicitly treated as a separate function related to risk reduction and emergency preparedness.

Article 21 of the Constitution establishes that public security is a shared function of federal, state, municipal, and the Federal District governments in accordance with the distribution of powers according to the Constitution and other related laws. The same article also mandates that these governments must form the National Public Security System (Sistema Nacional de Seguridad Pública, SNSP) to coordinate their work in:

- Regulating civil service processes, such as recruitment, selection, training, promotion, evaluation, promotion, and certification of law enforcement personnel;
- Establishing national databases of criminal records and police personnel;
- Formulating crime-prevention policy;
- Creating opportunities and mechanisms for citizens' participation in the evaluation of public policies and security agencies performance; and
- Disbursing federal funds among state and municipal agencies.

Article 115 of the Constitution grants municipalities specific authority over public security, preventive policing, and traffic enforcement in their territories. This article was reformed in 2008 to include a provision that gives governors the capacity to assume command of municipal

2 In Spanish, both *safety* and *security* translate as "seguridad."

forces under cases of emergencies or large public disorder. Furthermore, it gives governors the power to decide when a situation constitutes an emergency or a large public disorder.

All three levels of government have legislative powers over public security and civil protection. The Federal Congress has the authority to legislate with regards to the coordination of systems, both in public security and civil protection, and to organize federal agencies in these sectors (Article 73). It also has jurisdiction over criminal law regarding federal crimes. Equally, the state legislatures and the Federal District Assembly have the authority to legislate on the coordination within the state public security and civil protection systems and to organize state agencies. States also have authority over criminal law (except for federal crimes). Finally, municipal councils have the power to make by-laws (*reglamentos*) and organize their own agencies.

Mexico's federal judicial system has jurisdiction over federal crimes,[3] while local crimes are the competency of the state judiciary systems. As a result, the country used to have thirty-three judicial systems (one federal and thirty-two state systems), each with its own criminal code. Judicial reform started in 2008, generated a single uniform national criminal code in 2014, and is scheduled to be completed by 2016. It pivots from Mexico's traditional inquisitorial system to a new oral, adversarial system. This reform emphasizes due process and will deeply change criminal procedure both at the federal and state levels, including the role of police in criminal investigations.

The General Law of the SNSP (Ley General del Sistema Nacional de Seguridad Pública, 2009) is the legal framework for the Public Security Systems, according to Article 21 of the Constitution. It addresses, inter alia, the basic standards for the civil service in law enforcement institutions, the internal organization of police departments, general duties for all police officers, and the operation of the national databases and registries.[4] This law also creates several intergovernmental relations bodies:

- The National Public Security Council (CNSP), composed of all relevant cabinet ministries,[5] the thirty-one state governors, and the head of the Federal District's government;

3 Such as terrorism, drug trafficking, possession of heavy weaponry, etc.

4 Police personnel, stolen vehicles, firearms and equipment, criminal records, among others.

5 Ministry of Defence (SEDENA), Ministry of Public Security (SSP), Ministry of the Navy (SEMAR), Attorney General (PGR), Ministry of the Interior (SEGOB), among others.

- The Attorneys Generals Conference, the Ministers of Public Security Conference, and the Prisons or Penitentiary Conference, each formed by the respective federal minister and thirty-two local counterparts;[6]
- The Municipal Public Security Conference, with the participation of two mayors (*presidentes municipales*) from each state; and
- The local and regional councils, created within each state and some municipalities, replicating the composition of the national council at a local level.

An Executive Secretariat, controlled by the Ministry of the Interior, is responsible for coordinating the work of all intergovernmental mechanisms, tools, and bodies of the National Public Security System.

Most states have adapted, or are in the process of adapting, their own legislation in response to the new SNSP law, designed to reflect the new mandates. This will liken state and municipal public security systems, as well as their respective institutional structures, to that of the federal government in a number ways. Likewise, the General Law of Civil Protection (*Ley General de Protección Civil*, 2012) is the legal framework for the Civil Protection Systems (federal, state, and municipal) and creates similar mechanisms for coordination among authorities in the three levels of government.

Institutions at the Federal Level

Federal Ministerial Police (Policía Federal Ministerial) is in charge of the investigation of federal crimes, in support of the federal public minister (*Ministerio Público Federal*), and both are part of the Federal Attorney General's Office (Procuraduría General de la República, PGR).

Federal Police (Policía Federal, PF) now falls under the Secretariat of the Interior (Secretaría de Gobernación), after the former Secretariat of Public Security (SSP) was disbanded in January 2013. Although it was originally a preventive police, its investigative powers now overlap with those of the Ministerial Police. PF's original mandate was to protect critical infrastructure, patrol federal highways, and prevent federal crimes, as well as assist local governments when requested, but with the new investigative powers they are also actively involved in organized crime investigations.

---

6 Thirty-one states and the Federal District.

The **Centre for Research and National Security** (CISEN) is a civil entity also under the control of the minister of the interior. Its mandate is to generate intelligence to safeguard national security.

The **army** and the **navy**, under the control of the Secretariat of National Defence and the Secretariat of Navy respectively, are also actively involved in public security activities, particularly in areas with a strong presence of OCGs. The deployment of these federal forces has been said to be a temporary measure while the Federal Police reaches its projected capacities in personnel and tactical capabilities (Shirk 2011). Meanwhile, both forces have been used to surge capacity in areas of conflict. Nonetheless, they have also been deployed to function as municipal police in places where local law enforcement agencies have been dismantled after scandals of corruption and involvement with OCGs. The appointment of military personnel to lead local police forces is becoming common (Sabet 2010). These two institutions are often deployed and are well prepared to support relief efforts in regions affected by disasters.

The new federal government that took office in December 2012 has announced the creation of a new federal paramilitary police: the **National Gendarmerie** (*Gendarmería Nacional*). The new police force will be of a military nature but under civilian control. Its functions and how they will complement those of the other two federal police forces remain to be determined.

The **Civil Protection National Coordination** is the federal agency in charge of disaster reduction and emergency management policy. It is also the agency responsible for horizontal coordination of all federal agencies for federal interventions and emergency management, and vertical coordination with state and municipal emergency management agencies.

Institutions at the State Level

At the state level, public security structures are organized according to local constitutions and laws. Nevertheless, states have often opted to mirror the structure of the federal government. Most states have two police services: an investigative police, commonly known as state judicial or ministerial police, and a preventive police. State investigative police departments have a mandate to investigate local crime. State preventive police departments, by contrast, do not always have a clear mandate. Normally, they patrol state highways and have specialized teams for major incidents, but they are also found doing municipal police work, such as responding to emergency calls.

Institutions at the Municipal Level

Municipalities have only a preventive police, sometimes divided into traffic enforcement and preventive police. Their principal mandate is to enforce municipal by-laws, including those related to traffic, as well as crime prevention and preventive patrol. Although most mayor cities have a municipal police, approximately 800 of more than 2,400 municipalities in Mexico have no police force. These are mostly rural municipalities with small populations, but there are some exceptions, like Morelia, the capital city of the state of Michoacan, with a population over 700,000, which is served by the state police.

Historical Development of Federal Arrangements

Mexico has been a federation for almost two centuries, but for most of the twentieth century it was characterized by a strong central government, dominated by a single hegemonic political party. In practice, the president had strong control over elected governors and mayors, and enjoys discretion over their appointment and removal.

The renaissance of Mexican federalism in the late twentieth century was spawned by the decentralization of public services and democratization at the municipal level. Political and democratic changes at the municipal and state levels precipitated constitutional changes in the mid-1990s that gave rise to the National Public Security System (SNSP). Such was the federal government's response to the new reality whereby, for the first time, it did not have control over local police forces.

At the same time, mayors of different state capitals wanted more control over police in their jurisdiction. Prior to this period of reform, the Constitution gave municipalities control over their police force, except in the state capitals, where they were subject to control by governors. Ergo, most large municipalities that were state capitals did not have a police service, and the ones that did exist were controlled by the state police yet paid for by the municipalities. Some municipal police departments were created in state capitals through legal agreements with the state governor, but by the late 1990s, a new constitutional reform of Article 115 gave municipal governments unlimited control over their own police departments.

With the creation of the SNSP and its financial mechanisms, the federal government was able to push reforms to professionalize state and municipal forces. Except for smaller municipalities, all other local police forces implemented minimum standards for hiring new policemen, such as a minimum secondary school education; at least six months of full-time training in academies; and a basic set of test and evaluations for the vetting process. The SNSP also created important instruments and tools for the collaborative work required to share functions, such as the national emergency call number 066. Operational and intelligence data sharing has also improved over recent years with Plataforma México, an information platform available to all law enforcement agencies with centralized databases on information, such as stolen vehicles, fingerprints, or police personnel, among others.

During this period of reform, drug cartels adapted their strategies and influence. Small-scale drug trafficking became a concern for authorities at all levels of government. Fights for control over local territory among cartels or their affiliated gangs began in different regions of the country. Soon local police departments became unintended protagonists, either as allies or targets of organized crime. Homicides and other violent crime began to soar in 2007, after years of sustained decline. While Mexico's homicide rate of 23.7 (2011) was still below the Latin American average of 25.9 per 100,000 (Molzahn, Rodríguez, and Shirk 2013), it was up sharply from 8.1 just four years earlier.

This crisis of violent criminal activity prompted the current second wave of reforms. These reforms are marked by a tendency for the federal government to expand its responsibilities in public security and re-centralize some powers and resources. Public concern has allowed support for increased investment and more powers for federal public security agencies. Even local and especially state governments of the more violent regions, such as Michoacán, Nuevo León, and Chihuahua, have been publicly endorsing a greater role for the federal government. The pace of change has hastened, but with less room for public discussion on the direction of these reforms.

Since its inception, the SNSP's design had little room for asymmetries. It failed to pay much attention to local differences and priorities and had no intention to incorporate local experience. Its focus has always been top-down. Since the outbreak of OCG violence, the tendency has been towards greater symmetry in government agencies. As part of its strategy to fight crime, the federal government has promoted new policies to standardize how the public security services are organized and delivered across the country. These polices are not limited to minimum standards as they were at the beginning of the SNSP; now they address protocols such as the colour of uniforms or departmental

Figure 6.1. Intentional Homicide Rate (1995–2011)

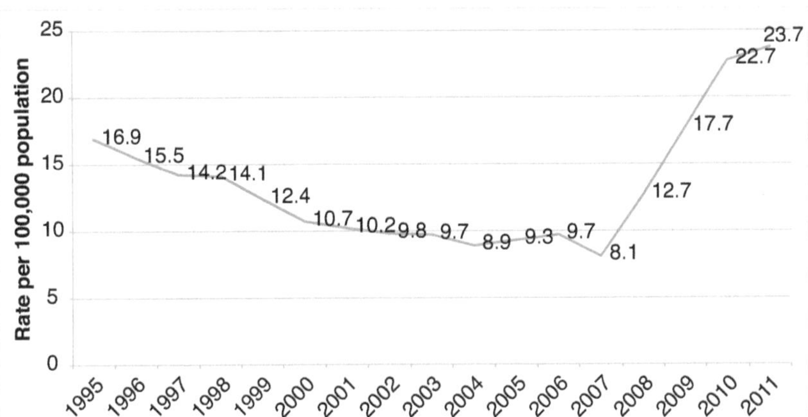

nomenclature. At the same time, some aspects that may be more relevant to the standardization of service, such as internal and external controls and accountability mechanisms, are poorly developed or altogether lacking.[7] In spite of the many legal bodies established to coordinate security policy among members of the SNSP, there has been little debate on what should be standardized, and what should remain under the control of each police force.

A proposed new reform will go even further, handing control over municipal police to each state governor. The proposition comes at a time of high-profile scandals within some municipal police forces, that have had a bearing on public perception. The National Victimization and Perception on Public Security Survey (ENVIPE) 2012 showed that the army and navy enjoy high levels of trust, around 80 per cent (55/25 said have much/some trust), while municipal police is the least trusted law enforcement institution, around 30 per cent (7/23 said have much/some trust). Security is the main concern for Mexicans, with economic conditions second. Yet the 2011 ENVIPE survey showed that up to 92 per cent of crimes are not reported to police or the public ministry. There is an evident lack of trust in governing authorities, with police among the least trusted.

7 The vetting process, an important internal control in every police, has been actively promoted and it is an important component of the federal government strategy. Nonetheless, other necessary internal and external controls have been neglected.

These findings are one impetus for reform. The tendency to centralize control of police is also horizontal, with federal and some state governments exploring the idea of having just one police agency at each level. Meanwhile, the resources and powers of federal agencies – particularly those of the army and the Federal Police – have increased substantially, compared to other federal agencies and all local police forces.

The same trend holds for civil protection. The country's vulnerabilities and high exposure to natural hydro-meteorological and geological hazards led the World Bank to rank it as "one of the world's 30 most exposed countries to three or more types of natural hazards" (Hofliger et al. 2012). The United Nations Office for Disaster Risk Reduction (UNISDR) maintains that "building the capacity of local institutions is key to sustaining disaster risk reduction." Yet the new General Law of Civil Protection (LGPC 2012) undermines local capacity by centralizing power in the Federal Ministry of the Interior. Under this new law, to be appointed to a state or municipal emergency preparedness agency, public servants must first be "certified" by an agency under the control of the Federal Ministry of the Interior. In addition, a municipal government cannot merge the security and emergency preparedness functions under a single agency, since the law also standardizes the nomenclature of local agencies – they must be named civil protection units – and the ministry that will control them.

All this is happening in tandem with an ambitious judicial reform. The adoption of oral and adversarial procedures will bring new challenges to police agencies and other institutions. So far, each state has its own criminal code, causing multiple problems for the judicial system, as well as for criminal lawyers, making it hard to compare data among states. The new federal administration has committed to creating a unified criminal code.[8]

Metrics and Fiscal Dimension

Spending on public security has grown steadily. Figures vary, depending on several factors,[9] but some approximations peg overall spending

8 Included in the Pact for Mexico agreement. Justice in Mexico (n.d.).

9 Differences in budgeting and accounting procedures among subnational governments in Mexico, the scope of the definition of public security, and the different mandates of the agencies involved. The army would be a good example. Its budget is often added to public security expenditure figures because it has been heavily involved in public security functions, yet still performs its traditional national defence activities with that budget.

Table 6.1. Change in the Size of the Federal Police Forces and Spending

	AFI	PFP	Total federal forces	PGR budget (millions of pesos)	SSP budget (millions of pesos)
2001	4,920	10,241	15,161	5,451.2	5,156.8
2002	5,525	10,830	16,355	6,991.9	6,389.0
2003	6,122	12,535	18,657	7,267.0	6,259.6
2004	8,078	14,415	22,493	7,521.3	6,397.6
2005	7,676	11,756	19,432	7,572.3	6,976.9
2006	8,127	12,907	21,034	8,862.4	8,676.0
2007	7,992	21,761	29,753	9,439.5	17,626.9
2008	5,996	31,936	37,932	8,950.2	21,140.3
2009	4,974	32,264	37,238	12,309.9	32,916.8

Source: Sabet (2010).

at up to 1.7 per cent of GDP in 2009 (Mendoza Mora 2009); and up to 6.3 per cent of all federal expenditure (Tapia 2011). Between 2001 and 2010, the now-defunct federal Ministry of Public Security's (SSP) annual budget increased from US$789 million (US$1:MXN9.70) to US$2.4 billion (US$1:MXN12.50). The army and other federal public security departments also saw their budgets grow. The number of Federal Police also increased sharply, as shown in table 6.1.

State and municipal expenditure in security has also increased, although figures are harder to obtain. Most of their own resources are used to pay police wages and other security personnel, as well as operating expenses. Similar to SSP, much of this increase has gone towards hiring more police. State and municipal resources potentially add up to 54 per cent of all national public security spending, compared to 39 per cent of the federal budget and the 7 per cent in federal funds, transfers and subsidies for subnational governments (Tapia 2011).

About 90 per cent of police personnel come from state and municipal forces. There are around 450,000 police in Mexico (see table 6.3).

The comparison among states also shows interesting results. The homicide rate differs significantly from one state to another (see figure 6.2). Despite the spike in violence and crime in some parts of the country, some states have homicide rates that can be compared to very safe countries.

Table 6.2. Spending on Public Security, Prosecution of Justice, and Prisons

	Municipal and state budgets (millions of pesos)	Federal budget (millions of pesos)	Total budget (millions of pesos)	% of government budget	% of GDP
2007	84,846.9	48,110.7	132,957.7	5.9	1.2
2008	100,804.0	58,982.7	159,786.7	6.2	1.3
2009	117,002.4	77,766.5	194,769.0	6.4	1.7

Source: Sabet (2010).

Table 6.3. Police Personnel by Type of Police Force

Federal Police	40,212	9.06%
Federal Ministerial Police	5,900	1.33%
State ministerial police	29,243	6.59%
State police (incl. the Federal District)	202,274	45.58%
Municipal police	166,147	37.44%
Total	443,776	

Sources: Federal Police (Bergman and Arango 2011); Federal Ministerial Police (Sabet 2010); state ministerial police, state police, and municipal police.

Some estimates attribute 45 to 60 per cent of all homicides to OCGs (Molzahn, Rodrígez, and Shirk 2013). The strong presence of OCGs explains why Chihuahua, Baja California, Tamaulipas, Sinaloa, and Michoacan lie well above the national average. Nonetheless, the analysis of all crimes presents a different picture. While Tamaulipas has a much higher homicide rate than the State of Mexico (29.53 and 7.52 respectively), the National Victimization and Perception on Public Security Survey (ENVIPE 2012)[10] shows that the overall crime rate for Tamaulipas (20,544 per 100,000 inhabitants) is almost half of the rate for the State of Mexico (39,905). According to the SNSP, Tamaulipas has 184 municipal and state police officers per 100,000 population, and the State of Mexico has 428. Ergo, factors unrelated to OCGs, such as fiscal resources, institutional capacity, or cultural differences, create differences among states.

---

10 A national annual survey made by the National Institute of Statistics and Geography (INEGI).

Figure 6.2. Homicides Rates per 100,000 by State

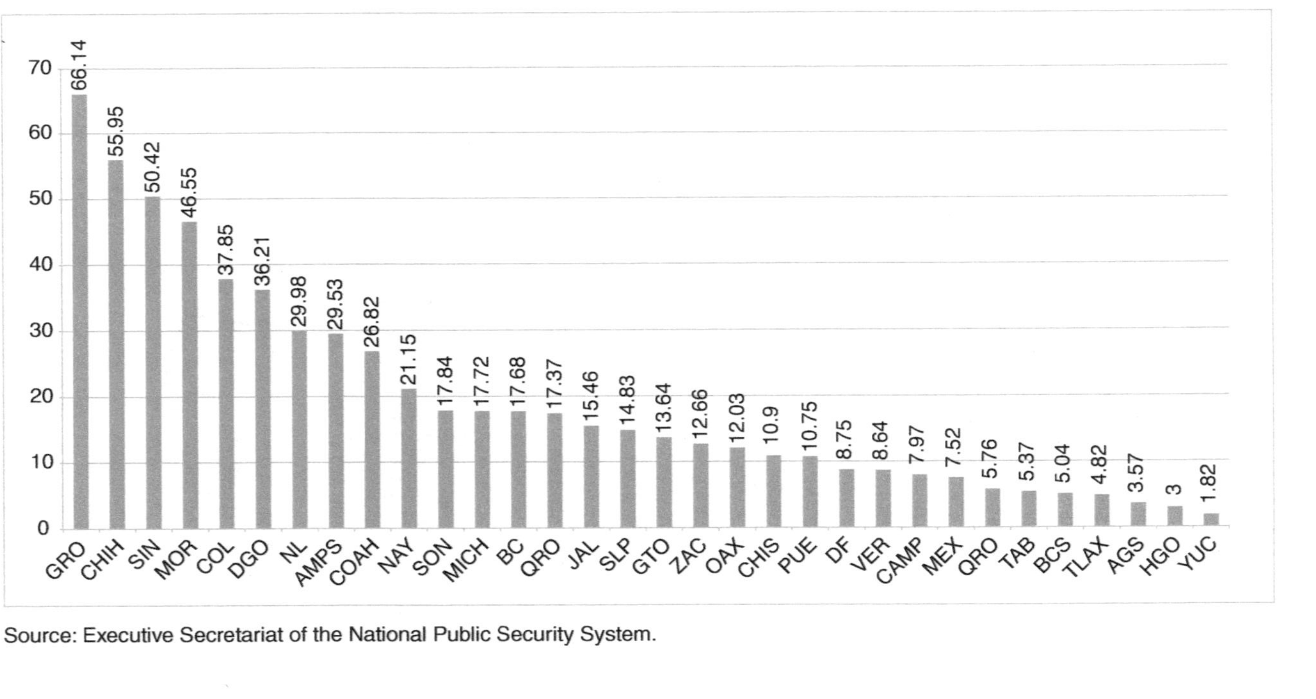

Source: Executive Secretariat of the National Public Security System.

Federal funds for public security have increased, and overall spending through this mechanism has also grown, from US$400 million in 2007 to US$1.3 billion in 2012. Among these conditional funds, the two most important[11] are the Public Security Contribution Fund (FASP)[12] and the Subsidy for Municipal Public Security (SUBSEMUN). The first is intended for states and the Federal District; the latter for a group of selected municipalities. Both funds are used mainly for new technologies, equipment, training and personnel evaluation, crime prevention, and special programs.

FASP, the first such fund, was also intended for municipalities, but in practice most of the resources are retained at the state level. The allocation formula has always been a subject of controversy among states and the federal government, since part of the formula criteria has reverse incentives: the funding allocation is a function of crime and inmates. To avoid controversy, the National Public Safety Council has opted, almost at every opportunity, to keep the same proportion of spending from year to year instead of actually reallocating spending using the formula.

SUBSEMUN is transferred to municipalities through the states, although the federal government works directly with municipalities to establish goals and evaluate compliance with funding rules. Although its formula has changed over time, population has remained an important criterion. Money is transferred to municipalities three times a year. If municipalities fail to meet the goals previously negotiated with the SNSP's Executive Secretariat, they lose the part that has not yet been transferred. The problem is that the process of setting goals and evaluating achievements and compliance lacks rigour and transparency, thus allowing discretion or even politically motivated intervention. In practice, a municipality may continue to receive funds irrespective of achieving goals or their relevance to the overall objectives.

These funding instruments suffer from lack of clarity, a problem that becomes worse at the subnational levels where the institutions with the mandate to grant access to public information are not as strong as at the federal government. Procurement processes are inefficient and affected

---

11 There are other funds conditioned to specific programs, such as Mando Único and Plataforma México.

12 Fondo de Aportaciones para la Seguridad de los Estados y el Distrito Federal, FASP.

by corruption at municipal and state levels, with little oversight from federal authorities. SUBSEMUN and FASP funds are considered federal funds, even after they have been transferred to the municipalities, so the federal auditor general can audit the way they are spent. Notwithstanding this authority, the auditor general lacks effective oversight of the way funds are spent.

Nonetheless, these conditional transfers raised important issues within the local public security agenda that have long been neglected by subnational governments, such as gender, domestic violence, human trafficking, and even crime prevention. These funding instruments also brought some positive results in a country with more than 1,600 police forces, such as the extension of the emergency calls service to every major city and town, as well as creating a state-of-the-art telecommunication network that allows interoperability among agencies of the three levels of government nationwide. These funds also enabled three levels of government to work together to establish minimum standards for professional career service within police departments, even though they have yet to be fully implemented; and police forces across the country are much better equipped than five years ago.

The federal government's funding instruments were essential to accomplishing most of the aforementioned changes. However, they also came at a cost to local priorities and principles. The lack of flexibility caused several states and municipalities to invest scarce resources in national priorities (special units, encrypted communication radios, etc.), even if they were far from being the most pressing issue or the right solutions for their communities. States facing an acute problem of domestic violence and with no kidnappings may end up with an anti-kidnapping special unit, instead of a domestic violence special unit. Furthermore, it undermined local capacity and forced an end to successful local practices and models, even if they were rare. These funds not only condition the priorities for investment, but also dictate organization, methods, etc.

But the biggest shortfall of these funding tools is that they have not delivered results in lower crime rates, or at least professional, trusted public security institutions for all Mexicans, since the SNSP and conditional transfers were set up in 1996. The federal government continues to intervene in all aspects of the design and organization of local police agencies. The lack of sound evaluation and accountability mechanisms, fundamental aspects in a federal system, may help explain these outcomes. Yet federal intervention is necessitated by the fact that states rarely use their own resources to support municipal public security. Doing so is at their discretion and political motivation.[13]

Risk and emergency management is extremely underfunded at the local level. States and municipalities that have suffered the consequences of disasters are prone to be better prepared and equipped, mostly as a result of their own means. There are two federal funding mechanisms in this area: FONDEN and FOPREDEN. The first is to respond to disasters and the latter is mostly to prevent disasters and has been used, inter alia, to conduct risks assessments. The Ministry of Social Development (SEDESOL) has also funded such assessments as well as projects for adapting to climate change and community resilience. Other emergency services, such as paramedics and firefighters, are still voluntary in most parts of the country. The new federal law mandates that state governments must also have emergency and preparedness funds, but implementation is lagging.

Case Studies

Policy Case Study 1: War on Drugs

Drug cartels have been operating in Mexico for decades, but their deleterious effects on local public security were long limited to a few cities or regions that served as their operational bases or strategic territories. Changes in the international drug market, along with a growing and more competitive domestic market, brought the attention of OCGs to territories outside their traditional places of interest, leading to violent confrontations among cartels and with authorities.

It is widely acknowledged that an important cause of this deteriorating environment is the result of weakness and corruption among local institutions. The negligence and sometimes complicity of local authorities has seen whole regions besieged by organized crime. The federal government responded by declaring the war on drugs in 2006, assuming a major role, and extending the role of the armed forces in the fight against these cartels, cognizant of the shortfalls of its own civilian police institutions for the role. At the same time, an ambitious reform of the security apparatus was undertaken at all three levels of government.

13 In practice, states choose which municipalities receive police equipment bought with state funds, as well as when and how much they get.

Homicide trends have since grown rapidly after years of steady decline. Other crimes, such as extortion and kidnapping, have also seen a sharp increase as drug cartels seek to diversify.

The initial reaction by the federal government was to create a National Police as a substitute for all other federal, state, and municipal police forces. After facing resistance from a variety of actors, including some governors, mayors, and members of congress, the strategy has morphed into the creation of thirty-two strong state police agencies with oversight and even control over municipalities.[14] Both strategies failed to recognize important regional differences in institutional capacity among states and municipalities, and other urgent local priorities. The challenges inherent to reforming a federalized security apparatus have not been properly addressed by the federal government in all cases. The federal government has assumed not only its own responsibility, but also that of state governments. It has not held governors and mayors to account for reforming their own security apparatus, made transparency and accountability its main tool to promote coordination and shared responsibility, or facilitated bottom-up solutions and local priorities.

This case shows that all the legal, operational, and financial instruments and mechanisms created over a decade of reforms to facilitate coordination among the different levels of government were not designed to work in times of urgent need. The lack of provisions to deal with exceptional circumstances is now an impetus for re-centralization that threatens to erode local public security institutions further.

Policy Case Study 2: Hurricane Wilma

Risk and emergency management or civil protection is a shared responsibility among all three levels of government. The first to respond to emergencies is the municipal government. It can then request state or federal help as needed. Likewise, state governments may request federal help in major emergencies. Assistance from the federal government

---

14 *Policía acreditable* is an initiative that seeks to adapt every state police to the new police model (*modelo policial*). In its first stage, the program aims is to create a police force of over 400 members in each state that will be staffed with certified personnel from the current police force and university students with degrees in criminology or similar disciplines. *Mando único* (unified command) seeks to bring municipal forces under the control of state police under special circumstances.

comes in the form of economic funds for disaster relief (FONDEN) and surge capacity, such as armed forces personnel.

In practice, every time a major disasters happens, all three levels of government become involved. Some public utilities, such as electricity, are under federal jurisdiction. The army deploys its disaster relief plan (DNIII) on the occasion of every major crisis. Health and schools fall under the control of the states. Water supply is either under state or municipal jurisdiction. Local emergency services, such as police, firefighters, and paramedics, are under municipal jurisdiction or coordinated by it.

In 2005, Wilma hit the Yucatan Peninsula as a Category 4 hurricane and moved on two days later as a Category 2 hurricane. The region has some of Mexico's most important international tourist destinations, such as Cancun (the main tourist destination in Mexico), Riviera Maya and Cozumel (the main cruise destination worldwide). In 2005, the state of Quintana Roo, where all three tourist centres are located, received 28 per cent of all international tourists arriving by airplane. The region is so important to the Mexican economy that Goldman Sachs revised Mexico's growth expectations for 2005 from 2.8 to 2.5 per cent because of the storm (SECTUR 2006). According to the Ministry of Tourism, Wilma damaged 80 per cent of the over 27,000 hotel rooms and 95 per cent of restaurants; marinas and shopping centres were forced to close, amounting to an estimated daily loss of US$15 million. Insured property damages were estimated at US$1.7 billion (CEPAL 2006).

The response to this disaster from three levels of government was well coordinated and effective. Before the storm, 35,000 tourists were evacuated and almost 40,000 were moved to temporary shelters. Schools and hospitals followed protocols. The work of local emergency preparedness agencies and emergency services, before and during the storm, paid off: no deaths were blamed directly on the storm. The Economic Commission for Latin America (CEPAL) reported that the protocols, alert systems, and shelters prepared in advance by municipal and state authorities played a significant role in protecting the life of people in the communities affected. One year later, the tourist infrastructure had not only recovered but also improved, and Quintana Roo remains one of the main international destinations, as well as one of the fastest growing states and an important economic region. Federal intervention not only brought services such as electricity back promptly, but also was crucial in reconstruction and long-term public and private investments after the storm.

This case illustrates that, irrespective of the underfunded mandate for emergency preparedness at local levels, the civil protection sector delivers better results in times of urgent need than the security sector. Both system designs are similar, yet the dynamics are very different.

For instance, a disaster such as Hurricane Wilma is a much more focalized problem than the violence generated by the OCGs. The area affected by a disaster is well delimited and, even more importantly, remains somehow the same. The authorities involved after a storm hits are the same during the months of recovery. The area affected by OCG violence is much more dynamic and can spread to large areas of the country and beyond, involving different authorities.

The time frame for coordination is also different. Most disaster relief takes place in a few months after the emergency, while the operations against OCGs continue for years.

Overall Assessment of the Adequacy of Public Security Arrangements

The creation of the SNSP to coordinate all levels of government on the shared function of public security made positive changes, and some of the current arrangements have proven adequate. Nonetheless, crime and violence have continued to grow and the security institutions are still far from being professional and trusted. Financial resources have increased steadily over the years. So is federalism an explanation for sluggish improvements and the lack of results? Are the current federal arrangements inadequate for the needed reforms? Is re-centralization of power the answer to progress in the professionalization of security institutions and the safety of communities? Many influential parts of the Mexican political class and society at large seem to think so, the former president Calderon being one main advocate. There have been attempts to eliminate municipal police departments, and still other considerations that will significantly reduce their powers and relevance. There is also frustration with how newfound democracy impedes important reforms in other sectors, since there is a need to build the necessary consensus.

Furthermore, the federal and state governments have been unable to professionalize their own police institutions, even though they are significantly smaller than what they would become if municipal police forces were to disappear. Corruption is more prevalent at the municipal level, but states and federal institutions, including the army, are not immune. So are state and federal agencies more resistant to infiltration by OCGs; or do they have less exposure? So far OCGs are interested in municipal police forces, because they are deployed within an easily exploitable territory. If the state police became the dominant force in those territories, would they do better? The same question applies to public trust in security institutions: does the public have more trust in federal agencies because they are better prepared and less prone to corruption; or because there is much less contact between federal agencies and the general population? What would happen if the federal or the state police started doing traffic enforcement and responding to domestic violence calls: are they more professional, allowing for more public trust? The answer to these questions may be affirmative in most cases, especially when comparing with police departments from small, rural municipalities. But compared to major municipal police departments in bigger cities (the minority of the total municipal police forces), the answer may be negative in many cases.

So is re-centralization the answer? Would it be better to adopt a more flexible system, such as one where municipalities with adequate resources and technical capacities could have a local police? Alternatively, municipalities and states could opt to contract services from the state or federal governments. By recognizing that there are significant differences among municipal police forces, federal and state governments would benefit from having more resources to exploit where they are needed most.

It is also important to keep strengthening public security federal institutions to restrict the armed forces' role in public security functions. A professional and trusted federal police is needed to provide equal security to all Mexicans, especially where security has been neglected by local authorities. At the same time, it is critical to limit federal intervention to periods when it is absolutely necessary, without political interference and after a transparent process ruled by the judiciary.

Nevertheless, such intervention should not occur at the expense of local institutions. A more balanced budget is needed, and states and municipalities should do their part to increase funding. An evaluation scheme is essential to determine the effectiveness of the federal structure in providing public security. The Evaluation National Council (CONEVAL) – a technical independent federal agency in charge of policy evaluation – should be mandated to evaluate the design, implementation, and results of all programs for local public security funded with federal monies. As a result, programs would be better designed and there would be relevant indicators to measure progress, putting the right incentives in place. The evaluation of results would reinforce accountability, showing clearly how everyone performed and making all results public, as with every other evaluation conducted by CONEVAL. This measure alone will change the dynamics of all aforementioned councils and intergovernmental relations, and will inform federal and local congress discussion about public security policies. Sound evaluation may obviate the need for reform of current arrangements.

This will also promote changes in the types of policies funded, allowing bottom-up and local initiatives to be considered in the funding alternatives. The system has been designed to allow such collaboration, but in practice it has worked hierarchically. Evaluation may also help established intergovernmental arrangements to accomplish this end by establishing clear responsibilities and goals to which every participant is held accountable.

Broader oversight, in areas such as human rights and corruption at an institutional level, will become an important matter of intergovernmental relations in the near future. Mexico lacks formal external oversight mechanisms for police, such as independent civilian agencies at the state level.

Conclusions

The public security system in Mexico is decentralized. The three levels of government have administrative and operational responsibilities, making public security a shared function. The democratization of the last two decades encouraged decentralization, and the need to coordinate became evident to avoid dispersion of effort and resources. Mexico created a complex system of institutionalized mechanisms, instruments, and bodies for the parties of the three levels of government to participate. It was designed to allow vertical and horizontal cooperation, and bottom-up and top-down collaboration in strategic and tactical matters; but in practice the system has operated in very hierarchically. The recent crisis of violence related to organized-crime groups presents important challenges to federal arrangements and pushes the system towards re-centralization of powers and resources. Evidence in Mexico and elsewhere suggests that by reforming structures alone it is difficult to obtain significantly different outcomes (Bayley 2001). Instead, Mexico may benefit more by making extant arrangements work better. A key element for this objective is evaluation, which has been neglected in the sector at all levels of government.

Mexico would benefit from a more flexible system, one that seeks standardization as a means to establish a minimum level of service to all Mexicans, and at the same time allow asymmetry to respond better to local priorities. By having this flexibility and recognizing the local differences, the federal government would be more effective in providing surge capacity and focalized intervention where needed. It is equally important to have provisions to allow crisis interventions without the need to reform the system, but always subject to controls and with clear limits.

References

Bayley, David H. 2001. *Democratizing the Police Abroad: What to Do and How to Do It. Issues in International Crime.* Washington: US Department of Justice.

Bergman, Marcelo, and Arturo Arango. 2011. *Mucho gasto y resultados inciertos. El creciente costo de nuestra Policía Federal.* https://www.casede.org/BibliotecaCasede/Muchogasto_resultadosinciertos_ElcostocrecientedenuestraPoliciaFederal.pdf.

CEPAL. 2006. *Características e impacto socioeconómico de los huracanes "Stan" y "Wilma" en la República Mexicana en el 2005.* https://www.cepal.org/es/publicaciones/25801-caracteristicas-impacto-socioeconomico-huracanes-stan-wilma-la-republica.

Crisis Group. 2013. *Peña Nieto's Challenge: Criminal Cartels and Rule of Law in Mexico.* Report no. 48. https://www.crisisgroup.org/latin-america-caribbean/mexico/pena-nieto-s-challenge-criminal-cartels-and-rule-law-mexico.

Encuesta Nacional de Victimización y Percepción sobre Seguridad Pública (ENVIPE). 2012. http://www.beta.inegi.org.mx/proyectos/enchogares/regulares/envipe/2012/.

Hofliger, Rubem, Olivier Mahul, Francis Ghesquiere, and Salvador Perez. 2012. *FONDEN: Mexico's Natural Disaster Fund – A Review.* Washington: International Bank for Reconstruction and Development/The World Bank. http://www.proteccioncivil.gob.mx/work/models/ProteccionCivil/Almacen/libro_fonden.pdf.

Justice in Mexico. n.d. "SEGOB Will Prioritize Oral Trials." https://justiceinmexico.org/segob-will-prioritize-oral-trials/.

Mendoza Mora, Carlos. 2009. *El Costo de la Inseguridad en México.* Mexico City: Instituto Ciudadano de Estudios sobre la Inseguridad.

Molzahn, Cory, Octavio Rodríguez, and David A. Shirk. 2013. *Drug Violence in Mexico: Data and Analysis through 2013.* Trans-Border Institute, Joan B. Kroc https://justiceinmexico.files.wordpress.com/2014/07/dvm-2014-final.pdf.

Sabet, Daniel. 2010. *Police Reform in Mexico: Advances and Persistent Obstacles*. Working Paper Series on U.S.-Mexico Security Collaboration. Washington: Mexico Institute at the Woodrow Wilson Center and the Trans-Border Institute at the University of San Diego. https://www.wilsoncenter.org/sites/default/files/Chapter%208-Police%20Reform%20in%20Mexico%2C%20Advances%20and%20PErsistent%20Obstacles.pdf.

SECTUR. 2006. "A un año de Wilma, sus impactos en el turismo del caribe mexicano." *Boletín cuatrimestral de turismo* 17. Mexico.

Shirk, David A. 2011. *The Drug War in Mexico: Confronting a Shared Threat*. Council Special Report No. 60. New York: Council on Foreign Relations.

Tapia, José. 2011. *El gasto en seguridad: Observaciones de la ASF a la gestión y usode recursos*. México Evalúa, Centro de Análisis en Políticas Públicas, A.C. http://mexicoevalua.org/2011/06/01/el-gasto-en-seguridad-observaciones-de-la-asf-a-la-gestion-y-uso-de-recursos/.

7 South Africa

NICO STEYTLER AND LUKAS MUNTINGH

Introduction

South Africa is facing a major public safety crisis threatening its constitutional democracy. Personal violent crime (murder,[1] rape and robbery) remains among the highest in the world; corruption in the public service is rife; public protests about poor service delivery are frequent (Powell, O'Donovan, and De Visser 2015), widespread, and often turn violent; xenophobic attacks occur frequently (South African History Online 2015); and industrial strike action has also resulted in violence.[2] Devastating natural disasters have, fortunately, been infrequent.

The state institutions concerned with public safety and corruption are located mainly at the national level, but perform poorly to meet these diverse challenges. Moreover, the national government's response to crime has focused almost exclusively on law enforcement, neglecting primary, secondary and tertiary crime prevention of a socio-economic nature. The South African Police Service (SAPS), despite its size (nearly 194,000) (SAPS 2015, 309), has been demoralized by corruption from the top to the bottom, it has been politicized, and its public order policing is ill-equipped and inadequately trained to deal with frequent public disturbances. The National Prosecuting Authority (NPA), too, has been politicized, and its success rate is declining (Redpath 2012). The national court system has run up huge backlogs in trying cases and the national

1 According to the World Bank the intentional homicide rate for South Africa and Columbia (2011/12) is the same at 32 per 100,000 population. See World Bank (2017).

2 The Marikana massacre is the worst incident in recent history. It was investigated by the Farlam Commission of Inquiry. See Marikana Commission of Inquiry (n.d.).

Department of Correctional Services does little more than warehousing a large and growing prison population of some 42,000 people awaiting trial.[3] Sentenced prisoners seldom receive the necessary services to reduce the risk of reoffending after release.

Against this backdrop, the provinces play a very limited supervisory role over the SAPS, but metropolitan municipalities are emerging as state institutions that are increasing their complementary role to the SAPS's efforts to combat crime through their own police forces.

However, the public, living in fear and defenceless, has sought protection elsewhere; there are now three private security personnel for every police officer (News24Wire 2015), and for those who cannot afford the privatized security, mob justice is often an attractive option.

It is thus argued that the public safety state apparatus is in crisis, as it is experiencing "a relatively strong decline in (followed by unusually low levels of) legitimacy" (Boin and T'Hart 2000, 13). It will be further argued that, given the crisis in the national public safety institutions, a more decentralized response is emerging from the bottom. The opposition-held Western Cape province and City of Cape Town (but also other metropolitan municipalities) are forging ahead, exploring the limited constitutional space they have with a more independent stance on public safety, initiatives opposed by the national government that seeks to centralize all public safety institutions. However, further decentralization will not by itself provide the answer; the transformation of the central institutions as non-political, professional institutions providing a public service will have the greatest impact, along with a coherent all-of-government approach to addressing the root causes of poverty and inequality.

Nomenclature

A number of terms are used in the broad field of public security. In the first democratic government, the old name of Minister of Police was replaced by the "Minister of Safety and Security," a title that lasted fifteen years, when the name reverted to the old, as a sign of being tough on crime. The provincial ministries responsible for policing oversight are often referred to as "Community Safety." The private "security"

3 During 2014/15, the department had an annual average of 42,077 unsentenced inmates. See DCS (2015, 9).

sector is also concerned principally with crime. The general trend is thus that references to "public security" or "public safety" (often used interchangeably, or jointly) have a narrow meaning, focusing directly on crime. Disaster management, dealing with natural and man-made disasters, are usually not included in either concept, and in practice are handled exclusively under the national and provincial departments concerned with local government. In this chapter, then, we use the term *public security* to encompass matters that are linked to crime, which is also our main focus.

Main Public Safety Risks

Crime and the fear of crime occupy significant space in the South African discourse, and with good reason. Since 1990 there has been a dramatic increase in violent as well as property crimes. Reflecting on crime levels post-1994 Altbeker (2007, 12) concludes, "Every piece of reliable data we have tells us that South Africa ranks at the very top of the world's league tables for violent crime ... [It is] an exceptionally, possibly uniquely, violent society."

From four victimization surveys between 1998 and 2010, perceptions of safety revealed, first, that more than 40 per cent of households surveyed believed that crime had come down in their area from 2008 to 2010, but 32 per cent believed it increased, and 26 per cent that it remained the same. Therefore, even though a notable proportion perceived an improvement in the crime situation in their area of residence, nearly 60 per cent saw no change or deterioration. Second, 63 per cent of South Africans feel unsafe when walking in their neighbourhoods after sunset, primarily for fear of being robbed. Undoubtedly this fear affects people's behaviour and the extent to which they can enjoy life in the area in which they reside. This reality of fear is recognized by the national government (National Planning Commission 2011a, 245).

The high levels of crime are, no doubt, attributable to South Africa's socio-economic conditions – not general poverty, but rather one of the highest levels of income disparity (income Gini coefficient 57.8) (UNDP 2014, 170), with nearly half of its 50 million population living in poverty evenly spread across urban and rural areas. Public protests about poor service delivery, as well as a lack of housing and jobs, are almost a weekly occurrence throughout the country, with the trend that they turn increasingly violent (Karamoko 2011). Labour disputes are increasingly accompanied by violence. Adding to the woes of the poor are the millions of undocumented migrants from neighbouring countries, notably Zimbabwe, who compete for scarce jobs, boiling over in 2008 in widespread violent and often fatal xenophobic attacks, threatening to erupt again following the economic downturn since 2008, which saw the loss of over a million jobs.

With crime rampant and public order ever under threat, the SAPS and other national institutions in the criminal justice system are making slow progress in the battle against crime. The SAPS, reflecting much of the civil service, is riven with corruption from top to bottom. Two national commissioners have lost their positions as the result of corruption, and the last one is being investigated to determine if she is fit to hold office.[4] In 2011/12 more than 600 police officers were arrested in Gauteng province alone on criminal charges (*Legal Briefs* 2012). Not only is the police service marked by corruption, but also with ineptitude and lack of training. Crime detection rates are abysmal, as a fifth of the 25,000 detectives are untrained (Essop 2012, 2), resulting in low conviction rates.[5] Public order policing is also inept, as evidenced by the police killing of thirty-four striking mineworkers on 16 August 2012 at Marikana in the North West province. However, the police arrest some 1.6 million people annually, but the majority of these arrests are for crimes less serious than shoplifting (SAPS 2011, 66) – a practice that suggests that arrest targets are chased to demonstrate impact, rather than tackling major crime problem areas that would show effectiveness. The SAPS is consequently spending significant time and resources on crimes that do not pose a serious threat to public safety.

The NPA does not engender much confidence either. In recent years the performance of the NPA has seen a decline, as measured by the number of prosecutions and the number of offenders sentenced to

4 The former police commissioner, Jackie Selebi, was given a fifteen-year prison sentence in December 2011 for corruption, because he received cash from a known mobster in exchange for information and protection. He was released on medical parole in early 2012 and died in January 2015. His successor, Bheki Cele, did not fare much better and was dismissed after for maladministration. The appointed head of Crime Intelligence, Richard Mdluli, was suspended and under investigation for using a crime intelligence slush fund to fund his family and girlfriend (apart from a murder charge, which was inexplicably dropped by the NPA). Following the Marikana massacre, the national commissioner, Riah Phiyega, was suspended and was subsequently found not fit to hold office (Khoza 2017).

5 For example, in a number of Cape Town townships, 1,469 murders cases were opened over five years, but only 11.8 per cent resulted in convictions (De Wee 2012, 5).

imprisonment. From 2004/5 to 2010/11 the number of cases finalized by the NPA (obtaining a verdict) declined by 13 per cent, or just more than 50,000 cases. The decline occurred whilst the change in the rate of violent crime showed negligible variations.

Against the backdrop of an ineffective state, the safety needs of communities, individuals, and businesses have created an enormous demand for private security. Armed with guns and flak jackets, private security officers patrol streets, respond to alarms, and provide a sense of security for walled-in communities. The demand for public safety created a high growth sector in the otherwise sluggish economy, and there are now 2.5 private security operatives for every police officer. For the majority of the population who cannot afford privatized police, self-help becomes the only option. Unlike private sector security, which can legally provide only preventive services, community justice includes punishment as well. In a three-month period (May to July 2012) in impoverished Cape Town townships, which are also poorly policed, fourteen suspected criminals were most brutally executed in vigilante actions (Maregele 2012, 3; *Cape Times* editorial 2012b, 10). In this sorry tale of institutional failures, crumbling social cohesion, and the unravelling of the constitutional state, South Africa's constitutional system of devolved government hardly features; provinces have no police force of their own and may only perform a limited role in supervising the SAPS. Most of the metropolitan municipalities have established metropolitan police forces with restricted powers, and even these powers are under the threat of centralization.

It is argued that the roots of the centralized criminal justice system are to be traced to the repressive and ignominious policing practices of the apartheid past. The negotiated "revolution" that led to the creation of the system of multilevel government (national, government, provinces, and local government) established a unique system in which provinces have no policing powers: they have the power to monitor national policing but without any sanctions. This "federal" design has showed no fruit yet and is unlikely to do so. What is of general significance, however, is the response to the failure of centralized policing: first, a victimized population has turned to private security or to vigilantism. Second, there are limited but telling signs that metropolitan police forces are increasingly picking up the slack and going even beyond their constitutional mandate. It is further argued that in a situation of poor performing provinces and the majority of municipalities, the decentralization of policing does not provide the answer to better public security. Greater effectiveness of the national police force and increasing the role of local police forces may provide a partial solution, but most importantly, a disconnect between combating and preventing crime should be bridged. This would bring provinces into a whole-of-government approach to crime.

Historical Roots of the Centralized Public Safety System

The design of the security state in the 1993 and 1996 Constitutions was firmly embedded in the context of the pre-1994 history of the repressive South African state. During the apartheid era the national security establishment, comprising the South African Police (SAP), the South African Defence Force, and intelligence agencies, supported by the courts, was central to keeping the apartheid state afloat. In the 1980s the main focus of national security was on the low-intensity civil war and uprisings in the black townships. The repressive apartheid security apparatus was complemented and bolstered by black ethnic-based police forces of the four "independent" homelands and ten self-governing territories. Being under the control and in the service of the South African security apparatus, they, too, became targets of the liberation movements and black communities.

Among the principal features of public safety during this period are first, very tight control exercised by the centre over all security matters. This control did not lie with the national cabinet but with an inner group of "securocrats," the State Security Council – a case of centralizing the centre. Second, within the closed community of securocrats, secrecy and the absence of accountability were the order of the day. The impunity that followed led to the emergence of covert and clandestine operations that mirrored the death squads of Chile and Argentina (Steytler 1990). Third, the role distinctions between the SAP and the Defence Force disappeared. When the police failed to quell internal protest, their efforts were complemented by the Defence Force in patrolling the black townships with white conscripts. At the same time the SAP drifted into a militarized mode of functioning. Fourth, the police and defence forces in the black homelands were an integral part of the apartheid state, and their defence of their meagre spoils of the apartheid system was as repressive as those of their white counterparts. The emergence of local security forces in black townships added to the toxic mix. The illegitimate local councils in black urban townships were allowed and encouraged to employ ill-trained and poorly equipped armed personnel to suppress popular revolts. The outcome of these features was the narrow construction of public safety, focusing largely on white interest and homeland survival, thereby failing to serve the security concerns of the majority of the population, and ignoring the socio-economic drivers of crime and a lack of safety.

The unbanning of the liberation movements in 1990 saw the negotiations towards an inclusive democratic South Africa. Responding to the apartheid regime that sought to establish a type of ethnic divided-and-rule federalism through "independent" homelands and self-governing territories, the liberation movements (the African National Congress [ANC] in particular) fought for a centrist state that could build national unity and redress the ravages of apartheid. The white minority government, along with some ethnic homeland leaders, sought to retain a grip on some levers of power through a federal system. The outcome of the "negotiated revolution" was a hybrid state, displaying some federal elements within a strong central state structure; nine provincial governments were established with allocated powers, but a strong central supervisory hand was secured. The federal elements in the Constitutions were, paradoxically, the result of a process of devolution. Although, on paper, South Africa was in 1990 a fractured state, comprising a white-dominated state, in addition to fourteen self-governing black territories, the very object of the liberation war was to establish a united, non-racial state. The constitutional settlement of 1994 was thus at one and the same time a unification of ethnic and racial structures into a single non-racial South Africa, and a devolution of limited power to nine provinces. The same scenario also played itself out in the security arrangements.

From 1990 the major policy imperative about the reshaping of public safety was the need to democratize policing, by making the police transparent and accountable to the communities they served. "Community involvement" in decision-making became the mantra of reform during the 1990s. As to suitable methods, opinions differed. On the one hand, there was the fear of a centralized police force that could be abused for narrow political ends. Arguments were thus advanced for the unbundling of the SAP, and mooting the model of the fragmented police force in England and Wales. This model was not, as in England, coupled to a federal state structure. The countervailing argument was the need for central control to ensure stability and peace in a country that was at war with itself. The notion of a provincial police force was out of the question. Given the high level of ongoing conflict at the time in KwaZulu-Natal (between supporters of the ANC and supporters of the Inkatha Freedom Party, which collaborated with the apartheid regime), the illegitimacy of all the homelands' security forces and the fear of renegade provinces with their own armed forces, one national police institution that exercises direct-line authority over all armed forces was the only real option on the table. The concept of community-based policing suited the overall project of democratizing the state and led, among other things, to changing the name of the SA Police to the SA Police *Service* (SAPS). These policy choices were reflected in the interim Constitution of 1993 as well as the final Constitution of 1996. However, a measure of path-dependency was apparent. The new democratic wine was poured in the old apartheid bottles; the past forms of centralist control and an emphasis on crime combatting at the expense of crime prevention, were never abandoned and shaped the range of changes during the next two decades.

Constitutional Landscape of Public Safety Institutions

The 1993 interim Constitution was in essence a peace agreement between the ANC and the white minority government. Provinces were established as a compromise, and consequently they received limited powers over the national police force. It provided that the South African Police Service (SAPS) would be "structured at both national and provincial levels" and would function under the direction of both the national and provincial governments (section 214(1) interim Constitution). The powers of provinces included approving the appointment of a provincial police commissioner, passing legislation not inconsistent with national legislation on the functioning of the police in the province, directing the activities of the police commissioner, and approving the establishment of local (municipal) police services, with powers limited to preventing crime and the enforcement of local by-laws.

The 1996 Constitution, adopted by the democratically elected Constitutional Assembly, watered down the provincial policing competency considerably. This was in line with an overall downgrading or hollowing out of provincial competencies, reflecting the ANC's reluctant compromise on provinces, and strengthening the role of local government. The point of departure was that "the security services of the Republic consist of a single defence force, a single police force and any intelligence services established in terms of the Constitution" (section 199(1) Constitution). Furthermore, "security services must be structured and regulated by national legislation" (section 199(4) Constitution). Responding to a legacy of impunity, a governing principle of national security is that it is "subject to the authority of Parliament and the national executive" (section 198(d) Constitution).

The shift to the centre affected provinces' role in and influence over policing. While policing remained a concurrent function of the national and provincial governments, provincial powers are limited. First, a consultative duty is imposed on the national executive to take into account "the policing needs and priorities of the provinces as determined by the provincial executives" (section 206(1) Constitution). A province has a reciprocal entitlement to liaise with the national minister responsible for police on crime and policing in the province.

Second, the main provincial function is that of oversight. A province is entitled:

(a) To monitor police conduct;
(b) To oversee the effectiveness and efficiency of the police service, including receiving reports on the police service; and
(c) To assess the effectiveness of visible policing (section 206(3) Constitution), which includes the establishment and maintenance of police stations, crime reaction units, and patrolling services (as defined in section 219(2d) interim Constitution).

To effect its oversight role, a province may also investigate complaints of police inefficiency or a breakdown in relations between the police and any community. It cannot act upon any findings with any sanctions, but is limited to making recommendations to the responsible national minister.

Third, on a more proactive level, a province may "promote good relations between the police and the community" (section 206(3) Constitution). The result is thus that the provincial role was designed to be a good, ineffectual, arm's-length away from the "hard side" of policing in South Africa.

In line with local government's enhanced status as a sphere of government alongside the national and provincial governments (section 40(1) Constitution), the Constitution also provides that national legislation must make provision for municipal police services. The South African Police Service Act of 1995 thus mandates any local or metropolitan government to seek the approval of the provincial government to establish a police service. Municipal and metropolitan police

Table 7.1. Competencies of Three Levels of Government

Level of government	Crime prevention: law and practice	Investigation and arrest: law and practice	Public order: law and practice	Oversight: law and practice
National	Policy	SAPS	SAPS	Civilian secretariat; Independent Police Investigations Inspectorate
Provincial	Social services	None	None	Department of Community Safety (limited in practice)
Local	Social Services	Some limited instances	Limited	None

forces are subject mutatis mutandis to any regulations that the minister of police may issue in respect of the SAPS under the SA Police Service Act. The functions of a municipal police service are traffic policing, subject to any legislation relating to road traffic; the policing of municipal by-laws and regulations that are the responsibility of the municipality in question; and the prevention of crime. The Act affords municipal police officers the legal powers of arrest, search, and seizure within their area of jurisdiction or with permission of another municipality outside their jurisdiction. They are allowed to make arrests but must hand over any arrested person to the SAPS. They cannot investigate crimes and are required to hand over any case to the SAPS. Table 7.1 sums up the competences of the three levels of government with respect of policing as well as the practice that is discussed below.

While the institutions of armed force reside at the national level, provinces and local government must address the socio-economic conditions that engender crime. The principal functions of provinces are education, health services, social development (including social services), housing, roads, and transport. Municipalities are mandated to provide basic municipal services such as water, sanitation, electricity, and municipal health services. While these levels of government have only their toes in the security waters, they must stem the social tide of crime. Although there is a constitutional disconnect between the two functions, some provinces and metropolitan municipalities (metros) are willing to wade a bit deeper into the muddy and treacherous crime waters, as described below.

Metrics, Fiscal Dimensions, and Developments

A policy linkage between crime and socio-economic conditions was the point of departure of the first democratic government of Nelson Mandela (Rauch 2001). There were great expectations from the 1996 National Crime Prevention Strategy (NCPS), and government departments and civil society would rally around it. The NCPS articulated a dual approach where more effective law enforcement would be balanced with addressing the social causes of crime. It would unavoidably require a long-term approach, but this long-term view resulted in diminished political support for the NCPS.

The high violent crime rate and public demands for action prompted the government to opt for more visible short-term strategies focusing on priority crimes as described in the National Crime Combating Strategy (NCCS) of 2000 (Du Plessis and Louw 2005). By the late 1990s the initial political support for the balanced approach of the NCPS had fizzled out.

While the NCPS was in substance and approach inclusive of the three spheres of government and non-governmental organizations, and balancing law enforcement with addressing the social causes of crime, the NCCS was exclusive in defining government's response to crime as a SAPS function. In effect, the national government had monopolized the policymaking on crime and safety, defining it as a law enforcement problem and marginalizing crime prevention (Frank 2003, 15).

A further consequence was that the overarching policy framework (the NCPS) to steer responses from the three spheres of government to crime and safety effectively disappeared. If a requirement for effective policymaking is that it should be joined-up by taking a holistic view looking beyond institutional boundaries to the government's strategic objectives and seeks to establish the ethical, moral, and legal base for policy (Bullock, Mountford, and Stanley 2001), the national government's response to crime and safety did not achieve this. Instead of overarching and cohesion-building strategic objectives, the emphasis on law enforcement and the prominence given to SAPS proved to be divisive and unable to guide responses to crime and safety.

With the emphasis on combatting crime, the SAPS has grown significantly over the last decade to nearly 200 000 employees, or 372 officers per 100,000 population. This is well below the recommended UN standard of one police official per 500 persons, but as already noted, there are serious concerns about their effectiveness and adherence to constitutional requirements for human rights and good governance.

The SAPS budget has grown by leaps and bounds, resulting in a more than four-fold increase since 2002/3, in a trend reflective of government's emphasis on law enforcement as the crime management strategy (National Treasury 2002, 2017). The increase in the SAPS budget was, however, not accompanied by a concomitant increase in provincial safety and security budgets. The centralization of control over safety and security was therefore very much reflected in a centralization of the budget by the national government. Comparatively, the Western Cape budget for public safety does not constitute even 0.5 per cent of the SAPS budget (Western Cape Provincial Legislature 2012).

The increased spending on national crime combatting is no doubt a result of the centralized nature of policing. Consequently, there has been no significant increase in provincial spending. As explained below, with provinces having hardly any of their own revenue, crime levels, which may differ between provinces, also do not feature as an element in determining the equitable share of each province. Although such a block grant is unconditional, the provinces' discretion is very much limited by expenditure constraints imposed by national standards and obligations in the key areas of education and health. The result is that there is hardly any revenue to improve public security significantly.

Oversight structures operate at a number of levels but without much tangible results. First, there are two civilian bodies, the Civilian Secretariat for Police (with a mandate to monitor and evaluate the functioning of the police) and the Independent Police Investigative Directorate (formerly Independent Complaints Directorate) to investigate serious allegations against police officials. Second, political oversight is performed by Parliament. Third, independent constitutional bodies – the auditor-general and the public protector, and the SA Human Rights Commission – perform oversight functions.

Provinces

Given the emphasis on combatting crime and the absence of an overall crime prevention strategy, the scope for provinces to play a meaningful role is minimal. Each province has established a department of public or community safety (often in combination with traffic police), but comprises civilian employees only. Little is publicly visible about how provinces exercise their oversight, and judging from their budgets, this is not surprising. The budgets of the departments responsible for policing comprise a minuscule item in the provincial budget. The Western Cape Department of Community Safety, perhaps the most active in the country, consumed 0.84 per cent of the 2010/11 provincial budget, of which 53 per cent was spent on traffic officers. These figures have not changed much over time, as little effect is given to the oversight mandate.

This limited budget is sourced from national transfers to provinces. In a case of extreme vertical fiscal imbalance, provinces receive on average 97 per cent of their income from national transfers through both untied block grants (80 per cent) and conditional grants (20 per cent). None of the conditional grants are linked to policing.

Local Government

As the crime combatting door is slightly ajar for local government, most of the metropolitan municipalities have established metro police services, and Cape Town is seeking concertedly to get its foot further through the door. Metropolitan police services were established in Johannesburg (2001), Cape Town (2001), Ethekwini (Durban) (2002), Ekurhuleni (East Rand) (2002), Tshwane (Pretoria) (2002), and Nelson Mandela Bay (Port Elizabeth) (2003). Only one local rural municipality, Swartland, has followed suit. The number of police officers is not insignificant. For example, Johannesburg has in excess of 4,400 officers, Cape Town 1,400, and Nelson Mandela Bay 720. The training of the metropolitan police is effected by the municipalities themselves, but in terms of regulations prescribed by the SAPS. The majority of metro police officials were absorbed from the municipal traffic departments, and concerns have been expressed about the quality of the training they receive. Discipline is at times suspect, illustrated by the temporary police officers of the Ethekwini Metro Police (Durban) who threatened in August 2012 to burn down city hall if their demand of permanent appointment was not met (IOL 2012b).[6]

Given the number of officers, the expenditure on metro policing is considerable. Having real police officers on the beat, the expenditure by the city of Cape Town, for example, on policing and fire protection was 7.8 per cent of their 2008/9 budget, with half of that on policing.

6 In 2008, when the Ekurhuleni Metropolitan Police Service went on strike and blockaded roads, a violent confrontation erupted between it and the SAPS with an exchange of fire.

Expenditure on social welfare (which falls outside the constitutional competence) was less at 2.3 per cent. The expenditure is covered by the municipality's own revenue collected mainly from property taxes. An additional expenditure is the employment by the municipality of private security companies to provide security in particular neighbourhoods, so-called city improvement districts. In a partnership with the ratepayers in a particular neighbourhood, who are willing to pay a surcharge on their property rates, the municipality contracts a security firm to provide additional security for that area. These have been popular in inner city districts as well as wealthier suburbs, although their impact has been little more than crime displacement.

Given the uneven service provided by the SAPS, metropolitan governments are seeking to fill the vacuum within the available constitutional space (and beyond). The city of Cape Town, under the control of the main opposition party, is at the forefront of such initiatives. It distinguishes between traffic officers, law enforcement officers, and metro police officers both by uniform and job description. While the law enforcement officers are concerned with the enforcement of municipal by-laws (and prevent illegal land invasions) and the traffic police with traffic, the metro police officers have bigger fish to fry. They, according to the city, "work closely with SAPS on serious criminal issues with a strong emphasis on crime prevention," which includes holding roadblocks to search vehicles for illegal firearms and drugs (*City News* 2012, 5). In 2012 it increased its budget for a Gang Task Force to crack down on gangs and the drug trade (Nicholson 2012, 5). The most audacious initiative yet was the establishment of a unit to fight abalone poachers along Cape Town's 300 km coastline, because nature conservation falls squarely in the lap of the provincial and national governments, both of which have shown an ineptness in preventing the decimation of this shellfish delicacy.

Unlike the lack of coordination between combatting and preventing crime, metropolitan governments are better placed to draw the linkages. For example, the city's anti-crime initiatives are broad; through by-laws on inner city dwellings, places of ill repute are closed down. Through the municipality's central strategic planning document, the Integrated Development Plan, anti-crime strategies are forged through proper township planning, the erection of street lighting, and nuisance legislation. A further example is the Violence Prevention through Urban Upgrading Project, initiated in 2006 by the city of Cape Town, which aimed to reduce crime and increase safety levels in designated areas of Khayelitsha, and to upgrade neighbourhoods, improve social standards, and introduce sustainable community projects to empower the local residents.

Other metropolitan governments also focus on the social side of crime prevention. One aspect has been the need for ex-prisoner reintegration. The city of Johannesburg has, for example, recognized reoffending as a significant threat to public safety. Under its Human Development Program, the city lists numerous services aimed at reducing vulnerability and could also benefit former prisoners, such as the vulnerable households support program, skills development program, and youth development program.

Whereas the national government is likely to resist further local government intrusions in the policing domain, the placement of the metro police forces under national control is in the cards. At the ANC's Policy Conference in 2012, the party resolved that there should be a single police service. The reasons advanced by the ANC Western Cape delegation was that there was no uniform training of officers, and serious crime scenes were botched because there were no prescribed and mutually agreed upon standards between the SAPS and metropolitan police on how to handle such scenes. It therefore called for the municipal, metropolitan, and traffic police to be placed under the command and control of the national commissioner of SAPS (Hartley 2012, 4). The Democratic Alliance (DA), which governs the city of Cape Town and Western Cape province, saw it as yet another attempt to seize powers of a functioning municipality in opposition hands (Ndenze 2012, 5). For commentators it was yet another example of the ruling party wanting to be in control of all law enforcement bodies (Johan Burger, quoted in Hartley 2012, 4).

Intergovernmental Relations

With no police force of their own, provinces' monitoring role of the SAPS is embedded in intergovernmental relations. This relationship must be played against the constitutional framework of cooperative government between the three spheres of government (see chapter 3, Constitution). More specifically, the Constitution provides for an intergovernmental committee (a MinMEC), consisting of the national minister and the members of the (provincial) Executive Committee (MECs) responsible for policing, with the aim to ensure "effective co-ordination of the police service and effective co-operation among spheres of governments" (section 206(8) Constitution). Such a committee has been established and meets regularly, but its impact on the functioning of the SAPS is limited. The MinMEC meets two to three times a year, and then nine MECs compete for space on the agenda and the ear of the minister of police. With such limited opportunity and time for discussion, it is unlikely that provincial, let alone local, crime and safety matters will receive adequate analysis and discussion. It is reported that, except for rare instances, there is little evidence that the SAPS has tailored its strategies to local needs (Paremoer, Africa, and Mattes 2012, 137).[7] As with MinMECs in other sectors, the national minister usually dominates his or her ANC colleagues in eight provinces. The Western Cape, the only province under the control of the main opposition party, the DA, has had little impact on strategic decisions. As there are no separate police forces whose coordination and cooperation must be secured, the forum is about the provinces' oversight function. This makes for fraught intergovernmental relations, because it is the only example in the Constitution where the usual hierarchical monitoring relationship is turned on its head – provinces monitoring the national government.

Although oversight includes the fairly intrusive appointment of an investigation or commission of inquiry, a province has few substantive remedies; it can make recommendations to the national police minister and introduce removal proceedings against a provincial commissioner, but it cannot fire the incumbent. A further dampener on vigorous monitoring is that if the province's good efforts pay off in improved policing, the SAPS, rather than the province, will garner the credit for improved performance. No evidence has emerged of any success of this model of reverse supervision.

Even where a province seeks to exploit the constitutional space of oversight, it's a rocky road. In ANC-controlled provinces, exercising this oversight role operates within a strong centralized party system. Even the DA-controlled Western Cape has encountered national resistance to its initiatives, as they are perceived as politically motivated. It

7 One example comes from the Western Cape. Nationally, the SAPS decided to abolish a number of specialized crime-fighting units, including one that focused on gang-related violence. While Cape Town has a very high murder rate, the location of these crimes is confined to a few townships where gang violence is rife, as mentioned above. The Western Cape minister for community safety thus decried the national decision to abolish the specialist gang unit, because it would prejudice local policing efforts to combat gang violence (De Wee 2012, 5).

makes, of course, political sense for the DA to improve policing in the Western Cape; its national platform for expansion is a record of better service delivery, and achieving more effective policing through its oversight activities could be received well by electorates in other provinces demoralized by ineffective policing. The Western Cape's first initiative was a draft bill in 2012 on community safety, which aimed to formalize the oversight function. On adoption in 2013, the law's constitutionality was questioned by the national minister, but this was overtaken by the province's third initiative described below. The second action was the call by Premier Helen Zille (the national leader of the DA) for President Zuma to deploy Defence Force troops in certain townships where gang warfare raged seemingly beyond the control of SAPS. The request was turned down as being unnecessary. The third initiative was the appointment by Premier Zille in August 2012, contrary to the wishes of the minister of police, of a provincial commission of inquiry into the poor state of policing in Khayelitsha, the largest black township in Cape Town and site of numerous incidents of mob justice. The minister sought unsuccessfully in the Western Cape High Court for an interdict to stop the commission because, among other claims, the province did not follow the appropriate intergovernmental procedures of consultation. The minister then took the matter to the Constitutional Court,[8] but was unsuccessful, and the commission went ahead. The judgment confirmed the powers of a provincial premier to establish a commission of inquiry as is provided for under the Constitution.

Policy Case Study: Disaster Management

In the field of disaster management, all three spheres of government are drawn into a single system to deal with threats to and breaches of public order. The prime example has been the widespread xenophobic attacks in 2008 against foreigners in black townships. The UN Special Rapporteur on the Promotion and Protection of Human Rights and Fundamental Freedoms while Countering Terrorism noted in 2007 that South Africa's undocumented immigrant community had grown rapidly since 1994 and could be regarded by some as a threat to security (Schenin 2007). Moreover, there were indeed notable xenophobic

---

8 *Minister of Police and Others v Premier of the Western Cape and Others* [2013] ZACC 33, 2013 (12) BCLR 1365 (CC), 2014 (1) SA 1 (CC) (1 October 2013).

sentiments, posing further threats to security. Six months after the special rapporteur published his report, widespread xenophobic attacks took place in Gauteng and Western Cape provinces in May 2008, and large numbers of immigrants from elsewhere in Africa were killed, injured, and internally displaced. Since 2008 xenophobic attacks have occurred sporadically in various parts of the country.

The xenophobic attacks brought provinces and local government to the foreground. While the restoration of law and order was the responsibility of the SAPS, municipalities, with the assistance of provinces, had to cope with large numbers of displaced foreigners, by providing food and shelter and commencing the long process of reintegrating them in communities. This brought to the fore the role of provinces and municipalities in managing a disaster, which was very different from the usual ones of drought, fire, and flooding.

"Disaster management" is a concurrent national and provincial competency. Some of the associated services such as ambulance services are an exclusive provincial competence, while firefighting services are again a municipal function. The national government has regulated this functional area through the Disaster Management Act of 2002. Coming into operation in 2004, it established a hierarchical system of disaster management centres. At the apex is the National Disaster Management Centre, located in the national department concerned with provincial and local government, responsible for the coordination of the system including provincial and local disaster management centres in metropolitan and district municipalities. The establishment of local centres is thus a result of a legislative assignment that municipalities have experienced as unfunded mandates. The Act also provides for the declaration of national, provincial, and local disasters.

The intergovernmental as well as hierarchical nature of the system is recognized also in the establishment of an Intergovernmental Committee on Disaster Management, which is appointed by the president and comprises the responsible national minister, provincial ministers, and representatives from the municipalities. With the national minister as the chairperson, the committee is accountable and must report to the national cabinet.

When it comes to the funding of the system, the principle established in the Act is that the national, provincial, and local organs may contribute to response efforts (including assisting one another), but repairing damage to public sector infrastructure is the responsibility of the affected organs of state. Requests by provinces and municipalities for financial assistance are considered by the national government, guided by a number of factors including the magnitude of the disaster and whether the provincial or local resources have been exhausted.

The disaster management system reflects at the same time a strong centralized element of coordination, but also the need for provincial and local involvement. As a national disaster is yet to be declared, the focus has been on provincial and local disasters. With almost no discretionary funding, provinces have become reliant on national financial assistance to cope with provincial disasters. Municipalities are more capable of dealing with disasters, but argue that this function was assigned to them without proper compensation. Again, with limited provincial discretionary funding, municipalities look at the national government for financial support.

Although there has been no declared national disaster, in every case of a provincial or municipal disaster, there is usually a combined response of the three levels of government. Except in cases such as drought relief where only the provincial and national government would be involved mostly through financial aid, disasters affecting human life, such as severe flooding, will draw in the national SAPS, provincial ambulance services, and local rescue services. Operations are managed at a local or provincial level through a coordinating committee comprising the parties involved.

Overall Assessment

By all accounts, the current, much centralized system to secure public safety is, euphemistically put, not working. A more accurate description is that South Africa is experiencing a public safety crisis. Not only do levels of violent and fear-inducing crime remain unacceptably high (although some declines are noted), the institutions of state responsible for addressing crime and public safety are experiencing rapidly declining levels of legitimacy. In particular, reference is made here to SAPS as the government embodiment of a "law and order" and "get tough on crime" strategy. Apart from this approach being ineffective, there is a growing chasm between the population in general, and specifically disgruntled communities with reference to their socio-economic position, and law enforcement. They have resorted to self-help by enlisting the private security where they can afford it and, on occasion, mob violence where they cannot. Some provincial governments, notably the opposition-held Western Cape, are seeking to take their monitoring mandate seriously, while metropolitan governments are devoting increasing resources to combatting crime through their metropolitan police services. The national government is contesting the expansive interpretation of the constitutional provisions.

The question then arises whether the very centrist nature of the state's efforts at securing public safety is the root cause of the problem. Does the answer, then, lie in the decentralization of policing?

Centralized policing in a broad sense would appear to be a major cause of the problem. First, there are fundamental problems with the substance of current policies addressing crime and safety, as well as the processes of policymaking. The national response to public security has been to combat crime, a policy conceived and implemented without an all-of-government (and society) approach. Second, there is evidence that the SAPS has been ignoring provincial and local priorities, and therefore has been unable to bring down specific manifestations of crime. Equally important, SAPS has essentially failed to engage constructively with community-based stakeholders, such as community-based organizations and thus aggravated its own legitimacy woes.

Is the decentralization of crime combating and prevention, then, the answer? For the National Planning Commission (NPC) the answer does not lie down this avenue, but rather in the reinvigoration of the national institutions. At a national level the various organs of state that constitute the criminal justice system do not cooperate well by effectively coordinating effort. Moreover, in many respects the SAPS lacks professionalism and is plagued by poor management and corruption. The specific accountability institutions are also failing in their task. In the NPC's analysis, the lack of effective provincial oversight is not a contributing factor. This is not surprising, as the NPC's *Diagnostic Report* decries the lack of capacity and abundance of corruption in provinces to perform even their basic functions of providing effective education and health services. The implicit view is that moves towards decentralizing some policing functions to provinces will exacerbate the problem in most provinces. Thus, in the NPC's *Vision 2030* the provinces feature only in the socio-economic responses to crime. The NPC's five priorities to achieve a crime-free South Africa are:

- Strengthening the national criminal justice system, by ensuring better cooperation between the police, prosecution, judiciary, and correctional services;
- Making the police service more professional;

- Demilitarizing the police service;
- Building safety by using an integrated approach, focusing on the fundamental socio-economic causes of crime; and
- Building community participation in community safety. On this score municipalities are expected to play an important role in establishing community safety centres to build safe and healthy communities.

The NPC's approach of double-tracking state endeavours to secure public safety (policing remaining a central responsibility, while tackling the socio-economic causes of crime is an all-of-government task) resuscitates the inclusive and context-sensitive approach of the 1996 NCPS in terms of which provinces and local government must intervene to deal with the roots of crime within their functional areas. We are in agreement with this approach, but would add the codicil that a modest asymmetrical devolution of policing powers to capable metropolitan governments may add some value to address localized crime conditions. This will also bolster the policing powers already claimed by provinces and cities who are responding to the needs of their fearful and despondent residents.

With respect to the second track of crime prevention, the need for a coordinated approach by all spheres cries out. The first step towards public safety will be to recognize that there is indeed a crisis at hand. Recognizing a crisis, and doing so quickly, would bring a number of advantages, the most important being that it creates the opportunity and the pressure for innovation – for policy decision-makers to consider options that have hitherto fallen outside the prevailing paradigm. The second step is the non-centralization of policy formation – an approach that emphasizes inclusivity of all spheres of government as well as the citizenry, in an effort to build a common vision of a more just South Africa.

The final question that should be addressed is the significance of the South African experience for an international audience, particularly for other developing countries experimenting with federalism. First, it was the correct approach to have adopted a strong centralized police force immediately after democratization of the state in 1994. State authority had to be established, and competing police forces may have contributed to the continuation of instability, which is usually the hallmark of national peace transitions. Furthermore, where constituent units are newly established, weak, and corruption-ridden, it is unlikely that they will be able to provide adequate public safety at all. Second, it is wrong, however, to exclude provinces from policing decisions altogether. In a large country where social and economic dynamics, manifested in crime rates and crime types, differ from province to province, close cooperation between the provinces and the national police force is essential. The position was appropriately reflected in the interim Constitution where the emphasis fell on the joint direction of the national police force by the national and provincial government. Third, the inclusion of the provincial governments in policing by vesting them with an oversight function (without sanctions) is bound to be largely ineffective. By turning the largely hierarchical relationship between the national government and provinces on its head, it may lead inevitably to a conflictual rather than a cooperative relationship. Fourth, when the national police force has almost the exclusive task of crime combatting, and they fail in that task, it follows that victimized citizens will seek to secure their own safety through private means, which leads to greater inequality (the wealthy buy their security) or greater lawlessness (the poor resort to vigilantism). Fifth, a further, more positive response is local governments can step into the breach to secure their communities. Such a development would, however, depend on breaking the centrist paradigm of the national government. Finally, as public insecurity is a multifaceted phenomenon, entailing political, social, and economic factors, federated states can produce public security only through a whole-of-government approach that deals with both combatting and preventing crime.

References

Altbeker, A. 2007. *A Country at War with Itself: South Africa's Crisis of Crime.* Cape Town: Jonathan Ball Publishers.

Boin, A., and P. T'Hart. 2000. "Institutional Crises and Reforms in Policy Sectors." In *Government Institutions: Effects, Changes and Normative Foundations,* ed. H. Wagenaar, 9–31. Dordrecht: Kluwer Academic Publishers. https://doi.org/10.1007/978-94-010-0963-8_1.

Bullock, H., J. Mountford, and R. Stanley. 2001. *Better Policy-Making.* London: Centre for Management and Policy Studies.

City News. 2012. "What the City's Peace Officers Do," 5 June.

Department of Correctional Services. 2015. *Annual Report.* Pretoria: DCS.

De Wee, Maygene. 2012. "Min Sukses teen Bendes." *Die Burger* 6 (September): 5.

Du Plessis, A., and A. Louw. 2005. "Crime and Crime Prevention in South Africa: 10 Years After." *Canadian Journal of Criminology and Criminal Justice* (April): 430–1.

Essop, Philda. 2012. "Kwart van Speurders in SA 'nie Opgelei.'" *Die Burger* 6 (September): 2.

Frank, C. 2003. "What Have We Learned? Social Crime Prevention in SA: A Critical Overview." *Crime Quarterly* 6 (15), 21–6.

Hartley, Aziz. 2012. "ANC in Bid for One Police Service." *Cape Times*, 3 July.

– 2012b. "Metro Cops Threaten to Burn City Hall." 21 August. http://www.iol.co.za/news/politics/metro-cops-threaten-to-burn-city-hall-1.1366647#.UEdFoqBNRTY.

Karamoko, Jelanie. 2011. "Community Protests in South Africa: Trends, Analysis and Explanations." Community Law Centre. https://www.sajr.co.za/docs/default-source/default-document-library/14-community-protests.pdf?sfvrsn=2.

Khoza, A. 2017. "The Riah End: Suspended Phiyega Completes Term as Police Boss." News24.com. http://www.news24.com/SouthAfrica/News/the-riah-end-suspended-phiyega-completes-term-as-police-boss-20170612.

Legal Briefs. 2012. "600 Gauteng Police Arrested in a Year: Petros." 3 May.

Maregele, Barbara. 2012. "14th Vigilante Murder as Mob Kills Robbery Suspect." *Cape Times*, 11 July.

Marikana Commission of Inquiry. n.d. "About the Commission." http://www.marikanacomm.org.za.

National Planning Commission. 2011a. *Diagnostic Report*. Pretoria: National Planning Commission.

National Treasury. 2002. *Estimates of National Expenditure Vote 24. Safety and Security*. Pretoria: National Treasury. http://www.treasury.gov.za/documents/mtbps/2002/estimates_02.pdf.

– 2017. *Estimates of National Expenditure Vote 23. Police*. Pretoria: National Treasury. http://www.treasury.gov.za/documents/mtbps/2017/aene/Vote%2023%20Police.pdf.

Ndenze, Babalo. 2012. "DA Slams ANC's Plan for Single Police Service." *Cape Times*, 4 July.

News24Wire. 2015. "Private Security Officers in SA Outnumber Police and Army." BusinessTech. https://businesstech.co.za/news/general/99248/private-security-officers-outnumber-sa-police-and-army-combined/.

Nicholson, Zara. 2012. "City Sets aside R20m to Fight Gangs, Drugs." *Cape Times*, 1 September.

Paremoer, Laureen, Cherrel Africa, and Robert Mattes. 2012. *Open Society Monitoring Index: Dimensions, Indicators and Available Evidence*. Report for Open Society Foundation of South Africa.

Powell, Derek, Michael O'Donovan, and Jaap De Visser. 2015. *Civic Protests Barometer 2007–2014*. Cape Town: Dullah Omar Institute.

Rauch, Janine. 2001. *The 1996 National Crime Prevention Strategy*. Johannesburg: CSVR.

Redpath, Jean. 2012. *Failing to Prosecute? Assessing the State of the National Prosecuting Authority in South Africa*. Institute for South Africa Studies. https://issafrica.org/research/monographs/failing-to-prosecute-assessing-the-state-of-the-national-prosecuting-authority-in-south-africa.

South African Police Service. 2011. *Annual Report 2010/11*. Pretoria: SAPS.

– 2015. *Annual Report 2014/15*. Pretoria: SAPS.

Schenin, Martin. 2007. *Report of the Special Rapporteur on the Promotion and Protection of Human Rights and Fundamental Freedoms while Countering Terrorism: Mission to South Africa*. A/HRC/6/17/Add.2.

South African History Online. 2015. "Xenophobic Violence in Democratic South Africa." http://www.sahistory.org.za/article/xenophobic-violence-democratic-south-africa.

Steytler, Nico. 1990. "Policing Political Opponents: Death Squads and Cop Culture." In *Towards Justice? Crime and State Control in South Africa*, ed. Desiree Hansson and Smit Dirk van Zyl, 106–34. Cape Town: Oxford University Press.

UNDP. 2014. *Human Development Report 2014. Sustaining Human Progress: Reducing Vulnerabilities and Building Resilience.* New York: UNDP. http://hdr.undp.org/sites/default/files/hdr14-report-en-1.pdf.

Western Cape Provincial Legislature. 2012. "Western Cape Provincial Budget 2012 Highlights." https://www.westerncape.gov.za/other/2012/3/2012_wc_provincial_budget_highlights.pdf.

World Bank. 2017. "Intentional Homicides per 100,000 People)." https://data.worldbank.org/indicator/VC.IHR.PSRC.P5?end=2012&start=2012&view=chart&year_high_desc=false.

8 Spain

MARIO KÖLLING

Introduction

The Kingdom of Spain is one of the most decentralized countries in the world. Decentralization started after the Franco dictatorship, in parallel with the transition to democracy during the second half of the 1970s. The original objectives included the accommodation of Basque and Catalan nationalists, reform of the concept of public order to public security, and a redefinition of the role of police, which had been one of the most visible elements and representatives of the totalitarian regime. However, self-government enjoyed broad support, and practically all Spanish constituent units – autonomous communities (ACs) – strove for it. Although the transition to democracy was characterized by a broad compromise among all political forces, the increased violence by the terrorist group Basque Fatherland and Liberty (ETA) made terrorism an important public security problem for the new democratic state. Nevertheless, the impact of terrorism on the debate about the distribution of responsibilities has been limited. The recent economic and institutional crisis had a more decisive effect and may lead to necessary constitutional reforms to increase the efficiency and effectiveness of the model.

Even though the Spanish Constitution of 1978 circumnavigated the label of a federation, Spain has come to exhibit the basic structures and processes typical of federations and could be defined as a federation in practice, if not in name (Watts 2010). Political power in Spain is organized around a central government, seventeen autonomous communities, as well as two autonomous cities, and 8,112 local councils. All three levels have their own legal status; nevertheless the local level has only administrative – no legislative – autonomy.

Four central dimensions describe the evolution and the functioning of the Spanish state and explain the distribution of responsibilities related to public security issues. The first is a vertical one between the ACs and the central government: the ACs seek more powers and resources from the central government, mainly through bilateral negotiations, and the central government tries to maintain its role in coordinating state-wide policymaking. The second dimension is horizontal and characterized by lack of institutionalized cooperation and coordination mechanisms among the ACs. The third dimension makes reference to heterogeneous responsibilities at the regional level, because power has been devolved from the centre to the ACs asymmetrically, according to the aspirations of the ACs, some of which are seeking a more specific relationship with the central government. And the fourth (new) dimension is related to economic questions, with some ACs backtracking on demands for their own security forces because of budgetary constraints due to the consequences of the economic and financial crisis. Others insist on greater fiscal autonomy to cover their responsibilities, which includes their responsibilities in public security, while the central state tries to reduce spending on public security to reduce the public deficit.

Spain's population (46.5 million) density is less than that of most European countries. Following a long-standing pattern in Western Europe, rural populations have been moving to cities. Urban areas are also experiencing a significant increase in immigrant population, mainly from South America and North Africa. However, recently the immigration flow has declined and more Spaniards are emigrating because of high unemployment. A primary sector of the Spanish economy with an important impact on the organization of public security in the Mediterranean ACs is tourism.[1] The State Secretariat of Security of the Ministry of Home Affairs launches special annual plans during the

1 Safety and security is an important factor for tourism. Tourism demand has also been affected by lower oil prices and currency fluctuations. In general terms, the total contribution of travel and tourism to the Spanish GDP was in 2014 16 per cent. During the same year Spain received close to 65 million visitors (UNWTO 2015).

summers to provide tourists with a safer environment during their stay and travel in Spain.

Analysing the surveys of the Spanish Centre for Sociological Research (CIS) on the problems perceived as most important by Spanish citizens, there are three issues closely linked to public security: terrorism, immigration, and public insecurity. Nevertheless the perception of insecurity as one of the main problems in Spain is on the wane and reached a historical nadir in 2014. This is not only related to the decrease in crime in recent years, but also to the economic and financial problems the country has been facing, which are perceived as more important than in the past.

With regard to the territorial distribution of crime, we can find a broad asymmetry among ACs. Traditionally the police forces register higher levels in the capital region of Madrid, among the Mediterranean ACs, and the border cities of Ceuta and Melilla in the north of Africa. During recent years, the police recorded an increase in crime related to domestic burglary and drug trafficking. Armed violence is rare. The incidence of homicides is one of the lowest rates in the European Union (EU). While in 2003 police forces recorded 1,366 murders, in 2014 the number of homicides went down to 300. There was a general tendency for all levels of recorded crime to decrease in recent years, and the number of most types of crimes recorded fell between 2007 and 2015[2] (Gobierno de España 2015).

The government of Spain has been embroiled in a long-term conflict with the terrorist organization ETA, founded in 1959 and dedicated to Basque independence. In the past, ETA has targeted Spanish security forces, military personnel, Spanish government officials, and business people, as well as civilian institutions. The Spanish government attributes over 800 deaths to ETA terrorism since its campaign of violence began. In recent years, the government has made inroads against ETA, in part as the result of increased security cooperation with French authorities, robust application of Spanish post-9/11 criminal law, and a slow but powerful mobilization of civil society against it.

In 2011 ETA declared a permanent ceasefire, but the government called for ETA to announce unilaterally a definite end to its violence.

2 The total number of recorded crimes cover a wider range of offences than those detailed in the analyses that follow – namely, for the selected offences of violent crime, homicide, robbery, property crime, and drugs offences.

Although no direct negotiation took place and no peace agreement was signed, the terrorist organization announced the start of a unilateral disarmament program in early 2014 with the help of the International Verification Commission. This process has not officially recognized by the Spanish government.

Spain has also been a target of international terrorism. On 11 March 2004, only three days before national elections, several bombs detonated on passenger trains in Madrid. Evidence quickly surfaced that jihadist terrorists were responsible for the attack that killed 191 people. Spanish investigative services and the judicial system arrested and prosecuted Al Qaeda–linked members and have since been cooperating with foreign governments to diminish the international terrorist threat.

Constitutional and Legal Landscape

While transitioning to democracy during the second half of the 1970s, the democratization and modernization of public security was a primary goal. During this process the traditional legal and political notion of *public order* – deemed as a general operating clause of government intervention – was formally being replaced by the new notion of public security (Bas Vilafranca 2009, 39). The preamble of the Spanish Constitution (SC) proclaims that security, justice, and liberty are common goods of all Spanish citizens and specify the mission of security forces and bodies "to protect the free undertaking of rights and liberties and to guarantee citizen security" (Article 104.1). Although in terms of guaranteeing rights and freedoms the concept of public security attained consensus, when it came to discussing the territorial and political model of organization it became controversial. The constituent debate, and subsequently the debate on the statutes of the ACs, reflected the conflict among the various perspectives on the territorial organization of the Spanish state, and consequently the degree of decentralization of responsibilities in public security. To find a compromise, decentralization was designed as an open process in which responsibilities have been transferred from the central state government to the ACs asymmetrically, according to the aspirations of the ACs.

As a result of this asymmetric territorial distribution of power and sectorial responsibilities in Spain, politics related to public security comprises exclusive responsibilities, shared responsibilities, and concurrent responsibilities among the different administrative levels. This is the result of both top-down decentralization of state sovereignty and bottom-up decentralization in accordance with aspirations of individual ACs. According to Article 149.1.29, the central government has exclusive jurisdiction over public security, but without prejudice for autonomous communities to create their own police forces according to their respective statutes. The Constitution thus provides a framework for a system of public security based on three levels: the local, the constituent units, and the central state. The Spanish model is also defined by two other characteristics: the plurality of police forces, and the diversity of their roles and degrees of competence. In light of this asymmetry, since the beginning of decentralization, the challenge has been to maintain a coherent and homogeneous framework that could provide comparable policy outcomes across Spain.

The distribution of powers between the central government and the ACs regarding public security is specified by the Organic Law 2/1986[3] and the different Statutes of Autonomy.[4] The Organic Law 2/1986 established the main framework of the current Spanish police model and specified the institutional structure for cooperation and coordination of all activities of police forces. According to this constitutional and legal framework, the mandate to guarantee democratic coexistence and to protect citizens in the free exercise of their rights and public freedoms is facilitated by a public security system based chiefly on two state forces: regional and local police. The security forces of the central state are the Civil Guard and the National Police Force (NPF). Both forces fall under the Ministry of the Interior. The Civil Guard also reports to the Ministry of Defence in military missions as well as with regard to its equipment and accommodations. The Civil Guard was founded as a national police force in 1844 and initially was charged with putting an end to frequent attacks on the nation's highways. Subsequently, the Civil Guard was transformed into a paramilitary force of high mobility that patrolled large swathes of the countryside. In general, while the Civil Guard is still responsible for the development of security functions and the prevention and repression of crimes in rural areas, as well

3 Organic Law 2/1986, of 13 March, of the Security Forces and Bodies.

4 Statute of Autonomy is a law hierarchically located under the Spanish Constitution, and over any other form of legislation. This legislative corpus usually mimics the form of a constitution, establishing the organization of the autonomous government, the electoral rules, the distribution of competences between different levels of governance, and other regional-specific provisions, like the protection of cultural or lingual realities.

Table 8.1. Competences of the Security Forces of the Central State

National level	
Civil Guard	National Police Force
• Highway patrol • Drug operations • Anti-smuggling operations • Customs control • Weapons licences and arms control • Security of border areas and coast guard • Enforcement of environmental law	• Issuing of identity documents • Entry and exit controls of foreigners and Spaniards • Immigration law, refugee and asylum, extradition and expulsion • Gambling enforcement • Drug enforcement • Collaboration with Interpol and Europol • Overseeing private security companies
Subnational level	
General system	Special system
• Custody of buildings belonging to the autonomous community • Protection of the regional government • Coordination and control of private security companies • Inspection and control of gambling	• Citizen security and operational resources • Traffic control • Counterterrorism • Criminal police • Internal affairs – administrative
Local level	
• Custody of buildings belonging to the local government • Protection of the local government • Monitoring public spaces • Traffic control • Resolution of private disputes	

as within the territorial seas, the National Police Force operates in larger urban centres. The NPF can be traced back to the beginning of the nineteenth century and currently deals with more than 75 per cent of crime and police activity in Spain.

Article 148.1.22 SC allows ACs to create their own police forces to protect the buildings and institutions of the AC, as well as to coordinate the local police forces. Furthermore Article 1.1 of the Organic Law 2/1986 states, "The maintenance of public security shall be exercised by all public administrations throughout the security forces ... The autonomous communities participate in maintaining the public security in the terms established by their statutes and under this law." During decentralization, only ACs with a desire to assume responsibilities in public security through their statutes acquired competencies in this field after bilateral negotiations with the central government. The result is a heterogeneous system where different groups of ACs have different levels of competencies:

1 Autonomous communities with their own police forces:

The Ertzaintza in the Basque country – After a relatively short period of transition in the early 1990s the Ertzaintza took over the competences of the National Police and the Civil Guard in the Basque country where it covers the full spectrum of policing duties, except for border control, specific issues related to counterterrorism, identity documents, and immigration. The short transition period caused serious coordination problems with the national police forces, which led the central government to adopt different strategies in other ACs. The Ertzaintza now has 8,000 agents across five branches: citizen security and operational resources, traffic control, counterterrorism, criminal police, and internal affairs – administrative.

The *Mozos d'Esquadra* is the police force of Catalonia. Founded in the eighteenth century, the *Esquadres de Catalunya* was to support the army in the surveillance of roads. The Statute of Catalonia, approved in 1933, led to the creation of the Security Committee of Catalonia, which coordinated public security issues until 1939. During the Franco dictatorship, in 1950 the Deputation of Barcelona was authorized to create a section of *Mozos d'Esquadra*. Since the return of democracy to Spain, the *Mozos d'Esquadra* have been under the authority of the *Generalitat* of Catalonia and progressively replaced the National Police and Civil Guard across Catalonia. This substitution began in 1994, starting with traffic control in small villages, and was completed in the whole territory of the AC in November 2008 (including the transfer of responsibilities for criminal investigation, judicial police, and the fight against organized crime and counterterrorism).

Policía Foral in Navarre. In 1979, the police force began to protect official buildings and authorities. In 1986 the police force assumed jurisdiction over gambling and public entertainment. Since the 1990s, and after assuming the responsibilities of a full security force, it has gradually been extended its activities across the entire AC. It currently has 1,084 agents and is expected to reach 1,200 police officers in the coming years when the force will assume all responsibilities for policing Navarre. As in Catalonia and in the Basque country, the national police forces accompany the decentralization process and keep officers in the AC to handle terrorism, identity documents, immigration and other responsibilities of the central government.

In 2008 the *ACs of Canarias and Galicia* approved new laws to create their own police forces.[5] However, the creation of these two autonomous police forces has not fully materialized, mainly because of budgetary constraints.

2 The ACs whose statutes provide for the possibility of the creation of their own police forces but have not set up their own police: Andalusia, Asturias, Aragon, Extremadura, Castilla y Leon, Balearic Islands, and Valencia. In these cases the ACs can exercise their police powers by contracting units of the national police. Although they technically belong to the Interior Ministry, they report to the AC governments.

3 Some ACs do not foresee in their statutes the creation of an independent autonomous police force: Cantabria, Castilla–La Mancha, Ceuta, La Rioja, Murcia, and Melilla. By a specific agreement of cooperation, the national police covers the security competencies of these AC (Article 148.1.22).

Autonomous police forces can act only within the territorial boundaries of the relevant autonomous community, except in emergencies, when central state authorities can ask them to act outside their territory. Nevertheless in collaboration with the national police forces the ACs' police forces have to

- assure the compliance of central state laws;
- ensure the proper functioning of essential public services;
- collaborate with the judicial police;
- protect and monitor public spaces along with protecting legal demonstrations;
- cooperate in the settlement of private disputes;
- assist in cases of accident or catastrophe as well as in the implementation of civil protection plans; and
- assure compliance of regulations for the conservation of nature and the environment.

---

5 Ley de la Comunidad Autónoma de Canarias 2/2008, de 28 de mayo, del Cuerpo General de la Policía Canaria y Ley de la Comunidad Autónoma de Galicia 8/2007, de 13 de junio, de Policía de Galicia.

The exercise of these responsibilities should be carried out principally by the police forces of the autonomous communities without compromising the ability of the security forces of the central state to intervene, at the request of the authorities of the AC or central state authorities.

Local police forces. Since the 1980s the evolution of the local police has been continuous, and municipal police forces have become a major player in the public security in Spain: there are about 8,100 municipalities, of which approximately 1,800 have local police units whose members serve more than 85 per cent of the population. As a result of growth in urban areas during the 1990s, local police forces proliferated, grew, and assumed greater responsibilities, many of which have little to do with their conventional tasks of traffic control.

The central government, the governments of the autonomous communities and of the municipalities have their own administrative systems for hiring and promoting human resources. The central government runs the education and training centres for the national police forces and oversees the centres of the ACs. Although the ACs train their police agents autonomously in the use of their own weapons and technical equipment, the central government sets some minimum national standards.

In general, civil servants must pass the civil service exam of the government for which they want to work. Language requirements further limit movement among different levels of government. In the past, better salaries and working conditions have motivated some movement from the national police forces to autonomous or local police. However, during the past few years, budgetary constraints of constituent units limited such incentives.

Historical Developments

The general asymmetry of competencies within the ACs has been accompanied by an asymmetry of responsibilities for public security. The current arrangements have historical and political, but also economical and socio-demographic reasons.

Historically, certain ACs were at the forefront of decentralization. After the transition to democracy and before the Organic Law 2/1986 was approved, the Basque and Catalonian statutes of autonomy were the only ones that referred to their own police forces. That is because both ACs had already had their own police forces in the past, and more importantly, during the Second Republic.[6] The restoration of these forces was among their most important demands during this transition period. The national police forces were also seen as a symbol of the security forces of the Franco dictatorship, which used to suppress the cultural and ethnic identities of these ACs and were considered equally critical of self-government of constituent units. In fact the failed coup d'état in Spain on 23 February 1981 was led by a group of 200 armed officers of the Civil Guard. In other ACs the national police forces enjoyed greater support and legitimacy. Navarre, although not ethno-culturally distinct per se, had also had its own police force prior to the Franco dictatorship. The historical dimension is closely related to the symbolic character of police forces. In this regard some ACs had specific interests in having their own police forces, considering their language and culture distinct. They are not just functional institutions but representatives and symbols of a unique regional identity. To this end, these three ACs sought to distinguish their forces clearly by name and uniform (from the national police forces) and initially refused to have their autonomous police recruit members of the national police forces.

Politically, the Basque and the Catalonian nationalist parties played a crucial role in supporting different central governments. Their claims for more competences in general and regarding public security became part of political negotiations. During the centrifugal trend of the 1990s, several ACs were "encouraged" to acquire a higher degree of self-government. As a result, the issue of public security has gained in importance in most of them, and all ACs included in their statutes of autonomy references to public security and adopted respective laws. These laws differ significantly in scope and detail, but reflect the general political willingness of ACs to assume greater autonomy. Galicia, Andalusia, Valencia, and the Canary Islands initiated organizational structures for public security forces. The most recent reform of the statutes (2006–10) represents a further step towards decentralizing responsibilities, as exemplified by public security.[7]

Economically, ACs that built up their own police forces at the end of the 1980s and beginning of the 1990s – the Basque country, Navarre, and Catalonia – negotiated favourable agreements with the central

6 The Second Spanish Republic – from 14 April 1931 to 1 April 1939.

7 Comunidad Valenciana, Andalucía, Canaria, Galicia, Islas Baleares, Aragón y Castilla y León.

government to finance their police forces. Those three ACs are also the most economically prosperous Spanish regions, representing in this sense an "ideal model" for other ACs to emulate. The favourable financing agreements and extra income from traffic control provided economic incentives for other ACs to set up their own police force.

These historical, political, and economic reasons for the current arrangements are not a function of trying to provide better security to the population. In most ACs there is no electoral pressure for the creation of autonomous police forces, nor is it a priority or public concern. Public security is an important issue, but who is in charge is not.

During decentralization the central government provided the general legal framework for all activities related to public security. Although the central government transferred competences to the AC governments, it continues to monitor service delivery. The Coordination and Studies Office within the Secretary of State for Security assumes the coordination and supervision of activities of security forces and collects data from all security forces.

Furthermore the accession of Spain to the EU in 1986 has been a turning point in the country's recent history. Democratization and Europeanization can be considered the two major achievements of the development of Spain over the last three decades. The impact in economic, political, and social terms has been extraordinary. Besides a stronger social cohesion and modernization of the administration, the active commitment of the Spanish to a more open, more equitable, and more democratic world has given rise to a scenario radically different from that seen in the introverted and isolated Spain of the past. With regard to specific consequences for public security, there has been an important step forward in the fight against terrorism. Shortly after accession, the terrorist organization ETA was listed as a foreign terrorist organization by the United States and the European Union. Moreover the bilateral cross-border cooperation with France has been crucial in the fight against ETA terrorism. Already at the end of the eighties the Spanish and French governments had signed a pact against terrorism and drug traffic. Moreover Spain's counterterrorism was reinforced by essential cooperation from France. Moreover, Spain's work in counterterrorism for decades also allowed it to gain considerable experience, and in this sense the effectiveness of the Spanish model for managing terrorist threats provided considerable added value to international collaboration in counterterrorism. During the past years the counterterrorist police cooperation has defined North Africa as a priority area, especially Morocco – from where most Muslim immigrants to Spain come, as do most prisoners jailed in Spain for offences linked to jihadist terrorism – but also other Islamic countries, which led to the bilateral cooperation agreements on Islamic-oriented terrorism (Reinares and García-Calvo 2015). Spain fostered common security in the Mediterranean, not only bilaterally but also through broader cooperation frameworks such as the Union for the Mediterranean, the European Neighbourhood Policy, and other forums like the 5 + 5 Initiative, the Mediterranean Dialogue of the NATO and the Istanbul Cooperation Initiative.

Since the nineties there have been several initiatives to adapt Spanish domestic security structures to the threat posed by international terrorism and crime. The mandatory transposition to Spanish law of European law implied a considerable Europeanization of Spain's counterterrorism policy in general, and of the programs developed to combat terrorism in particular.

At the political level, the Spanish strongly identify with and support European integration (more strongly than other countries), and for some time the government has shown great enthusiasm for creating a European area of security and justice, and for fostering relations with Mediterranean countries. Through its Interior Ministry, Spain has participated in enhancing cooperation within the framework of the European area of freedom, security, and justice, as well as within the framework of the European Justice and Home Affairs Council.

Although the Spanish accession to the EU had important positive economic consequences, after decades of economic growth, a deep recession in Spain began with the end of the housing boom in 2007 and the international financial crisis in the second quarter of 2008. Since then, in response to the budget deficit and public debt, the central government and the ACs governments were forced to cut public spending to meet the Eurozone public deficit targets, which also affected the financial resources dedicated to public security forces. Since the onset of the economic crisis and cuts in public spending, the central government and several ACs have shown less interest in assuming the additional financial burden of autonomous police units.

Metrics and the Fiscal Dimension

Metrics

Although there are different police forces at the local, constituent unit, and central state level, the public security system still emulates that of a centralized state: 35 per cent of the staff are local and police of the ACs, and 65 per cent are state police. Although the newly created police forces at the level of constituent units have progressively taken over responsibilities of the national police forces, neither the numbers of the national police forces nor their organizational structure has changed much; on the contrary, these forces have also increased their numbers. While the number of police officers has remained virtually unchanged in most EU member states, in Spain they rose by over 22 per cent between 2000 and 2009. According to the director of the Civil Guard, at 5.3 police per 1,000 population in 2012, Spain's rate is among the highest in the EU and internationally. However, during the past years, in times of budgetary restraint, the government of Spain was under pressure to reduce its public spending (Fernández de Mesa, 2012). Bringing the ratio in line with the EU average of 3.27 would mean reducing the number of police by 73,339 – which is a rough equivalent of eliminating one national police force.

With regard to the territorial distribution of the security forces, according to figures from 2015, Ceuta and Melilla have by far the highest density of police officers: for every 100,000 inhabitants (neither city has a population of that size) there are 1,368 police officers in Ceuta and 1,264 in Melilla. No European country has such a large number of police officers in proportion to its population.

Other ACs with a high proportion of police officers are Madrid (748) and the Basque country (669). Compared to the 233 Mossos d'Esquadra per

Figure 8.1. Total Number of Police Officers

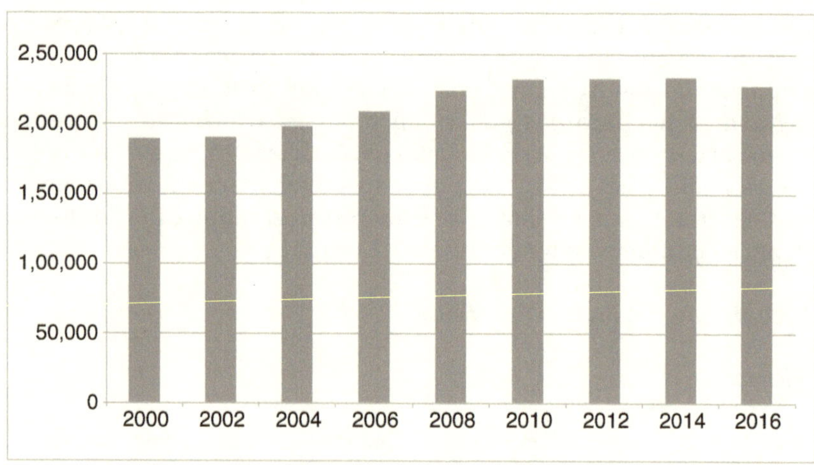

Source: Calculations based on Gobierno de España (2016).

Figure 8.2. Number of Police Agents, 2016

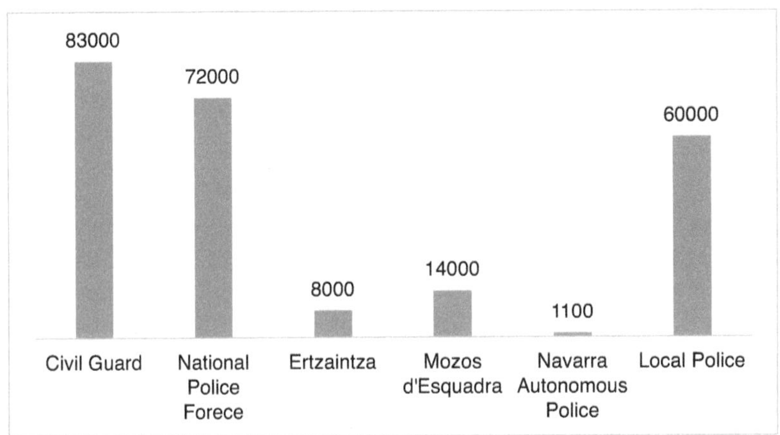

Source: Calculations based on Gobierno de España (2016).

Figure 8.3. Police Officers (per 1,000 inhabitants)

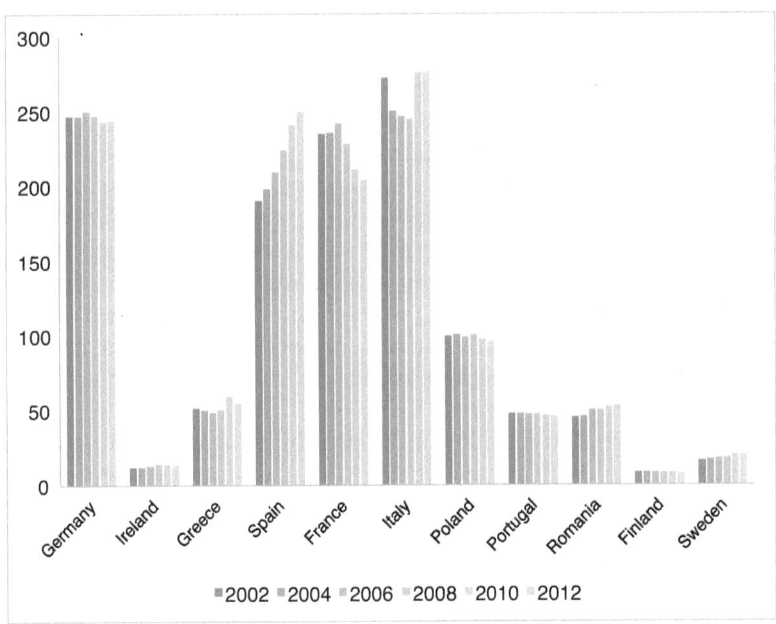

Source: Eurostat (2012).

100,000 inhabitants in Catalonia, there are 362 Ertzaintzas in the Basque country. In Navarre there are 169 police officers per 100,000 citizens.

After Madrid and the Basque country, the islands have the highest rates of agents per 100,000 population. The Balearic archipelago has 567 police officers per 100,000 inhabitants while the Canary Islands have 499.

Fiscal Dimension

The increased spending on public security during the past decades is a result of the growing challenge of international terrorism and the important role that it plays in the Spanish economy. Nevertheless there are also factors related to the decentralization policing. As already mentioned, the economic and debt crisis has an impact on development of the public security structure in Spain, since austerity during the past years has affected government spending at all levels. Funding and fiscal arrangements are thus critical to the decentralization of public security; for example, the ACs of the Canaries and Galicia have been negotiating with the central government financial agreements to establish their own police forces. However budgetary constraints have put these negotiations on hold.

In 2014, public administration total expenditures on public order and safety stood at 2 per cent of GDP, 0.2 per cent above the EU average. Within the 2014 budget, the equivalent of 1.3 per cent of GDP was spent on police services (0.3 per cent above the EU average), 0.4 per cent of GDP on law courts, 0.2 per cent of GDP on fire protection services (including in fact all civil protection operations), and 0.2 per cent of GDP for prisons. There are three different funding and fiscal arrangements:

1 ACs that opted to create their own police forces receive specific, earmarked transfers negotiated in bilateral agreements with the central government according to the number of agents and the level of services offered by the regional police. Depending on these agreements, extra costs, such as salary increase and specific resources, are paid by the ACs.
2 In ACs whose statutes include the possibility of establishing their own police forces, but have yet to do so, the central government pays half of the salary of the members of the units attached to the ACs, and the ACs assume the other half as well as the equipment.
3 In ACs whose statutes do not foresee the creation of an independent autonomous police force, the central government pays for public security.

Figure 8.4. Government Expenditure for Public Order and Safety in Euros (Millions)

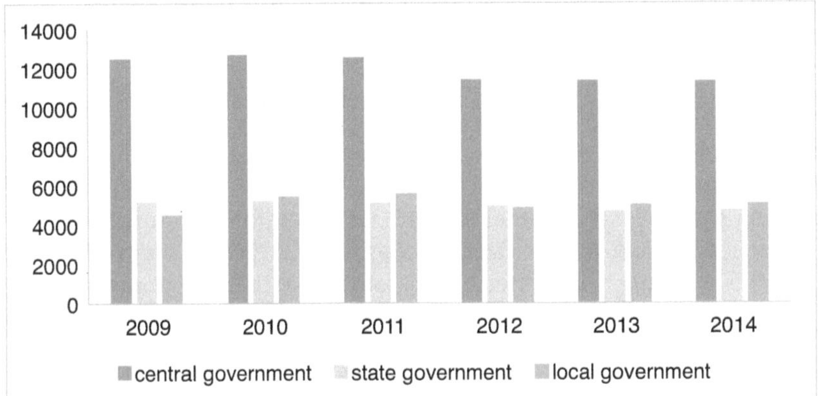

Note: Expenditure on public order and safety comprises police services, fire protection services, law courts, prisons, and R&D related to public order and safety.

Source: Eurostat (2016).

Intergovernmental Assessment

Vertical and horizontal cooperation among different tiers of government, and technical coordination are the key challenges for public security systems in decentralized countries. Especially in a system where different police forces operate with partly overlapping competences, cooperation is a basic element for a well-functioning service. In this sense Spanish legislation emphasizes the principles of mutual cooperation and institutional coordination among different security forces and levels of administration. Despite this normative and legal emphasis on cooperation and coordination, the Spanish model lacks an institutional framework to structure and encourage horizontal and vertical relations among the national, constituent unit, and local police forces. Lack of an institutional framework is exacerbated by competition, and consequently an unwillingness to cooperate and share information, not only between different police forces, but even between the two national police forces.

The Council for Security Policy,[8] chaired by the minister of the interior and composed of representatives of the Ministry of the Interior,

8 Organic Law 2/1986.

along with representatives of the governments of the ACs, is meant to spur institutional coordination. This council is supported by an expert committee of four representatives of the central government and another four of the ACs. This form of cooperation is typical in the Spanish state and reflects the absence of an upper chamber with territorial representation. The so-called sectoral conferences are bodies based on multilateral cooperation that work on specific issues, bringing together representatives of the central government and of the governments of the ACs. Despite the formal importance given to the council in establishing a vertical and horizontal coordination, it has met only once: in 2005 – twenty years after it was set up. Neither the minister of the interior, who can formally convoke a meeting, nor representatives of the governments of the ACs asked for further meetings. The asymmetric distribution of competences among the ACs as well as the fact that the council is made up of politicians, and not police officers, obviated its usefulness for coordination. In this sense multilateral coordination between police forces depends on informal rather than formal mechanisms for collaboration and exchange of information.

At the horizontal level, in 2013 the Spanish government set up the National Security Council. The council meets periodically at the invitation of the prime minister, who also chairs the meetings. The deputy prime minister, other members of the government, secretaries of state, and the director of the Prime Minister's Office participate at the meeting. The prime minister decides if other ministerial departments as well as other authorities, senior public officials, and experts may be convened to attend. There have been thirteen meetings – without direct participation of security forces of the constituent units.

Absent formal mechanisms of coordination, ACs coordinate their activities with the central government within bilateral cooperation mechanisms. Bilateral cooperation has been a constant in the Spanish model since the beginning of decentralizations. Bilateral cooperation can be useful for specific situations; however, it puts the ACs in a weak negotiation position and subjects them to political will and election cycles. For example, in 2011, when the Basque country and the central government were both governed by the Socialist Party, the Spanish cycling race passed through the Basque country under the responsibility of the Ertzaintza. However, in 2012, when the Basque country and the central government were governed by different parties, the central government claimed the Civil Guard for the competence of monitoring the race. The government of the Basque country argued that the Ertzaintza is responsible for "coordinating and directing" the security of the two stages that take place in the Basque country. Both sides called on the bilateral security board to reconcile these positions and find a solution.

To coordinate police action, autonomous communities with their own police forces have created security boards,"[9] which consist of an equal number of representatives of the national, constituent unit, and local police forces. Although formal strategic cooperation mechanisms are lacking, tactically police actually coordinate well, as exemplified by the Emergency System 112 that integrates all police forces.

Cooperation with foreign police forces is better than that among domestic ones, as measures against jihadist terrorists and ETA terrorists illustrate. Several incidents provoked by lack of coordination have given rise to initiatives to improve cooperation, through standardizing databases and facilitating access by all police forces.

Policy Case Study: Counterterrorism

The Madrid terror bombings of 11 March 2004 led to improved coordination through the creation of central institutions and increased staff for national police forces. Although Spain had mature internal security structures that were highly effective against ETA terrorism, at the time of the Madrid bombings the country's internal security structures were not as well adapted to international terrorism (Reinares 2009). In general terms, all police forces are involved in counterterrorism and report to the Interior Ministry. After the events of 11 March, the Executive Committee for the Unified Command of the National Security Forces (CEMU) was created inside the Interior Ministry. This committee approved a wide-ranging counterterrorism plan, which sets the standards for terrorism prevention and protection, and foresees the extraordinary mobilization of a large number of police, including regional and local police forces, by decision of the minister of the interior. In addition, the new unified command unit should concentrate and improve

9 Article 54.1, Organic Law 2/1986.

the coordination of information and intelligence sharing among police forces. Local information groups within the National Police and the Civil Guard were created in specific boarder regions, such as Ceuta and Melilla. The police forces of Catalonia and the Basque country have also shown clear interest in developing their know-how in global terrorism and have carried out such operations in their jurisdictions.

Furthermore the National Antiterrorism Coordination Centre (CNCA) was created to improve counterterrorism efforts among security forces. At the CNCA, agents from the National Police and the Civil Guard work alongside agents from the National Intelligence Centre and other police and security forces. Despite the catalyst effect of 11 March to enhance cooperation among Spain's police forces, the results have yet to materialize. There is a tradition of intense inter-service rivalry between the National Intelligence Centre, the Civil Guard, and the National Police. Furthermore there is an added layer of conflict between the national security services and the police forces of constituent units.

Overall Assessment

The decentralization of responsibilities in public security in Spain has been a direct consequence of the territorial model designed by the Constitution of 1978, namely the establishment of a politically decentralized state without a clearly defined territorial organization. This has given rise to a litany of problems: the highly complex distribution of responsibilities, the lack of institutionalized intergovernmental relations, and the inefficiency of the model.

In the distribution of responsibilities, the open character of decentralization led to an uncertainty about the models that would be adopted by the ACs, and to a long transition period. Citizens and regional and national police forces are confused about the distribution of responsibilities. But the level of public security has remained unaffected.

The lack of institutionalized government relations is a function of a high degree of politicization of relations among police forces. This led not only to agreements constrained by electoral cycles but also to considerable uncertainty after elections. Demand for an autonomous police is stronger in ACs with nationalist parties. Since these ACs have their own representation at the national parliament, they can lobby for specific solutions when the national government needs the support of these parties. However, the prevalence of bilateral negotiations between the central government and constituent units puts AC governments in a position of weakness and results in diverse outcomes. Politicization of the debate on public security leads to disputes among administrations and to no solutions for ACs with governments composed of parties that make up the opposition at the national level.

Effectiveness has not been a goal of decentralization. Still, the annual crime rate in Spain is well below the European average, and the perception of security among citizens is positive. However, the relation between the crime rate and the existence of a regional police force among the ACs is indeterminate. Neither is there an obvious relation between more police and less crime. However, the model and the way it works are becoming increasingly complex. The diversity of police forces in Spain, their different responsibilities, their different degrees of training, and the influx in police officers has led to conflicts over responsibilities, overlapping services, and escalating costs. The lack of transparency makes it difficult for citizens to determine who is responsible for what.

Conclusion

The organization of the police structure in Spain is complex and ongoing, without a clearly specified end. The number of crimes recorded by the police is low within the context of the EU, and public security has not been prominent.

The Spanish model of public security has elements of both centralized and decentralized countries in which the maintenance of security is asymmetrically shared between the central state government and other territorial administrations. In some ACs their own governments assume most competencies in the field, while in other ACs the central state maintains the competencies. The coexistence of two national police forces with analogous responsibilities and a number of constituent unit police forces in some ACs as well as differences in operational capacity among various local police forces requires strong mechanisms for collaboration and coordination. Yet tasks and responsibilities among Spain's many police forces are not clearly delineated. The Spanish model lacks institutionalized cooperation mechanisms among administrative levels. That engenders problems of coordination and effective policing. Furthermore the model is opaque and increasingly complex, making it difficult for citizens to attribute responsibilities to the different police forces.

The model contains some imbalances that are the result of legacy structures from the formerly centralized organization of the country. Throughout decentralization important responsibilities have been transferred to constituent units and the local level, but without reducing capacity at the central level, which remains integral to the Spanish public security system.

The establishment of regional police forces was a specific demand of ACs, with different ethno-cultural characteristics and historical traditions of having already had their own police forces. These police forces have now been largely consolidated and, despite economic and technical difficulties, have become a mainstay of public security in Spain.

In other ACs, budget constraints and a general debate on the scope of decentralization tempered initial enthusiasm for them to set up their own police forces. Although the crime rate is close to the European average, the number of police officers per capita is among the highest in the (democratic) world. In times of budgetary constraints, reforms, such as a clear definition of responsibilities of each police force and the sharing of resources among them, seem necessary to increase the efficiency and effectiveness of the model. In addition to the impact of the economic and financial crisis on the model, the Madrid bombings of 2004 provided an impetus for more central coordination and cooperation among police forces.

One lesson of the Spanish case is the speed of decentralization. In the Basque country, responsibilities have been transferred in blocks, which led to coordination problems among different security forces. In Catalonia, this process took fourteen years, starting in 1994 with traffic control in small villages and covering the whole territory of the AC by November 2008. Decentralization should also be accompanied by increased institutionalized cooperation and coordination. Efficiency concerns should also play an important role in guaranteeing sustainability of regional security forces. In this sense an increase of capacities at the level of constituent units should be offset by a reduction of capacities at the national level. The fact that it is not compromises decentralization and regional autonomy.

The Spanish State of Autonomies is in flux, and consolidation is necessary, to increase efficiency and to explain its benefits to the citizenry. The ingenuity and complexity of the formula involved have made Spain an interesting case study in the decentralization of public policies and its organization. Spain will remain an interesting case because the system needs to be reformed and adjusted to improve cooperation among the different levels of administration and to continue to produce positive outcomes with dwindling resources.

References

Bas Vilafranca, Alex. 2009. "39 *Activitat Parlamentària* 17:39–45.

Eurostat. 2016. "Crime and Criminal Justice Statistics." http://ec.europa.eu/eurostat/statistics-explained/index.php/Crime_and_criminal_justice_statistics.

– 2012. "Crime and Criminal Justice, 2006–2009." *Statistics in Focus* 6/2012.

Fernández de Mesa, Arsenio. 2012. Speech before the Spanish Parliament, 12 December.

Gobierno de España. 2015. "Balance de seguridad." Madrid.

– 2016. "Balance de seguridad." Madrid.

Reinares, Fernando. 2009. "After the Madrid Bombings: Internal Security Reforms and Prevention of Global Terrorism in Spain." *Studies in Conflict and Terrorism* 32 (5): 367–88. https://doi.org/10.1080/10576100902836767.

Reinares, Fernando, and Carola García-Calvo. 2015. "Cooperación antiterrorista entre España y Marruecos." Real Instituto Elcano. http://www.realinstitutoelcano.org/wps/portal/rielcano_es/contenido?WCM_GLOBAL_CONTEXT=/elcano/elcano_es/zonas_es/terrorismo+internacional/ari18-2015-reinares-garciacalvo-cooperacion-antiterrorista-entre-espana-y-marruecos.

World Tourism Organisation (UNWTO). 2015. "Tourism Highlights." Madrid.

Watts, Ronald L. 2010. "España ¿una federación multinacional encubierta?" In *España y modelos de federalismo*, ed. J. Tudela and F. Knüpling, 1–32. Madrid: CEPC/Fundación Manuel Giménez Abad.

Further Reading

Woodworth, Paddy. 2004. "The War against Terrorism: The Spanish Experience from ETA to al-Qaeda." *International Journal of Iberian Studies* 17 (3): 169–82. https://doi.org/10.1386/ijis.17.3.169/1.

9 Public Security and Safety According to Swiss Federalism

MARKUS H.F. MOHLER AND
RAINER J. SCHWEIZER

A. Introduction and Brief Survey of Swiss Polities

I. Brief Survey of Swiss Polities

Switzerland is a small country without noteworthy political aspirations abroad, and it provides a stable political system as well as prosperity in general, based on a (half) direct democratic, liberal, social, and federal political and legal order. It has adopted the *pluralist cooperative* federal system reflecting *diversity in unity* of languages, religions, cultures, and traditions. It also benefits from being surrounded by EU and NATO member states. Switzerland has not been affected by severe threats to its *security* in recent times (yet it has been affected by several terrorist acts since the 1970s). Therefore, the Swiss security policy has been perceived generally as being adequate, despite some puzzling disagreements as results of referenda. However, there are significant weaknesses: the number of police personnel of the federal as well as of the cantonal services is, despite having been increased slightly in the last four years, not sufficient to cope with the demographic development (particularly legal and illegal immigration and traffic), until recently increasing delinquency problems or other emergencies, and higher demands. The army, which has been drastically reduced in personnel and equipment since 1995, is – apart from delicate constitutional issues – legally limited in the assistance it can provide to the police for internal security. The criminal police services are considerably understaffed, particularly in identifying and investigating clandestine and complex criminal activities (Mohler 2013, 63–5). Finally, the competences between federal and cantonal authorities are not as clear as they used to be but flimsy and thus lead to uncertainties and conflicts of competence (negative and positive) (Mohler 2012; Schweizer and Mohler 2014).

II. General Remarks on Fundamental Security and Safety Regulations

Protecting and maintaining public security and public safety are fundamental political and constitutional purposes and obligations of Switzerland. The confederation and the federate states, i.e., the twenty-six cantons, bear the shared and *complementary responsibility* in fulfilling these obligations with the brunt of upholding public security and safety to be borne by the cantons.

The Swiss security and safety policy contains three basic features:

(1) policing, which comprises the tasks of the police services (either predominantly cantonal or, in special domains only, federal): security and safety, criminal, traffic, border and customs (federal) police, search and rescue services;

(2) the army, which falls entirely into the confederation's competence, which is responsible for preventing war, maintaining peace, and defending the country and its population, and can be deployed for police tasks as *subsidiary* assistance to cantonal police services if they cannot cope alone or with the help of other police services, furthermore to help to protect the population (in case of war or other emergencies);

(3) organizations/entities responsible for protection of the population and charged with preventing or coping with threats or damages to people and animals, cultural goods, or nature. Whereas the protection during an armed conflict falls into the competence of the federal authorities, the other tasks (*safety*, related to natural or technological causes) have to be taken care of by the cantons and municipalities in the first place.

In all these fields the confederation and the cantons cooperate actively and closely with all neighbouring countries and through the institutions of numerous security/safety-related European and further international organizations.

Although Switzerland with its special neutrality is neither a member state of the European Economy Area (EEA), the European Union (EU), or NATO, it is a member state of the Council of Europe, the European Free Trade Association (EFTA), the Organisation for Security and Cooperation in Europe (OSCE), and INTERPOL. Furthermore, it has concluded numerous bilateral treaties with the EU and belongs to the Schengen[1] area (association treaty for security cooperation with the EU stipulating the obligation to adapt Swiss legislation according to the Schengen development, the Schengen acquis – or drop out). It is an associated member of EUROPOL (operational partnership including exchange of personal data) and EUROJUST. It joined the NATO Partnership for Peace Program (PfP). Switzerland has also concluded special bilateral treaties designed to ensure close cooperation in police and criminal justice matters with all five neighbouring countries. With an emphasis on fighting terrorism and organized crime, Switzerland has engaged in close cooperation, based on treaties, with many other countries as well. Focusing on maintaining security on a supranational level, Schengen, EUROPOL, and the bilateral treaties with the neighbours are the most effective relations.

III. The EU-Swiss Legal Relations as a Stretched Federalist System

The EU itself is constructed as a *multi-level governmental system sui generis* with strong federalist elements, though far from being a federalist state. The EU comprises three levels: the EU level with its own organs (parliament, council, commission/administration, court), the national level of the member states (parliament, governments, courts), and the subnational

1 The Schengen area is the geographical European space based upon the original agreement *on the gradual abolition of checks at their common borders* of 14 June 1985 signed in Schengen/Luxemburg between the states of the Benelux Economic Union, the Federal Republic of Germany, and the French Republic, made effective by the Convention Implementing the Schengen Agreement of 19 June 1990 ratified by the same states. Meanwhile twenty-one EU member states (EU-MS) are full Schengen member states (Schengen-MS); Denmark is Schengen-MS with opt-out/opt-in possibility re further developments; Bulgaria, Croatia, and Romania are "future Schengen-MS" with partial implementation of the acquis; the United Kingdom and Ireland are not Schengen-MS but enjoy a special status allowing cooperation on criminal law matters (police and criminal justice) including the use of the Schengen Information System (SIS); Cyprus as EU-MS is not Schengen-MS as the result of a split between the northern Turkish and southern Greek part with a demarcation line (although Turkish Cypriots living in the northern part count as EU citizens). Four non-EU-members (Iceland, Liechtenstein, Norway, and Switzerland) are associated full Schengen-MS (status as of July 2016). Whereas the initial strategy was to compensate for the lesser standard of security by the abolition of the internal border police checks with certain measures, the permanent *development* of the *acquis* now aims to fight terrorism and organized crime as well as counter illegal migration with an increasing number of highly complex and complicated binding provisions of various legal forms, which recently proved to be anything but effective in view of the mass migration crisis.

level (regions, municipalities, citizens) (Kesting 2013, 27). Whereas these three-level relations are bound in a common legal framework, i.e., the Treaty on the European Union and the Treaty on the Functioning of the European Union, this is not the case for Switzerland, with its bilateral relations with EU in general, and the association agreements with regard to the Schengen acquis, and to the so-called Dublin scheme[2] in particular. Therefore, in addition to the EU two top levels of governance, any change of legal acts affecting the Schengen or the Dublin acquis is in Switzerland subject to the federalist two-level scheme – and the optional referendum clause. As an example, the EU authorities notify the adoption (by the parliament and the council) of a new ordinance, e.g., in the field of anti-terrorism measures, the Swiss federal authorities check whether the legal text is either self-executing also in Switzerland, or has to be integrated by the normal legislative procedures into Swiss law. In the first case, the new ordinance is published.[3] In the second case, the respective federal law has to be amended by the national parliament, subject to an optional referendum. If the new regulations concern the field of police law falling within the competence of the cantons, then all cantons have to adapt their respective legislation (by the cantonal parliaments, again subject to an optional referendum on the cantonal level) as well.

B. Nomenclature and Public Security–Related Legal Issues

I. Nomenclature

As it appears that there are no globally consistent definitions of the terms *safety* and *security*, for this analysis we use the following distinction, which is prevalent worldwide, especially in the field of civil aviation: *security* relates to (fighting) *intentional* threats or attempts to violate individual or collective rights and disrupt the public order, whereas *safety* relates to protecting people as well as operational systems against *unintended dangers* such as natural disasters or technological (non-natural) incidents. In the realm of aviation, measures of security aim primarily to prevent terrorist attacks, whereas safety regulations are concerned with the proper handling and functioning of operational systems.

2 EC Convention of 15 June 1990 determining the state responsible for examining the application for asylum lodged in one of the member states of the European Communities. "Dublin" indicates where this treaty has been signed.

3 More precisely: referred to the publication of the official text in the *Official Journal of the EU* (*OJ*).

II. Public Security–Related (International) Legal Issues

In the first instance, *public security* is a fundamental strategic *objective* and tactical *goal* of national (as well as subnational) and international policy. Furthermore, security is the corresponding *primary obligation* of states, as a result of the responsibility under international law to permanently try to comply with. However, it will never be fully achieved. Public *security* comprises acts ranging from the ordinary measures taken by law enforcement authorities within the framework of constitutional and relevant special laws, to extraordinary measures taken in emergencies to safeguard human rights and fundamental freedoms. This wide range of measures reveals *two different legal subsystems*: (a) the (national) *legal framework of law enforcement* respecting several international conventions (e.g., International Covenant on Civil and Political rights of 1966 [ICCPR], the American and European Conventions on Human Rights of 1969 and 1950 respectively [ACHR, ECHR]), and (b) *the law concerning the limitation of hostilities*, i.e., the "body of rules and principles specifically designed to regulate the conduct of states and individuals actively involved in situations of *international or non-international armed conflict*," referred to as the *international humanitarian law (IHL)* (Crawshaw, Delvin, and Williamson 1998, 66; Melzer 2008, 140). IHL, which aims to prevent arbitrariness when using lethal force, *complements* in fact – and *not replaces!* – the legal framework governing law enforcement (Crawshaw, Delvin, and Williamson 1998, 67; Melzer, 2008, 140). The *use of force* to uphold or restore public security is therefore not only governed by the national legislation but also *determined, justified, and limited by international law* (Crashaw, Delvin, and Williamson 1998, 64–6).

The two international covenants (International Covenant on Economic, Social, and Cultural Rights [ICESCR], and the ICCPR) apply in principle in times of peace as well as in times of armed conflicts and war (Crawshaw, Delvin, and Williamson 1998, 68). In many countries human rights set out in international conventions as well as the principles and rules of international humanitarian law are considered to be part of the national constitutional law.

Hostilities – as defined by international law – are non-international and international armed conflicts. *Non*-international armed conflicts are defined in the Protocol II to the Geneva Conventions.[4] Non-international

4 Additional Protocol of 1977 to the Geneva Conventions of 1949 relating to the Protection of Victims of Non-International Armed Conflicts, article 1.

armed conflicts are characterized by a higher intensity of violence than the one with regard to international conflicts requiring more than riots, sporadic acts of violence, or other acts of a similar nature (see paragraph 2 of article 1 of Protocol II). The conflicts are attributable to an identifiable and organized belligerent group and take a form and intensity of violence that cannot be handled anymore by regular law enforcement means (Melzer 2008, 256, 261). In such a situation the government has not only to declare the exceptional state of hostilities but also to *inform* the other member states, as well as the competent entities mentioned in the treaties (see article 4, paragraph 3, ICCPR; article 15, paragraph 4, ECHR; article 27, paragraph 3, ACHR). The government is also specifically obliged to provide precise instructions to the operational forces in accordance with IHL (see article 4 ff. of Protocol II; Melzer 2008, 403 ff.). In Switzerland, such a highly crucial decision is vested in the federal government alone.

Many national constitutions contain provisions on the *state of emergency*. Yet declaring the state of emergency does not simultaneously mean a shift from the legal framework of law enforcement to the *law concerning the limitation of hostilities* and, therefore the *IHL*, particularly not with regard to the use of (lethal) force. A state of emergency can also be caused by natural or technological disasters and, on the basis of national law, allows, for example the requisition of private property, which would otherwise violate the right to property, or the recruitment of people for emergency services, which would otherwise violate the prohibition of forced labour, or allocate extraordinary financial assistance beyond budgetary limits. However, the *use of force* that is not legitimate under the legal system of law enforcement requires a separate decision and follow-up procedure requiring necessary justifications.

Finally, it has to be remembered that any use of force that is *not* justified under the pertinent legal system calls for criminal investigation and prosecution of the individuals accountable for these acts (e.g., ECHR; for hostilities: Rome Statute on the International Criminal Court of 1998).

C. Selected Statistical Data for Switzerland

I. Selected Demographic Data

After a long period of weak to moderate increase of the inhabitants of Switzerland, the population has grown remarkably during the last ten years, primarily as the result of immigration.

Figure 9.1. Population Development in millions

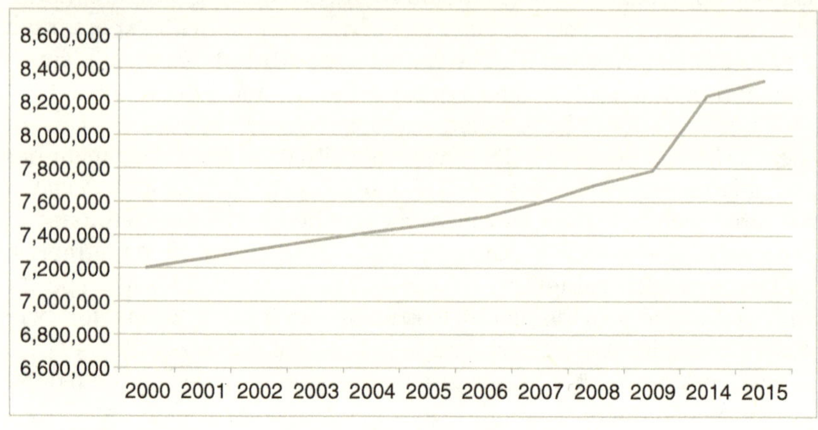

Figure 9.2. Percentage of Non-Swiss Residents*

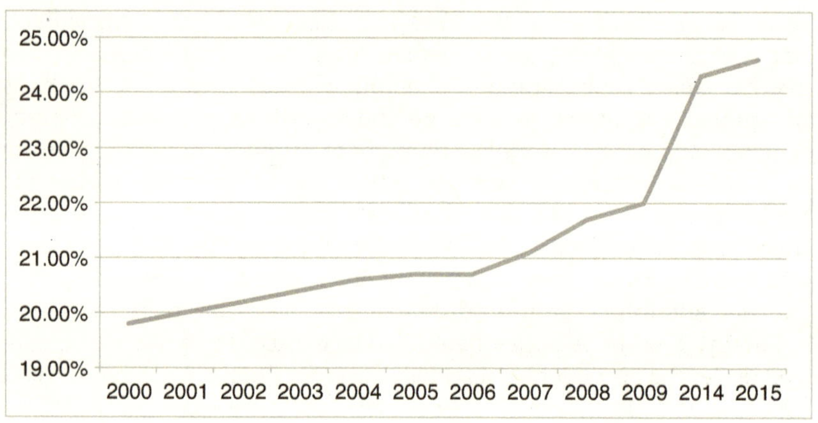

*Not comprising foreign officials, employees of international governmental organizations, asylum seekers, and violence refugees

II. Selected Crime Data

For a long time, crime rates were rather low, comparwith those of many other countries. Whereas violent crimes (homicides, serious assault) remain relatively moderate, property crimes, particularly burglary, were on the increase until 2013 but show remarkable decreases for 2014 (-8 per cent) and again for 2015 (-19 per cent) as the result of effective police prevention.

Table 9.1. Homicide Rates 2013–2015

	2013			2014			2015			2016		
Homicide offences	Number	%	Per 100,000	Number	%	Per 100,000	Number	%	Per 100,000	Number	%	Per 100,000
Attempted homicides	152	92.8	1.97	132	94.7	1.6	141	95.7	1.7	187	97.7	2.26
Accomplished homicides	58	94.8	0.71	41	97.6	0.5	57	84.2	0.68	45	100	0.53
Total intent. homicide offences	210		2.60	173		2.1	198		2.38	232		

Source: Swiss Police Criminal Statistics, Neuchâtel March 2014 and 2017. Graphics: Mohler.

Foreign nationals are overrepresented – as compared to their share of residents in the country – as perpetrators of crimes known to the police. Of the crimes committed, 34 per cent are by identified foreigners not residing in Switzerland ("criminal tourists").

III. Selected Rating of the Police Work

The police services in Switzerland enjoy a rather high rate of confidence by the people, as compared to other public authorities and social agents of and in the country (as well as on an international scale).

Table 9.2. Nationality and Resident Status of Foreigners of All Identified Perpetrators, Penal Code Only (as of 11 February 2016)

Swiss	Foreign residents	Asylum-seekers	Foreign non-residents
48%	31%	3%	18%

Source: Swiss Police Criminal Statistics (2015); Neuchâtel (2016, 26).

Table 9.3. Violation of the Federal Act on Narcotics and Psychotropic Substances

Swiss	Foreign residents	Asylum-seekers	Foreign non-residents
57%	21%	3%	8%

Source: Swiss Police Criminal Statistics (2015), Neuchâtel (2016, 26).

Table 9.4. Confidence in Public Authorities and Social Actors, Comparison (%)

	2017	2007–2017
Police	79	74
Courts	74	70
Federal government	71*	66
Federal parliament	66	62
Army	67	63
Economy	68	66
Political parties	55	52
Media	55	51

*According to the OECD (2015), confidence in the Swiss national government ranks with 78 per cent at the top of the assessed forty countries, with an increase of 12 per cent since 2007.

Source: Szvrcsev Tresch, Wenger (2017, 84).

Table 9.5. Service Orientation of Police Services (%)

The police are servingthe people ...	Average	M	F	Swiss	Non-Swiss
Very well	23.2	21.2	25.7	21.9	33.1
Rather well	53.5	51.8	55.5	54.3	48.0
➢ *Positive*	*78.7*	*73.6*	*81.2*	*76.2*	*81.2*
Insufficiently	20.8	23.6	17.5	21.2	17.1
Not at all	2.5	3.4	1.3	2.6	1.7
➢ *Negative*	*23.2*	*27.0*	*18.8*	*23.8*	*18.8*

Source: Killias et al. (2011, 20–1).

Table 9.6. Quality of Police Work

The quality of the police work is ...	%
Very good	16.2
(Rather) good	72.2
➢ *Positive*	*88.4*
(Rather) bad	9.9
Very bad	1.6

Source: Killias et al. (2011, 19).

D. History and Current Status of Safety and Security Related Federalism

I. A Short Historical Survey

Since the end of the thirteenth century, the forerunners of today's Switzerland, the so-called *federation of the eight old "localities,"* i.e., entities (later: cantons), have combined their primary objective of maintaining security (meaning defence against foreign powers) with maintenance of their respective autonomy. Any centralized authority was refused. After the Reformation, this single-minded determination to preserve their sovereignty over troops was reinforced for several reasons. In fact, the entities were on the brink of a major civil war, which – in a first phase – could be avoided only at the very last moment (1530), whereas later, two short wars between the confessional enemies (1652 and 1712) were inevitable.

The devastation of the Thirty Years War between the Protestant states of North and Middle Europe against the Catholic Habsburg emperor and confederate Catholic states (1618–48) at various places showed that staying away, remaining neutral, kept the entities safe. This was a first mindset for the later neutrality. However, the entities' opposition to a defence monopoly lasted throughout the following hundred years, even when Napoleon conquered and occupied the Swiss territory in 1798. After the Peace of Paris (1815) granting and *requesting* the status of armed Swiss neutrality, the delegates of twenty-two cantons concluded the *Bundesvertrag* (Federal Contract) to maintain their freedom, independence, and security against attacks of foreign powers and to ensure public peace and order within the country, yet without a permanent federal authority. Police in the current sense were part (and symbol) of the cantonal "sovereignty." Most cantonal police organizations were established in the first half of the nineteenth century following the Federal Contract of 1815 after the end of the short French domination.

The political conviction that policing remained the matter of the cantons has persisted ever since, yet with some fissions appearing during the last ten years related to public security management.

According to the first Constitution (1848), the army consisted of the cantonal contingents (three soldiers per 100 inhabitants) only. Later on (1874) the confederation got the right to legislate on and manage the army, but it still consisted predominantly of the (infantry) troops of the cantons. However, the cantons disposed of their infantry regiments and battalions, which could be deployed in their own territory when necessary. This last army-related cantonal residue of competence to engage their "own" cantonal troops was abolished in 2004 only.

Politics have reacted and adapted rather slowly to the changing security parameters, especially the globally pressing threats of organized crime in new forms: there are uncertainties about the future functions of the army and understaffed police services due to financial constraints, and there is only little pressure from the population (since organized crime does not usually affect the average citizen directly). Pragmatism overriding the respect for constitutional regulations and the corresponding boundaries between competences and responsibilities of federal and cantonal authorities, as well as a tendency to use inter-cantonal treaties (concordats) as a "fourth level" of the Swiss federalism to compensate for shortcomings, contribute to this current situation.

A further "development" of the army, including a major change of the respective legislation, has been passed by parliament.[5] Basically, the majority of the army (with fewer troops) shall now assist civil authorities of the cantons (i.e., reinforce the cantonal police services), and the principle of subsidiarity shall be handled less strictly. This concept may lead to some sort of a gendarmerie that can be called in by cantons before the actual – still valid – criteria are fulfilled. This has no basis in the federal constitution.

II. Current Status of Safety and Security-Related Federalism

1. GENERAL REGULATION

The Swiss Constitution does not grant the federal authorities comprehensive powers in police matters. Thus, each of the twenty-six cantons exercises police sovereignty within the constitutional framework. Although the cantons are in charge of maintaining or restoring public security and order, the confederation has a *subsidiary* ultimate responsibility in the following cases:

(a) It shall intervene when existential fundamental rights of its inhabitants are *in the entire country or in wider areas of it* under threat.

(b) It shall intervene when public order in a canton is disrupted or under threat of being disrupted and the canton in question is not able to cope with such a situation alone and with the aid of other cantons.

(c) Furthermore, foreign relations fall within the competence of the federal authorities (including treaties on police matters); reserved are the competences of the cantons concerning cooperation with their immediate neighbours (below the national state level on both sides).

(d) The confederation is responsible for safeguarding the country's existence and sovereignty in armed conflicts.

The competences of the confederation in regard to public security and safety are governed by the constitutional *principle of subsidiarity* and the *principle of the autonomy of the cantons*, and both must be observed in the allocation and execution of tasks. Yet the confederation has an ultimate competence concerning the protection of the *constitutional order*

---

5 A referendum of people opposing this bill failed.

(article 52, Federal Constitution, see above), the independence of the country, and the protection of the population in exceptional situations or a state of emergency.

In the exercise of their competences the cantons shall *cooperate with each other and with the confederation (horizontal and vertical federalism)* in protecting the liberty and rights of the people and safeguard the independence and security of the country. Besides, they are both bound to respect international law.

2. FEDERAL COMPETENCES

(a) Defence. The confederation is exclusively responsible for national defence and protection of the population in armed conflicts. Furthermore, the confederation is responsible for international cooperation in security matters and for cross-border judicial assistance, even if these tasks are partly delegated to cantonal authorities.

(b) International Public Law. The confederation is also responsible for protection of interests prescribed by international public law. Given the presence of about eighty international organizations, hundreds of diplomatic and consular missions in Switzerland, and permanent missions to international organizations in Geneva, the confederation and the cantons concerned are entrusted with important international security responsibilities (in Geneva alone there are more than 35,000 international officials registered).

(c) Penal Law. The Penal Code and the Penal Procedure Code are enacted by the confederation (according to this legislative power vested in the confederation by the Constitution). The cantons, however, are entitled to issue penal provisions of lesser severity (misdemeanours only) against violations of the public order.

(d) Judiciary. Whereas the *organization* of the penal, civil, and administrative jurisdiction as well as criminal investigation and prosecution dealing with cases at first or second instance falls predominantly[6] within the competence of the cantons, the *Swiss Federal Court* is the court of highest instance for the civil, penal, and public law

6 There are several crimes and offences that fall, according to articles 23–4 Swiss Penal Code Procedure, under federal jurisdiction, including investigation.

jurisdiction, including the constitutional review of cantonal legislation and federal ordinances. Besides, there is a federal administrative court and a federal penal court charged to judge on precisely defined cases.

(e) Special Police Tasks. Certain tasks assigned to federal and cantonal police services are entrusted to special agencies of the federal administration for *coordination* (e.g., to combat trafficking in persons and slavery, arms, and drugs, money laundering, and counterfeiting money). The confederation provides several important databases and information systems that are used by the cantons (e.g., criminal records, identification systems, databases containing details of wanted or missing people, and – since 2008 – the Schengen Information System). The Federal Police Office runs the international databases (Interpol, Schengen).

The confederation's activities in security police matters have increased over the last years: the former Border Guard and Customs Service, which previously acted exclusively at the national highway borders and had further tasks with regard to traffic, security, and administrative police matters (import/export), has been transformed into a sort of federal border police acting in a wider area. Moreover, a public transport police (mandatory for the Swiss Federal Railways as well as private passenger transport enterprises) – lacking a constitutional basis – was set up. And finally, private security services are mandated with certain tasks on behalf of federal authorities, and a "private" air traffic control company (owned by the confederation) ensures the tasks of the air police, together with the air force.

(f) Intelligence Services. Furthermore, the confederation is responsible for the foreign intelligence service and – albeit not exclusively – the domestic intelligence service, including fighting espionage. A new law on the intelligence service has been adopted by the (federal) parliament. It was approved by a public vote (65.5 per cent in favour) in a referendum in fall 2016.

3. CANTONAL COMPETENCES

(a) Policing Legislation. All cantons have enacted comprehensive acts – as legal basis and limits – with *regard to police matters* governing the tasks and duties of the police services, ranging from *security measures designed to prevent* violent tensions in society or other violence, to the maintenance of the public security, safety, and order or the protection

of families against violence. Furthermore, the cantons legislate on their own catastrophe management organization.

(b) Enforcement of Federal and Cantonal Laws. The cantons are in charge of *specific tasks* according to federal and cantonal law. For example, the cantonal police and prosecution services enforce the vast majority of the (federal) penal code provisions (see below); cantonal authorities are in charge of tasks of the health police, which is governed by federal acts. Furthermore, the cantonal police services enforce federal traffic rules on Swiss roads and navigable waters and implement parts of the Swiss Aliens Act. In case of natural or technological disasters, the cantons and the municipalities are responsible for the protection of the population, the fire and rescue services, medical and social care, technical support, and protection of cultural goods.

With regard to *criminal investigation and prosecution*, the federal and the cantonal authorities share competences according to the Swiss Penal Procedure Code (PPC, see above).

E. Federal, Cantonal, and Municipal Law Enforcement and Civil Protection Institutions

As mentioned before, the main competences with regard to maintaining and restoring public security and safety are vested in the cantons according to the Constitution. Yet this task is considered not only as a competence but also as an *obligation and responsibility* prescribed by national and international law.

I. Agencies within a Canton

1. CANTONAL SERVICES

(a) Cantonal Police Services. The twenty-six *cantonal police services* are still the backbone of security/safety policing in Switzerland. They vary widely in size according to population and territory and thus range from about 2,600 to some 25 employees. Basically all these services are organized according to the functions of security/safety police, criminal police, and traffic police.

They perform their duties primarily on the basis of the respective cantonal police law but cooperate closely with federal authorities (foremost with the Federal Office of Police, fedpol), other cantonal police services, and on request or spontaneously (as laid down in international conventions and treaties) with police forces of other countries, Interpol, and Europol. Except for urgent or neighbourhood cases, the international police cooperation is channelled through and shaped by fedpol, whereas with Schengen states, the Swiss police services render assistance the same way as in domestic cases.

(b) Cantonal Prosecution Authority. The cantons are also obliged to have a *prosecution authority* that is assisted by the cantonal criminal police. The prosecution authority decides whether to proceed with an investigation or not, leads the investigation if opened, and decides on abandoning a case, on a summary penalty, or on bringing charges (indictment) against the defendant(s) before the competent court. Furthermore, it is in close cooperation with the Federal Office of Justice responsible for the international judicial assistance.[7]

(c) Civil Protection. The main components (field organization, personnel) of this nationwide civil protection matrix network are with the communities and the cantons. They dispose of the personnel on the basis of the respective federal act and according to cantonal regulations, including devolutions to communities.

According to the pertinent federal law, all male Swiss citizens who are not eligible for the compulsory military service or have not served in the military or done (substitute) civilian service for a certain number of days, it is mandatory to serve in the civil protection service for a given amount of time.

Civil protection is organized in the cantons to improve the protection of cultural property in the event of armed conflict, too, according to the obligations set forth in the Hague Convention of 1954 and its additional protocols.

2. MUNICIPAL POLICE SERVICES

In many cantons the municipalities are entitled to their own municipal police. The most important and biggest municipal police service is the City Police of Zurich.[8] With the exception of the City Police of Zurich, the municipal police services have in general no competences with

7 Except for the competences of the police under the Schengen regime and specific police competences.

8 The City Police of Zurich also runs an important scientific department serving federal as well as cantonal police services for forensic examinations.

regard to criminal investigations.[9] They are concerned mainly with traffic control (on municipal streets, limited on cantonal roads) and maintenance of the public order within the municipal borders. However, they dispose of what belongs to the civil protections service: the fire brigade and either an own or contracted ambulance service.

Over the last few years, several cantons have integrated municipal police services into the cantonal police.[10]

II. Federal Agencies

1. OFFICE OF THE FEDERAL ATTORNEY GENERAL

The Office of the Attorney General is, first and foremost, the confederation's investigation and prosecution authority. It is competent for the prosecution of criminal acts that fall under federal jurisdiction. Moreover, it assures coordination with the respective cantonal authorities. It has – within its jurisdiction – the same tasks and competences as the cantonal prosecution authorities.

2. FEDERAL OFFICE OF POLICE (FEDPOL)

Fedpol is the most important police organization of the federal authorities. With the exception of a special task force for "hostage taking and blackmail" and some protection units (dignitaries, foreign guests, federal buildings), it has *no* operational *security police officers* in the field.

Part of fedpol are the federal *criminal* police services, which are composed of the Federal Criminal Police and other units of fedpol concerned with international cooperation (most important its 24/365 communication unit) and domestic coordination in various crime fields. Under certain conditions cantonal police officers may act on behalf of, and as part of, fedpol.

3. INTELLIGENCE SERVICES OF THE CONFEDERATION

(a) (General) Intelligence Service of the Confederation. The Intelligence Service of the Confederation (astonishingly part of the Defence Ministry) is primarily but (so far) not exclusively responsible for gathering, analysing, assessing, and sharing information related – among other

---

9 Except for the Canton of Vaud with other regulations.

10 Most important example: the more than 200-year-old City Police of Berne, the Swiss "Federal City" (Capital), was integrated into the Cantonal Police of Berne in 2008.

threats against the country such as, for example, espionage – to terrorism and violent extremism. It cooperates closely with the cantonal police services, which (still) have their own responsibilities, mainly under the leadership of the federal agency, and maintains the information exchange with partner services of other countries.[11]

(b) Financial Intelligence Unit. In order to combat money laundering, organized crime, and financing of terrorism, the Money Laundering Reporting Office Switzerland (MROS), the financial intelligence unit within fedpol, deals with the mandatory information provided by banks and other financial intermediaries. MROS is a member of the Egmont Group.[12]

4. BORDER GUARD

The Swiss Border Guard is the armed and uniformed corps of the Federal Customs Administration and is part of the Federal Department of Finance. It fulfils, together with the civilian part of the administration, a great number of responsibilities relating to customs and excise as well as to trading of certain goods (e.g., legal and illegal drugs, weapons, animals, plants, dual use goods etc.). Furthermore, it performed routine immigration control at the border crossing points and the field. With the Schengen regime, the task of these routine immigration checks was abolished. Instead, a zone of approximately twenty kilometres along the national border has been established for immigration control based on suspicion (within Schengen regulation limits) area. Yet these controls fall also into the competence of the respective cantonal police.

5. FEDERAL OFFICE FOR POPULATION PROTECTION

Regulation of protection of the population reflects the Swiss federal system in the most classical way. Under article 61 of the Constitution, *legislation* on the *civil defence* (protection) of persons and property against the effects of *armed conflicts* shall be the responsibility of the confederation, it shall legislate on deployment of civil defence units in the event

11 See above, II, 2, e.

12 The Egmont Group is an informal organization of national financial intelligence units facilitating the identification of suspected proceeds of crime and potential financing of terrorism. Currently (2017) it comprises 156 members (i.e. financial intelligence units [FIUs]. See Edgmont Group (2017).

of armed conflicts, and may declare civil defence service to be compulsory for men (voluntary for women). Furthermore, the confederation shall legislate on fair compensation for loss of income and on insurance for, and support of, those suffering damage to their health or lose their lives while performing civil defence service.

That means that the confederation has the *general (but not exclusive) competence to legislate* on civil defence only in case of armed conflicts. In case of other disasters or other emergencies, the confederation sets forth the principles of cooperation between civil protection agencies. Legislation on engagement of civil protection does not mean that federal authorities decide themselves in any case of emergencies or disasters. In fact, the Constitution, as well as the relevant federal laws, reserves the competence to organize the agencies and the engagement of the personnel to the cantons and communities. The pertinent federal act also proscribes the *cooperation* between the protection services, i.e., police, firefighters including rescue, the health system including ambulances and medical care, technical services etc. Therefore, the Federal Office for Population Protection is a predominantly administrative service, and there are only two operational units (the NBC[13]-Laboratory and the national alarm centre), in addition to the divisions for planning and support.

In short, *civil defence in case of armed conflicts* falls into the competence of the *federal authorities*, but is implemented by the cantons and municipalities, whereas *population protection* (in cases of *natural or technological emergencies*) is a *concern of the cantons and communities* with subsidiary assistance of federal staff if needed.

6. ARMY

(a) Militia System. The Swiss Army (including the Air Force) is in principle a militia organization. That means that it consists mostly of *non*-professional soldiers. Under article 58 of the Constitution, "The armed forces shall serve to prevent war and to maintain peace; they shall defend the country and its population. They shall support the civilian authorities in safeguarding the country against serious threats to internal security and in dealing with exceptional situations. Further duties may be provided for by law." A popular initiative to abolish the

---

13 Nuclear, Biological, Chemical.

compulsory militia system for men was turned down in a referendum in September 2013 by 73.2 per cent of the voters. On the other hand the federal act to buy twenty-two fighter planes to replace outdated ones, adopted by the National Council with 119 to 71 and by the Council of States by 25 to 17 was rejected in a referendum in May 2014 with 53.4 per cent of the voters.

(b) Main Tasks of the Army. According to the Constitution the foremost objective is to prevent war and to maintain peace. Of course, defending the country and the population is equally important if the primary objective cannot be achieved. Maintaining peace is not limited to crises with Switzerland (subsidiary assistance of police services in extraordinary situations; see following paragraph) but comprises also the support of such endeavours by the international community (e.g., peace support missions of the UN).

(c) Subsidiary Assistance to the Cantons. More pertinent in this context is the second phrase: supporting civilian authorities in safeguarding against serious threats to the internal security and in dealing with exceptional situations. There is some controversy about the meaning of some of these words. The majority takes the view that the threats need to be very serious and affect a larger part of the country (not just one canton) and that it is deemed an extraordinary situation only if public security is severely disturbed and the canton appears to be unable to cope with the situation, even with the support of police services of the cantons (Mohler 2012, 1193–1201). However, the reality appears to be different. Army units are deployed – on request of a canton only – in many situations that do not match these criteria (Mohler 2013, 67–74). Such requested interventions by army troops might become more frequent after the revised military law is implemented (see above). Such a change, not according to the Constitution as mentioned, would be a step towards a more centralistic concept of policing.

7. NATIONAL ECONOMIC SUPPLY

The national economic supply makes an important contribution to public safety and security. The confederation shall ensure that the country is supplied with essential goods and services if there is a threat of politico-military strife or war, or of severe shortages that the economy cannot counteract by itself. It shall take precautionary measures to address these matters. The Federal Act on National Economic Provision contains the relevant provisions.

F. Intergovernmental Mechanisms

I. Constitutional Regulation

The Constitution sets forth the criteria for intergovernmental cooperation between the confederation and the cantons (vertical) as well as among the cantons (horizontal). The confederation and the cantons are called upon to support each other and generally cooperate with, and support, each other (article 44). They shall provide each other with administrative assistance and mutual judicial assistance. In addition, the cantons may enter into agreements (*inter-cantonal* treaties called "concordats") with each other and establish common organizations and institutions. In particular, they may jointly undertake tasks of regional importance. On the other hand, the confederation may participate in such organizations or institutions within the scope of its competences.

Both provisions are equally important for maintaining and restoring public security and safety. According to the Swiss federal polities, *the horizontal cooperation* and (mutual) assistance *comes first*. In principle, only if these combined cantonal capacities are exhausted, the confederation may – on request – come to assist with its means, i.e., army units.[14]

II. Practical Implementation

Sophisticated mechanisms have been developed to translate the constitutional requirements into reality, resulting in qualified services. The necessity of *harmonizing regulations* and combining services has surged with the increase in population mobility as well as higher legal demands.

1. MECHANISM OF THE INTER-CANTONAL CONFERENCES

(a) Conference of Cantonal Governments. This conference aims to harmonize inter-cantonal cooperation and cooperation with the federal au-

14 This constitutional regulation may now be "softened," i.e. more frequent army units deployments in order to assist individual cantons.

thorities in general, yet particularly in foreign policy matters such as the bilateral treaties with the EU as well as tax issues.

(b) Conference of Cantonal Justice and Police Ministers (CCJPM). The Conference of Cantonal Justice and Police Ministers – more than a hundred years old – has set up several subject oriented working groups. Permanent "guests" at the meetings are the federal minister for justice and police, the head of the Federal Ministry for Defence, Population Protection, and Sport, as well as the president of the Conference of the Cantonal Police Commandants (see below). High-ranking representatives of the federal administration and specialists are invited if the agenda so requires. The aim of the conference is to *coordinate endeavours* on the *political level* vertically as well as horizontally (see above) in the fields falling into the cantonal competence. In recent years the fight against terrorism has been a prominent topic. However, this body has no legislative power. It may propose concordats" (see below) or share financial burdens, but the respective cantonal political bodies must approve its proposals.[15]

(c) Governmental Conference on Military Matters, Civil Protection, and Fire Brigades. The term *military* is strictly historical and has no significance anymore. The conference is responsible for *planning coordination* in emergencies, public alarm systems, protection of the population and their basic resources, rescue, assistance and emergency reconstruction of infrastructures, maintaining "lifeline" infrastructures, and provision of strategic goods. The conference's area of responsibility is limited, since many of these services are municipal (e.g., fire brigades) or even private (many ambulance services).

(d) Conference of Cantonal Police Commandants. The commandants' conference is the highest *coordination body* on the administrative, i.e., sub-political, level. It is responsible for techniques and means of regular cooperation between federal and cantonal as well as among cantonal police services, for harmonizing policing endeavours as far as possible, for research and development of tactics and techniques, and it

15 There is also a Conference of the Municipal Police "directors" (i.e., politically responsible councils). Its mission is the exchange of experiences and best practices on urban policing problems.

suggests changes to the ministerial conferences if political decisions are necessary.[16]

2. CONCORDATS RELATED TO POLICING

(a) Regional Concordats. Police services in Switzerland have formed *four regional groups*: Central, East, Northwest, and West. In all these regions, regional concordats have been concluded in order to regulate the mutual assistance in extraordinary situations. *With the exception of the Cantons of Zurich and Ticino* – Zurich as the largest canton and Ticino as the one south of the Alps – *all* cantonal police services belong to their regional concordat. They have binding legal character and they proved to be very effective, allowing fast reactions and support without much red tape, be it with material only, specialists, or units.[17]

There are also three concordats on *inter-cantonal police schools* providing basic training and some promotional training for the respective police services.

(b) Police Concordat Binding All Swiss Cantons. The provisions of the *nationwide Police Concordat of 2006* (IKAPOL)[18] are far more complicated, precisely reflecting Swiss federalism. First, the *operational concordat* body[19] can be addressed only if the regional services cannot cope with a given situation. If this operational body approves the request, it transmits it to the *political coordination* body,[20] which then decides. If it also approves of the request, it *invites* the cantons to assist the requesting police service with determined strengths of police units.[21] This "invitation"

16 A Municipal Police Chief Association serves, as on the sub-political level, to improve policing tactics for urban policing by exchange of experiences.

17 Most of them regulate the sending of police officers within minutes to a neighbouring canton in case of necessity and on request. The competence to decide on requesting or providing assistance is with the cantonal police commandants at least for a defined strength of manpower and a fixed period of time.

18 Literally translated: Intercantonal police assistance on the national level.

19 Consisting of appointed police commandants.

20 Consisting of appointed cantonal police ministers.

21 The number of police officers to be sent is fixed according to three criteria: situation provoking the request, sizes of the requesting and the requested police services, and possible necessity to be able to dispose over the own police for the requested services.

Figure 9.3. IKAPOL – Decision Procedure

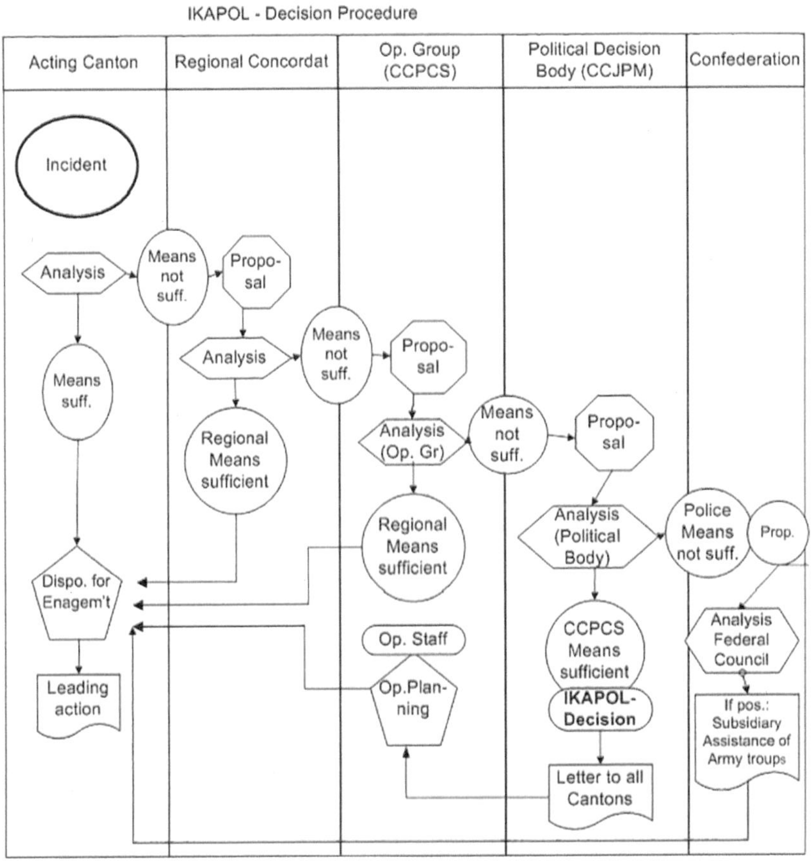

is not formally binding, but according to the constitutional obligation to assist each other it is a "must."

G. Fiscal Dimensions

In 2011, spending of the confederation, cantons, and communities to maintain public security has reached nearly CHF 5bn, roughly CHF 625 per capita, or 4.7 per cent of all tax-funded expenditures (on all three levels).

Table 9.7. Expenditures for Public Security/Safety

	1990	2000	2011	2015
Population (registered inhabitants)	6.8m	7.2m	8m	8.3m
Expenditures in absolute figures CHF	351m	514m	711m	1046m
% of all federal expenditures	1.13	1.09	1.14	1.60
Expenditures per capita in CHF/year	51.6	71.3	88.8	126

Source: Federal Department of Finances (2016).

Development of *Public Security* Expenditures of "the State," i.e., Confederation, Cantons, and Municipalities following classification of the functions of government COFOG of the UN.[22]

However, the various public security–related organizations and tax-funded activities are not congruent among all cantons and municipalities.

The rather massive increase in spending on public security over the last twenty years has less to do with the surge of criminality than with other factors, such as the extension of the federal jurisdiction, the rapid growth in the number of international treaties related to preventing and investigating specific (partly new) crimes, the Schengen association as well as bilateral treaties on police cooperation, and the new PPC expanding the rights of suspects and requiring an enhanced protection of witnesses and consequently higher personnel resources in order to comply with these legal requirements.

New provisions in cantonal police acts contributed also to an increased workload of the cantonal police services, which have been compensated much less, if at all.

In recent times questions were raised about sharing police competences between the cantonal police services and municipal police organizations which, of course, has to do with how to split the costs for

22 Public security according to COFOG contains police services, fire-protection services, law courts, prisons, R&D public order and safety, and public order and safety not elsewhere classified.

policing. Municipalities are not allowed to use measures of constraint except for those communities disposing of a municipal police organization, which means that all their members need to have the national professional "police officer" diploma.

H. Case Studies

I. Counterterrorism

Although Switzerland has not agreed on an explicit counterterrorism strategy, there is a "tacit" strategy overarching federalism: several legal provisions on the international, national, and sub-national law level set the parameter and provide the basis for and limits (i.e., human rights and respective jurisdiction) to countering terrorism. The political and operational leaders are called upon to make the best of it, in order to maintain or restore public security in a given situation while respecting the limits prescribed by law (situational leadership). Yet one question might remain open for quite some time during such a situation: who is the overall leader and commanding officer?

In 2009, as an example, several cantonal police services recognized that LTTE (Tamil Tigers) members living in Switzerland again collected money (coercively) among their diaspora kin and distributed propaganda material. The information was passed to either the Federal Intelligence Service or directly to the Federal Criminal Police. The Federal Attorney General's Office then started formal criminal proceedings and coordinated the simultaneous arrest of ten suspects in January 2011 by several cantonal police services. Twelve suspects were indicted and brought before the Federal Penal Court. The court procedures start in January 2018.

1. INTERNATIONAL LAW

Switzerland has ratified numerous international conventions related to fighting terrorism and protecting people from terrorist attacks (most of these conventions under the guidance of the UN,[23] some within the

23 For example, International Convention for the Suppression of Terrorist Bombings (15 December 1997); International Convention for the Suppression of the Financing of Terrorism (9 December 1999); International Convention for the Suppression of Acts of Nuclear Terrorism (13 April 2004).

Council of Europe framework[24]). The country is, of course, member of Interpol and associated with Schengen and, by virtue of an operational treaty, part of the Europol network.

2. NATIONAL LAW

The Constitution obliges the confederation, i.e., the federal authorities and the cantons, to "ensure the security of the country and the protection of the population" (article 57, paragraph 1) and to cooperate to this end. They all are responsible to aim (legally and operationally) at whatever is necessary for the protection of the people and bear the corresponding liability to the limit of what can be reasonably expected. Several federal and cantonal acts provide the necessary detailed legislation. Furthermore, the constitutional *principle of the general police clause* – combined with the duty to protect human rights based on the ECHR and following the consistent practice of the European Court of Human Rights – allows the authorities to intervene (and infringe human rights of suspects) within the limits of the *principle of proportionality* if there is a serious and immediate threat to fundamental rights but no precise legal basis to act accordingly.

Whereas the legislation relative to criminal investigation and prosecution – despite the fact that there is no single statutory definition of terrorism – appears to be sufficient for fighting terrorism (including mutual judicial assistance and extradition regulations), the respective new legislation relative to the *prevention* of terrorist attacks (federal law on the intelligence service) as adopted by parliament has entered into force on 1 September 2017.[25] The provisions on *measures* of the Federal Intelligence Service foresees even *deep* (also electronic) penetrations into the private sphere if they are approved individually by the Federal Administrative Court and politically by the head of the Defence Department after consultation of the heads of the Foreign Affairs and the Justice Department.

24 For example, European Convention on the Suppression of Terrorism (21 January 1977); Protocol Amending the European Convention on the Suppression of Terrorism (15 May 2003); Council of Europe Convention on the Prevention of Terrorism (16 May 2005).

25 See above D, II, 2, E.

3. CONCRETE COOPERATION WITHIN SWITZERLAND

As mentioned above, coordination and cooperation between the confederation and the cantons, as well as among the cantons (including the municipalities), is prescribed by the Constitution itself. The cantons are held to implement the federal laws, if so regulated, by themselves. Thus cooperation is a daily routine. The concordats (see above, E) assure the immediate assistance in case of necessity. The specialized intervention units ("anti-terror units") receive basic and regular continued training on inter-cantonal courses provided by the Swiss Police Institute, resulting in high-level interoperability.

The federal authorities dispose of a special intervention unit being part of the Federal Office of Police (fedpol) and as a last resort of army units (also with a small special intervention team).

4. INTERNATIONAL COOPERATION

International cooperation with other countries and with international organizations such as Interpol and Europol falls within the competence of the fedpol (except for formal judicial assistance: Federal Office of Justice [with exceptions]). If required operational assistance actions fall within the police competence of one or several cantons, these cantons have to comply with the requests of fedpol. An urgent request by a neighbouring police authority of an adjacent country can be answered and complied with directly by the respective cantonal police immediately followed by the information of fedpol. Furthermore, the Schengen acquis establishes the same direct police cooperation such as in domestic relations.

II. Emergency Management

Not least because of its partly mountainous terrain, Switzerland has always been forced to cope with disasters like avalanches, landslips, storm damages to forests, inundations or fires, even earthquakes in some regions. Moreover, in former times the country faced famines as well as pandemics. For the last thirty years, the challenge of refugee flows due to armed conflicts in several theatres has led to difficult situations with the potential to overpower local human resources. Self-help has thus been a constant necessity in order to cope. Besides, well-established inter-cantonal and inter-municipal networks comprise medical emergency services, voluntary fire departments, or aid to needy individuals. Regular training is necessary to cope with damage and emergencies.

Following the federalist structure, a distinction is made between *protection of the population* and *civil protection*: whereas *civil protection* applies to *armed conflicts* in which the federal authorities have the lead, the wider-framed *protection of the population* (partner organizations, see scheme below) applies to non-armed conflicts, i.e., natural or technical emergencies. Thus, civil protection is part of the protection of the population scheme (see above).

The tasks of protection of the population are assumed only partly by officials of the concerned services and authorities. Often civil servants employed for municipalities, cantons, or (rarely) the confederation, but also private persons, are charged with such tasks. Some civic responsibilities are imposed by federal and cantonal acts. The composition of the various emergency service units reflects the decentralized system relying on close cooperation on three levels among many state organizations and private partners (see figure 9.4).

Over time, several strategies have been developed to overcome disasters and emergencies. The intervention tasks and those of prevention or reconstruction are diverse and far-reaching. Generally, after the initial rescue phase, the rebuilding approach dominates and requires employment of various services. The cantons set up a network system with modules adapted to the challenges comprising municipal (e.g., fire brigade, medical/social assistance) or cantonal entities, diverse public and private companies (e.g., transportation companies, public utility, builders) and units of the civil protection or of the assisting army.

It is of utmost importance that every canton relies on its own cantonal emergency executive staff, with representatives of all partner organizations of the integrated system, which is ultimately directed by the cantonal government.

An emergency on a cantonal or regional level will be handled by the respective cantonal emergency organizations with the support of the federal and the municipal services, as the situation requires.

Provided that the emergency affects an area of *above regional dimensions*, or if the hit canton is incapacitated by the disaster, the federal government, if necessary assisted by the army, may even assume control.

Figure 9.4. Scheme of the Partner Organizations

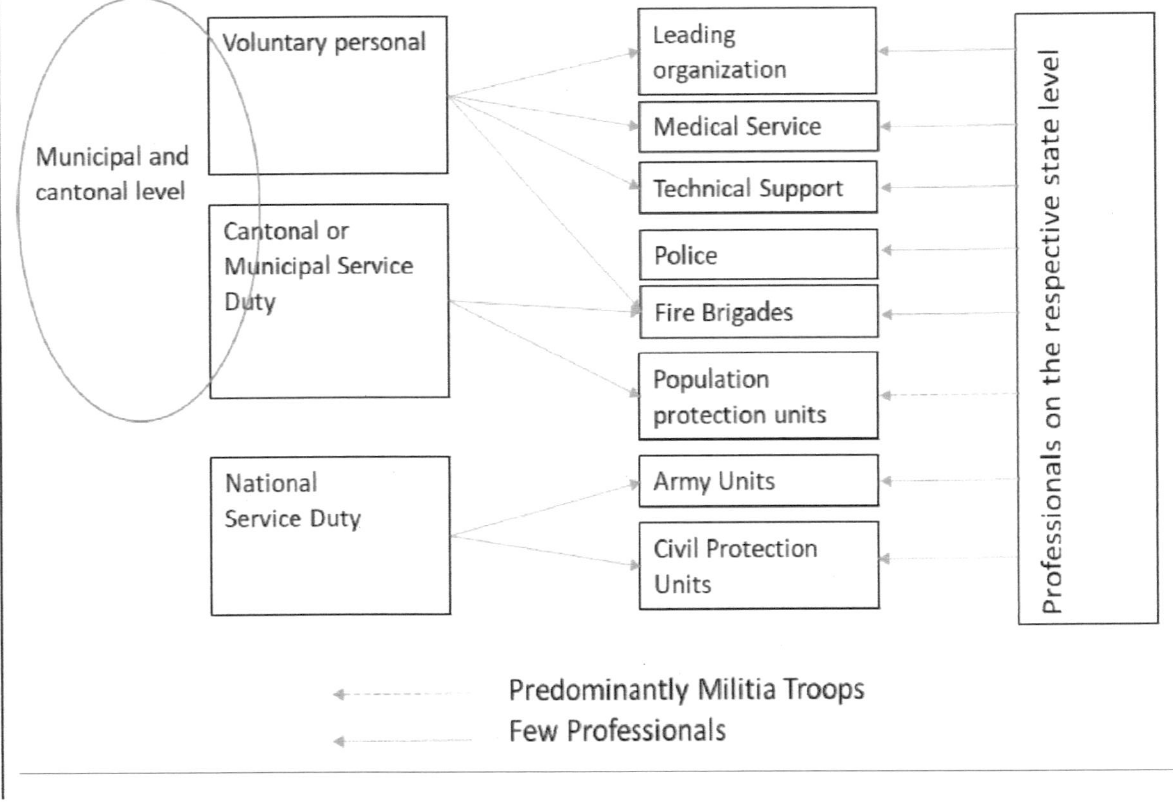

Source: Federal Council (2012, 5538), scheme slightly amended.

Figure 9.5. Cooperation Scheme

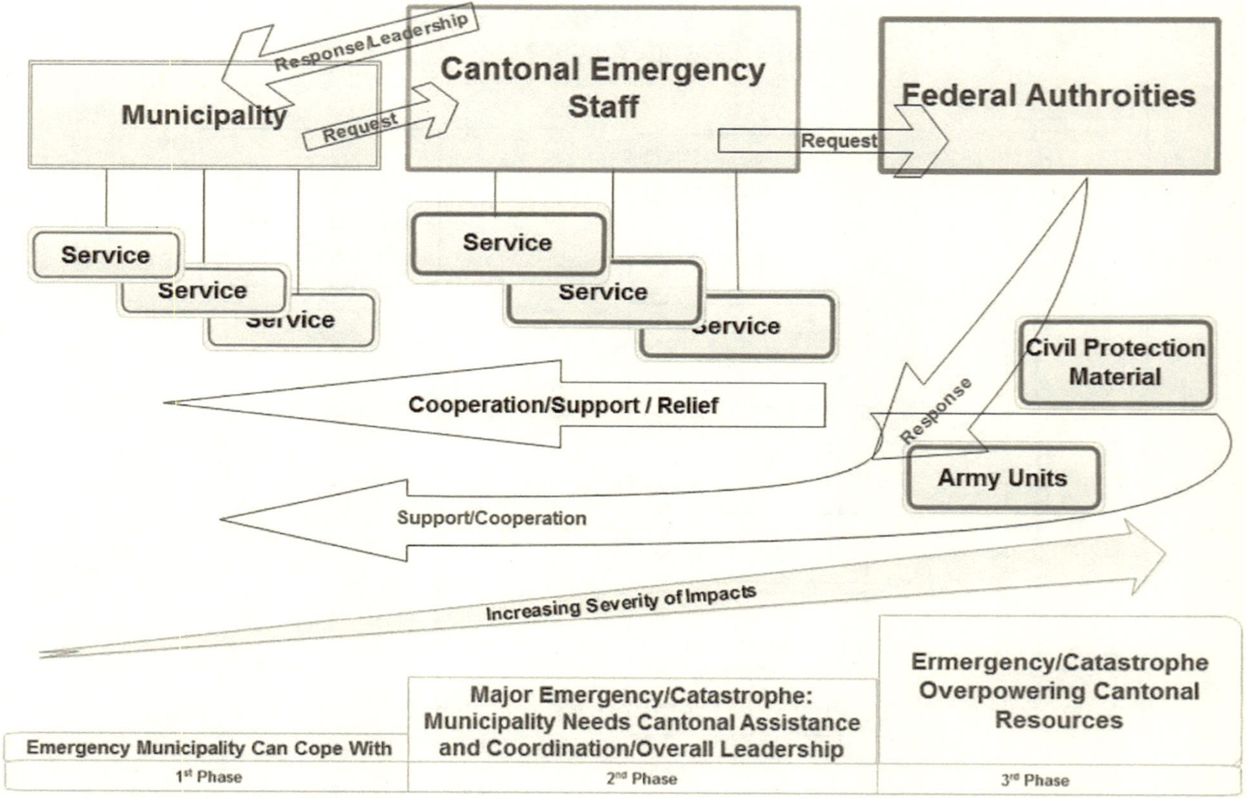

Municipality
Response/Leadership
Request
Cantonal Emergency Staff
Request
Federal Authroities
Service
Service
Service
Service
Service
Service
Civil Protection Material
Response
Army Units
Cooperation/Support / Relief
Support/Cooperation
Increasing Severity of Impacts
Emergency Municipality Can Cope With
1st Phase
Major Emergency/Catastrophe: Municipality Needs Cantonal Assistance and Coordination/Overall Leadership
2nd Phase
Ermergency/Catastrophe Overpowering Cantonal Resources
3rd Phase

I. Assessment

Although the picture of the cooperation mechanisms looks confusing for anyone not used to it, these mechanisms work well in practice.

I. General Effects

The Swiss system of legislative federalism is complex. Yet it has its merits: the constitutional principles are to (currently rather: should) be observed by all authorities, whether federal, cantonal, or municipal. The same is true for respect of fundamental rights and the obligation to protect people against violations of their fundamental rights.

Legislative competence in security matters is *shared between the confederation and the cantons* – with precedence of federal law according to constitutional regulations.

The *municipalities* have only limited legislative competences, but they do have important implementation duties in maintenance of public order and protection of the population and goods during disasters. Finally, inter-cantonal concordats are ranked "in between" the twenty-six cantons, including the 2,300 municipalities. The relation between cantonal and municipal regulations is also complementary, with precedence of cantonal law in case of conflict, whereas ratified inter-cantonal concordats precede mere cantonal law but are preceded by federal law.

Judicial powers are allocated to the confederation and the cantons with the Federal (Supreme) Court as the highest national judicial instance, which hears complaints against decisions by the two federal courts (the Federal Administrative Law Court and the Federal Penal Law Court) of first instance, and by the cantonal courts of last instance. The Federal (Supreme) Court functions also as a constitutional court, except for federal acts and international law.

The Swiss legal system is the result of the already mentioned "bottom-up" approach of the state structure and of direct democracy subjecting all (amendments to) acts to (optional or compulsory) referenda; it leads to an increased closeness between the legislature and judiciary to the populace.

II. Combating Crime

1. PREVENTION

On the strategic level the penal law serves as the main tool for general prevention. Although, like in most other countries, this is a far cry from being a well-working psycho-social mechanism, it is indispensable and depends on the resources for enforcement. Compared to other criminal law systems, the punitive sanctions of the Swiss Penal Code appear to be relatively lenient. Yet it can achieve its objective only if the perpetrators are identified and brought to justice.

The noblest task of the police is *to prevent* crimes and accidents. But such endeavours are strictly limited by respect for human rights and fundamental freedoms and therefore also by restricted competences of the police services. Any infringements of such rights and freedoms by police interventions are allowed only if there is a *specific legal basis* or under the narrow conditions of the *general police clause* or if there is an *immediate and definite severe risk of fundamental human rights violations* (see also below III).

2. PENAL REPRESSION: RE-SOCIALIZATION

According to the hierarchy of punitive sanctions of the penal code, the police services set their priorities for investigating reported or self-recognized offences. This means that there is a very high clearance rate for capital crimes (see table 9.1, homicides) and a modest one for shoplifting and the like. Bound by the *principle of proportionality,* the courts have to determine the *least punishment* (fine, pecuniary sanction, or prison term) *considered to be sufficient for the re-socialization* of the convicted person in relation to the committed offence. In general, a prison term not exceeding two years will be imposed on probation (if it's not a recidivist offender).[26] Currently, even a pecuniary sanction (as opposed to a fine) can be suspended conditionally (will probably be changed again). The insufficient human resources of the police services and the Border Guard pose a problem in fighting "criminal tourists" effectively (burglaries), yet with considerable progress in the last two years, thanks to revised tactics in border zone areas.

III. Combating Terrorism

The legal basis for criminal investigation of terrorist acts appears to be sufficient. However, the currently heated discussion focuses on where to draw the line between preventive infringements of fundamental

26 Therefore, comparisons of the relation between the numbers of the prison population and the general populace among various countries are not necessarily indicative for the overall criminality or the functioning of the criminal justice system of the compared countries.

freedoms and effective identification of suspects and dismantling terrorist groups *before* there is sufficient justifiable suspicion (probable cause) to start a criminal investigation based on the PPC (see above H, I, 2). According to the new federal law on the intelligence service, defined *preventive* invasions of privacy (protected by article 13, Constitution; article 8, ECHR) are allowed under restricting criteria and if approved by the Federal Administrative Court and politically agreed upon by the respective minister. However, the identification (and surveillance) of individuals who are either a "sleeping" terrorist or may soon turn into a potential terrorist or terrorists using cybercrime methods will remain a huge (and increasing) problem, yet *not* because of federalism.

IV. Emergency Management

The concept of emergency management is far-reaching: the starting points are the distinction between federal-level hazards and hazards limited to the cantonal or regional level, as well as the respective risk analysis. Moreover, there are activities aimed at damage containment and reduction of vulnerability. The geo-strategic changes of 1989–91 have caused not only a re-dimensioning of the army but also a review of the concept of protecting the population. A new strategy was implemented in 2001. Yet much has changed again since. Therefore the federal government prepared an updated strategy for the period 2015+ providing improvements (see above).

V. Drivers for and Resistance to Change

Recent years have shown that there are quite a number of drivers of change. However, two main factors offer resistance to far-reaching changes to fighting terrorism (and other types of organized crime) more effectively: the general political will to safeguard fundamental freedoms as far as possible, and a structural conservatism linked to the federalist polities of the country.[27] The first reason mentioned leads to

27 Any change or amendment of the Constitution requires a "double yes" in a compulsory referendum: not only the majority of the all voters is required but also the majority of all cantons (the vote of a canton follows the majority of voters in this canton). Thus, a majority of less-populated cantons may override the majority of all voters of the country. What was initially considered as protection of minorities has turned to the contrary: a minority may occasionally dominate the majority (since 1848 it happened nine times).

legal changes only if terrorist threats are *perceived* to be serious (such as the recent terrorist attacks in Paris, Brussels, or Germany), while the second is lessened by financial constraints of the cantons.

VI. Pragmatic Solutions Not Complying with the Constitution

Article 57 of the Constitution conceived to regulate cooperation between the confederation and the cantons on security matters has not matched this goal.[28] Despite the concurring opinion of legal scholars who deny new policing competences of the federal authorities based on this article, the federal parliament has passed several provisions enlarging precisely such federal powers and continues to do so, particularly with more possibilities of deploying army units according to the revised pertinent law.

VII. Conclusion

The constitutional structures in Switzerland, i.e., legislation on three political levels, in four languages, and the diversity and multitude of executive authorities and institutions, appear complex, and in fact are so. Yet the overarching common objectives and principles such as *federal fidelity*, a long-standing and intensively interpersonal relationship within the country (of small size) and beyond the national borders, enhance the proper functioning of public safety and security-related services. This has positive effects on the fight against terrorism or on coping with natural or technological disasters. Both fields, however, display an extraordinary character. Countering terrorism needs special secret preventive investigations; to safeguard the constitutional fundamental rights and freedoms, any invasion of the private sphere requires a credible judicial approval. Emergency management needs urgent and sometimes crucial decisions and actions, possibly even (in case of armed conflicts) beyond the constitutional framework. Both ways of action are very demanding to implement in the Swiss democratic federal system. But the federal system allows security to be maintained while citizens' rights are respected.

In emergencies the nationwide alarm system with the national alarm centre relying on direct separate and protected phone lines with all cantonal police headquarters (communications centres), amended now

28 Schweizer Mohler (2014, 1219–22).

by messages sent out by SMS to all those who have downloaded the appropriate app of the federal alarm unit, has worked well. Providing information and advice to the public during a disasters or emergency depends on the availability of facts and requires extensive coordination among the different operational partners (avoiding contradicting information). However, exercises as well as strong support from the population and – if necessary – from army units helps to overcome structural hurdles and the complex decision-making procedures.

References

Crawshaw, Ralph, Barry Delvin, and Tom Williamson. 1998. *Human Rights and Policing*. The Hague: Kluwer Law International.

Edgmont Group. 2017. "About." https://www.egmontgroup.org/en/content/about.

Federal Council. 2012. *Strategie Bevölkerungsschutz und Zivilschutz 2015+* (Strategy for protection of the population and civil protection 2015+), 9 May 2012. https://www.admin.ch/opc/de/federal-gazette/2012/5503.pdf.

Kesting, Martin. 2013. *Die Berliner Bezirke als Akteure im EU-Mehrebenensystem*. Munich: Herbert Utz Verlag.

Killias, Martin Silvia Staubli, Lorenz Biberstein, Matthias Bänziger, and Sandro Iadanza 2011. *Studie zur Kriminalität und Opfererfahrungen der Schweizer Bevölkerung: Analysen im Rahmen der schweizerischen Opferbefragung*. Zurich: University of Zurich.

Melzer, Nils. 2008. *Targeted Killing*. New York: Oxford University Press.

Mohler, Markus H.F. 2012. *Grundzüge des Polizeirechts in der Schweiz*. Basel: Helbing & Lichtenhahn.

– 2013. "Ungenügende Polizeibestände – Lösungsansatz unter Respektierung der verfassungsmässigen Kompetenzordnung." *Sichereit&Recht* 2:62–80.

OECD. 2015. "Government at a Glance 2015." http://www.oecd-ilibrary.org/sites/gov_glance-2015-en/11/01/index.html?contentType=%2fns%2fChapter%2c%2fns%2fStatisticalPublication&itemId=%2fcontent%2fchapter%2fgov_glance-2015-50-en&mimeType=text%2fhtml&containerItemId=%2fcontent%2fserial%2f22214399&accessItemIds=&option6=imprint&value6=http%3a%2f%2foecd.metastore.ingenta.com%2fcontent%2fimprint%2foecd.

Schweizer, Rainer J., and Markus H.F. Mohler. 2014. *St Gall Commentary to the Federal Constitution*. Vol. 1, *Remarks on the Security Constitution*. 3rd ed. Zurich: St Gallen, Dike Verlag.

Swiss Federal Department of Finances (Bundesamt für Statistik, Finanzstatistik der Schweiz 2014, Jahresbericht, 2016, https://www.bfs.admin.ch/bfs/de/home/aktuell/neue-veroeffentlichungen.assetdetail.1043529.html).

Swiss Police Criminal Statistics (2015; Neuchâtel 2016, https://www.bfs.admin.ch/bfs/de/home/statistiken/kataloge-datenbanken/publikationen.assetdetail.350887.html).

Szvrcsev Tresch, Tibor, and Andreas Wenger, eds. 2017. *Sicherheit 2017*. Zurich: Centre for Security Studies, ETH Zurich.

Further Reading

Albertini, Gianfranco, Thomas Armbruster, and Beat Spörri. 2016. *Militärisches Einsatzrecht*. Zurich: Schulthess.

Brunnengräber Achim, Heike Walk, ed. 2007. *Multi-Level-Governance: Klima-, Umwelt- und Sozialpolitik in einer interdependenten Welt*. Schriften zur Governance-Forschung. Baden-Baden: Nomos. https://doi.org/10.5771/9783845202990.

Foster, Marc. 2005. "Terroristischer Massenmord an Zivilisten als legitimer Freiheitskampf? (im Sinne von Art. 260quinquies Abs. 3 StGB) kraft Analogieverbot?" *Schweizerische Zeitschrift für Strafrecht* 123:458–70.

Gasser, Hans-Peter, and Nils Melzer. 2012. *Humanitäres Völkerrecht: Humanitäres Völkerrecht*. 2nd ed. Zurich: Schulthess.

Grabenwarter, Christoph, and Katharina Pabel. 2016. *Europäische Menschenrechtskonvention*. 6th ed. Munich: Beck.

Koller, Arnold, Daniel Thürer, Bernard Dafflon, Bernhard Ehrenzeller, Thomas Pfisterer, and Bernhard Waldmann. 2012. *Principles of Federalism*. Zurich: Dike.

Koller, Heinrich. 2006. "Kampf gegen den Terrorismus: Rechtliche Grundlagen und Schranken." *Zeitschrift für Schweizerisches Recht* 126:107 ff.

Mohler, Markus H.F. 2001. "Swiss Intercantonal and International Police Cooperation." In *International Police Cooperation*, ed. Daniel J. Koenig and Dilip Das, 271–87. Lanham, MD: Lexington Books.

– 2008. "'Raumsicherung': Verfassungsre chtliche Fragen zur jüngsten Entwicklung in Rechtsetzung, Doktrin und Reglementierung über den Einsatz der Armee." *LeGes* 3:437–64.

– 2013. "Polizeiliche Zusammenarbeit Schweiz-EU, eine Annäherung." *Sicherheit&Recht* 3:136–50.

– 2015. "Verfassungsrechtliche Ignoranz?" *Allgemeine Schweizerische Militärzeitschrift* 12:6–7.

– 2016. "Die EU hat mit dem Kernbereich von 'Schegen' und mit 'Dublin' den Stresstest bisher nicht bestanden." *Sicherheit&Recht* 1:3–26.

Mohler, Markus H.F., and Rainer J. Schweizer. 2009. "Sicherheitspolitik und Sicherheitsrecht – sicherheitsrechtliche Problemstellungen im Zusammenhang mit dem sicherheitspolitischen Bericht (des Bundesrates)." Jusletter of 7 December. Berne: Weblaw.

Müller, Reto Patrick. 2009. "Innere Sicherheit Schweiz, Rechtliche und tatsächliche Entwicklungen im Bund seit 1848." Egg b. Einsiedeln: Thesis-Verlag.

Pieth, Marc, Daniel Thelesklav, and Radha Yvory, eds. 2009. *Countering Terrorist Financing: The Practitioners Point of View*. Berne: Peter Lang.

Scheffler, Jan. 2012. "Einheitspolizei: Wegweisendes Modell oder falscher Reformeifer? Zur Diskussion um die Zentralisierung polizeilicher Organisationsstrukturen auf kantonaler Ebene." *Sicherheit&Recht*: 2:87–100.

Schweizer, Rainer J. 2012. "Bundesstaatliche Kompetenzverteilung im Polizei- und Sicherheitsrecht." *Sicherheit&Recht* 3:185–92.

Schweizer, Rainer J., and Lukas Gschwend. 2005. *Geschichte der KKJPD 1905–2005*. Zürich: Schulthess (in German, French, and Italian).

Schweizer, Rainer J., and Jan Scheffler. 2011. "Verfassungs- und völkerrechtliche Anforderungen an die Verteidigungskompetenz der schweizerischen Armee und an ihr zukünftiges Leistungsprofil." *Zeitschrift für öffentliches Recht* 66 (3): 299–365. https://doi.org/10.1007/s00708-011-0111-5.

Uster, Hanspeter. 2011. "Das Polizeikonkordat der Zentralschweiz." *Sicherheit&Recht* 3:154–62.

– 2012. "Das Polizeikonkordat der Zentralschweiz." *Sicherheit&Recht* 1:3–10.

10 Public Security in the United States of America: Challenges to Federalism from an All-Hazards Perspective

RICHARD J. KILROY JR

Introduction

The United States was founded on the principle of federalism, with its focus on both the separation and sharing of governmental powers. The challenges the Founders faced in the 1700s are, in many ways, the same challenges the country faces today: how to balance the need for national unity in light of the threats to public security, while at the same time respecting the need for autonomy among the individual states, and the need to protect civil liberties and civil rights.

Historically, security concerns have always trended towards an increased role played by the federal government at the expense of local communities and states. Federalist arguments in the 1700s for a stronger central government to defend the collective interests of the thirteen individual states from outside aggression, fragmentation, and even internal rebellion have been echoed in all subsequent centuries, based on the nature and imminence of the threat. In 2001, the terrorist attacks against the United States led to the largest reorganization of the federal government since the end of the Second World War, where the Homeland Security Act of 2002 would dwarf the National Security Act of 1947 in scope and complexity of federal government reorganization and response to security challenges.

This chapter examines the extent to which the concept of federalism and its institutional structures within the United States have been challenged by the events of the terrorist attacks of 11 September 2001 (9/11), in particular, and the reorganization of the federal government to deal with other threats to homeland security (an all-hazards perspective), such as natural disasters, after September 2005. The chapter provides a brief constitutional and historical context for the discussion of public security in the United States and describes the institutions established by local, state, and federal governments to respond to threats, whether they are natural (naturogenic) or caused by human beings (anthropogenic). The focusing events of the terrorist attacks in 2001 and natural disasters in 2005 provide the framework for analysis, with special attention drawn to a case study on disaster response after Hurricanes Katrina and Rita.[1] This case study provides unique insights in assessing how federalism and governance in the United States have been affected by the terrorist attacks of 9/11 and the consolidation of the federal government's response to public security challenges from both types of threats.

Constitutional and Legal Landscape

The United States was established in 1789 as a constitutional republic, based on a federal system of local, state, and national governments. An earlier experiment in governance after independence from Great Britain, under the Articles of Confederation, failed to unite the thirteen fiercely independent states into a unified nation with a central government capable of "providing for the common defense" of all the states.[2] The foundational values of independence, autonomy, and sovereignty that fuelled the Revolutionary War stoked the fires of debate in Philadelphia, Pennsylvania, in 1787 in forging a constitution built on a federal model of governance. A strong commitment to constitutionalism, federalism, and the separation of powers both vertically and horizontally would shape the new nation's political institutions and their roles and responsibilities to provide for the public safety and security of its citizens.

Today's system of governance is rooted in this strong federal democratic tradition and comprises fifty states, the District of Columbia, and

---

1 A *focusing event* is defined as "an event that is sudden, relatively rare, can be reasonably defined as harmful or revealing the possibility of potentially greater harms, inflicts harms or suggests potential harms that are or could be concentrated on a definable geographic area or community of interest, and that is known to policy makers and the public simultaneously" (Birkland 1997, 22). Kettl (2014) also uses the term *policy lightning* to describe such events.

2 Words quoted from the Preamble to the Constitution of the United States (1787).

fourteen dependent territories. The U.S government is responsible for securing the world's third-largest territory, at 9,826,675 square kilometres, and also the fourth-highest population, with 321,368,864 people (CIA 2016). To guarantee national security, the government relies on the Department of Defense, which consists of 1.3 million active-duty military service members and 800,000 Guard and Reserve personnel (Department of Defense 2016). In 2002, the Department of Homeland Security was created, contributing 216,000 employees and twenty-two additional federal agencies to provide domestic security (Department of Homeland Security 2012; White House 2012). As a total sum, no country in the world spends more on security than the United States (SIPRI 2015).

Public security programs are highly decentralized at the state and local level. Large cities (New York, Chicago, Los Angeles, etc.) have highly structured police organizations, while rural communities without dedicated police organizations depend on state police or county sheriff departments with limited resources to cover broad geographical areas. This has contributed to the nation's strong sense of individualism and protection of individual rights over personal security and gun ownership, thus creating an inherent tension in the United States. The demands individuals place on the federal government for increased security and protection from national security threats often conflict with their desires to preserve freedom and liberty over their own safety and security when facing local threats, such as violent crime.

In the federal system of government that has emerged in the United States, state and local governments enjoy a great deal of autonomy of action in public safety, provided they act within constitutional and legal authorities. The irony is that the Constitution does not explicitly mention local or municipal governments, which are considered subordinate to state governments, in a federal context. There is flexibility in the federal system that allows for this autonomy, yet the subsidiarity effect becomes evident when local and state resources are insufficient and federal support is required. Even then, the federal intervention is typically short-lived until the local authorities can take control of the situation (see later case study on natural disaster response).

Historical Developments

In Philadelphia, in 1787, the Constitutional Convention met to address the shortcomings of the young republic's first attempt at framing a new nation. The Articles of Confederation, signed ten years earlier, were a weak attempt to forge a minimal national consensus for governing the newly independent thirteen colonies. As such, it did not include a Bill of Rights, since these were left to the individual states to confer. Also, the Articles provided neither for a federal military, nor for the collective protection of the new republic, leaving this again to the state militias. At the time the Articles were signed, the Founders were more concerned with the potential for states entering into conflict with each other or other nations than the collective security of the United States. Internal threats of rebellion and division, as occurred in Massachusetts under Daniel Shay's leadership in 1786, spurred the Founders to reconvene the following year to forge a new Constitution.

Through a series of written discourses and exchanges, the federalists (Hamilton, Madison, and Jay) laid out an argument for a stronger central government to provide for the "common defense and general welfare" of the citizens (Constitution 1787). As James Madison noted in *Federalist 41*, "The means of security can only be regulated by the means and danger of attack ... They will in fact be ever determined by these rules and no others" (Hamilton, Madison, and Jay 1961, 257). National security and public safety were a major concern for both federalists and anti-federalists (e.g., Jefferson, Mason, Henry, and Gerry); however, each side differed on the solutions offered. In the end, the federalists won out and the Constitution ratified in 1789 by the thirteen colonies allowed for a much stronger central government, which would be empowered by the states to provide for a standing army and navy, though limited in size and mission by the central role the U.S. Congress would play in the separation of powers between the branches of government.

Under the U.S. Constitution, as intended by the Founders, the three main – albeit, at the time, unequal – branches of government (Executive, Legislative, and Judicial) (see table 10.1) had specific powers on issues of public security. Their ability to "check and balance" each other's powers would ensure that wars could not be entered into hastily and that the United States "goes not abroad in search of monsters to destroy" (Adams 1821).

Despite George Washington's request to the Continental Congress to keep a standing army of 2,600 regular troops and officers to face new threats after the Revolutionary War, the country was broke, and the Continental Army was reduced to eighty men under arms (Ayers et al. 2010, 152). During the country's early years, state militias continued to provide the main defence of the nation, as they had done during the

Table 10.1. Constitutional Authorities and Public Safety

Legislative	Executive	Judicial
Raise and support armies	Commander-in-chief	Admiralty and maritime jurisdiction
Provide and maintain navy	Enforce laws	Settle disputes between states
Call out militia	Commission officers	Judicial review of laws
Declare war	Make war	Try public officials

Source: Constitution of the United States (1787).

Revolutionary War. Although national security was clearly a domain of the federal government in defence of the collective states and national sovereignty, the federal government continued to struggle to raise funds and secure an army from the state militias, even during the War of 1812. Thomas Jefferson, a staunch anti-federalist, conceded this when he stated in a letter to Thomas Cooper in 1814,

> In the beginning of our government we were willing to introduce the least coercion possible on the will of the citizen. Hence a system of military duty was established too indulgent to his indolence. This [War of 1812] is the first opportunity we have had of trying it, and it has completely failed – an issue foreseen by many, and for which remedies have been proposed. That of classing the militia according to age and allotting each age to the particular kind of service to which it was competent was proposed to Congress in 1805 and subsequently; and on the last trial was lost, I believe, by a single vote. Had it prevailed, what has now happened would not have happened. Instead of burning our Capitol, we should have possessed theirs in Montreal and Quebec. We must now adopt it, and all will be safe. (Lipscomb and Bergh 1903–4, 185)

Domestically, with regard to public security, the role of state and local governments was clearly seen as pre-eminent, protected by the "reservation clause" of the Constitution, which stated that all powers not specifically delegated to the federal government were reserved for the individual states. Thus, local and state governments would be responsible for providing policing, law enforcement, and the prosecution of criminals (although some crimes, such as treason, would be enforced at the federal level).

Nowhere was this sentiment more evident than in the Posse Comitatus Act (1878). In this Act, Congress specifically prohibited the U.S.

military from being used as a domestic police force, preventing its role in conducting search and seizure, arrests, and or detention of U.S. citizens on U.S. soil. Congress did create federal agencies with law enforcement authorities (U.S. Secret Service in 1865; Federal Bureau of Investigation in 1908); however, their statutes were originally limited to very specific authorities, such as in the case of the Secret Service as part of the U.S. Treasury, to investigate and prosecute crimes against the nation's financial security (counterfeiters, etc.).

The one federal agency with law enforcement authority that has existed since the nation's founding is the U.S. Coast Guard. Begun as the U.S. Revenue Cutter Service in 1790, the Coast Guard's law enforcement role was limited to enforcing maritime law against smuggling and collecting customs duties. The Coast Guard was considered an "armed service," since, in wartime, it could come under the authority of the U.S. Navy and its fleet used to supplement naval vessels. The Coast Guard was originally part of the Department of Treasury, and later the Department of Transportation. After the terrorist attacks of 9/11, it was reassigned to the new Department of Homeland Security in 2002.

On the one hand, the domain of public security has primarily been a local issue, with individual communities empowered to provide self-protection or protective services. To this end, there are over 17,000 state and local law enforcement agencies, with police forces ranging in size from communities with one deputy to municipalities with organizations of 30,000 officers. The types of local law enforcement organizations include local police; state police and highway patrol, special jurisdictional police, and deputy sheriffs (Discoverpolicing 2013).[3] Governance can be conferred through mayor-councils, council-managers, commissions, or town meetings. Many counties have local sheriff's departments. State highway patrol officers enforce traffic laws on state roads, U.S. highways, and federal interstate highways within their state jurisdictions. Many states also have a State Bureau of Investigation (SBI) to augment local communities with their limited investigative capabilities. Historically, community policing has been a critical component of

3 Special jurisdictional police: "Officers for special jurisdictions provide police services for defined entities or areas within another jurisdiction. These include parks, schools, transportation assets (e.g., airports, subways), hospitals, housing authorities, and government buildings. Special jurisdiction police are generally full-service departments, offering the same services as local police" (Discoverpolicing 2013).

Table 10.2. Public Safety Agencies

Local	State	Federal
Municipal police	State police	Federal Bureau of Investigation
County sheriffs	Highway patrol	U.S. marshals
Tribal police	State bureau of investigation	U.S. Customs and Border Patrol
		Drug Enforcement Agency
		Bureau of Alcohol Tobacco and Firearms
		Secret Service

Source: Bureau of Justice Statistics (2017).

the federal system, with a very limited role for federal agencies, such as the FBI or even the Naval Criminal Investigative Services (NCIS) – despite Hollywood's portrayal of the latter.

On the other hand, national security has clearly been a federal responsibility. The five armed services (army, navy, air force, marines, and coast guard) provide for the defence of the nation against internal and external threats. The Second Amendment to the Constitution allows for the existence of a "well-regulated militia" and the right of citizens to "bear arms"; however, states are prohibited from waging war or conducting military actions against other nations, or even each other (Constitution 1787).

The state National Guard units, to a certain extent, continue to serve in the capacity of state militias. For example, the 181st Infantry Regiment of the Massachusetts Army National Guard dates its founding to 1636 and the establishment of the first militia in North America by the Massachusetts Bay Company (National Guard 2014). Some states, such as Texas and Virginia, still have a state militia structure apart from the National Guard. In Texas, the adjutant general of the state holds the rank of a two-star major general in the National Guard, and a three-star rank of lieutenant general in the Texas Militia. The Virginia Militia is unorganized, and military commissions are ceremonial, based on historical practices.[4]

4 For example, all U.S. citizens who serve in academic and cadre positions at the Virginia Military Institute in Lexington, VA, are commissioned in the Virginia Militia, which dates back to the institute's founding in 1844. Military rank is awarded on the basis of academic rank (e.g., a full professor is commissioned as a colonel, an associate professor is commissioned as a lieutenant colonel, etc.). The Citadel in Charleston, South Carolina, is another state military school that continues this same tradition.

Where the federal government came to play a larger role domestically in providing security was in the territorial expansion to the west and in the pacification of Indigenous tribes. Before and after the Civil War, the U.S. Army established a series of forts or garrisons that also served as economic hubs for western expansion (Faragher 1999). In these remote settlements, the army did provide a local public security role, to be augmented with local town sheriffs and U.S. marshals to provide law enforcement. As these territories later became states, they assumed more local jurisdictional control of public security, evident in the incorporation of towns and cities with their own police forces. For example, in Arizona today, over 140 different law enforcement agencies exist. The city of Phoenix alone has 16, including the Phoenix City Police, Maricopa County Sheriff's Office, and State Capitol Police (Discoverpolicing 2013).

Throughout the history of the United States, from Lincoln's suspension of habeas corpus during the Civil War, Franklin Delano Roosevelt's internment of Japanese-Americans during the World War, to Bush's Patriot Act after 9/11, an expansion of executive authority occurs during time of war, but typically contracts afterwards, depending on the nature of the threat. An example has been the constantly fluctuating size of the nation's military forces.[5]

Metrics and Fiscal Dimension

Since security and public safety are considered community goods in the United States, it has been the responsibility of the local community to provide these basic services. Police are public servants, thus towns and cities have municipal police departments paid for by taxes raised in those communities. Larger communities also fund other "first responder" services such as fire and rescue. In smaller communities, these services may still be voluntary, staffed by volunteer firefighters or emergency medical service (EMS) workers, or contracted out to private companies. For example, some private companies often provide emergency rescue-response services based on local county or municipal

5 After the withdrawal of forces from Iraq at the end of 2011 and the drawdown from Afghanistan in 2012, the active duty military decreased its size considerably as the result of a mandated budget cut of $487 billion over ten years (Department of Defense 2012).

agreements with the hospitals in those communities.[6] Funding for these services is often obtained through donations or grants.

The size of the police presence in the United States today varies by state and community, with cities having a larger police presence per population (2.5:1,000) compared to rural communities (1.8:1,000) (IACOP 2011). Aggregate figures for the nation as a whole, in 2011, reflect a police-to-population ratio for the entire country at 292:100,000 (Public Intelligence 2011). Yet that number has been questioned, after the impact of the economic downturn of 2008, where some municipalities have had to lay off as many as half of their full-time police officers.[7] The largest metropolitan area police force is in Washington, DC, with a ratio of 612:100,000 (Governing 2012).

The cost of local public safety and security has grown significantly for many communities, even though tax revenues have either declined or remained stagnant. There is an argument that the United States needs to reduce spending on public safety, as much as $100 billion annually, which would free up funds for other community programs such as education to reduce crime (Hughes 2012). A similar argument focuses on the high cost of incarceration in the United States, where the prisoner population has grown from 500,000 inmates to more than 2.3 million in the last thirty years. The United States is reported to lead the world with 25 per cent of the global prisoner population, despite having only 5 per cent of the world's population (Hawkins 2010). Incarceration costs taxpayers $80 billion annually (Forbes 2016). Some communities have turned to cost-savings programs in public safety and security to meet new fiscal demands to reduce spending on public safety. For example, in Sunnyvale, California, the cost of public safety went from $69 million

---

6 In Rockbridge County, Virginia, private EMS services are contracted by the local community hospital, Stonewall Jackson, in Lexington, VA, which is part of the Carillion Medical Group, with its primary hospital in Roanoke, VA. Any patient who did not want to be treated at a Carillion hospital would have to drive to Augusta County, then call 9-11, in order to be taken to the Augusta Medical Center, which then refers patients to the University of Virginia hospital in Charlottesville, VA (author's experience living in this community).

7 In January 2011, the Camden, New Jersey Police Department reported that 163 officers were laid off, leaving 204 officers to police a city with the population of 75,000 (DOJ 2011). Camden had to turn to more contracted police support from the county to provide safety to one of the most violent cities in the United States (Christie 2014).

in 2010 to $77 million in 2013, a 10 per cent increase. To address these rising costs, the city introduced a program whereby police, firefighters, and emergency management personnel are cross-trained to be able to perform each other's missions. This allows the city to offset costs by balancing personnel needs and not hiring individuals to perform one public safety or security role (CBS SF Bay Area 2013).

Federal and state funding for public safety and security is usually obtained through grants provided to local communities. Beginning in 1968, with the Omnibus Crime Control and Safe Streets Act, such spending is a prime means for the federal government to influence states and local communities.[8] For example, in 1994, President Clinton created the Community-Oriented Policing Services (COPS) program, which promised to fund the hiring of new police officers nationwide. In Massachusetts from 1994 to 2004, the state government received $215 million in COPS funding, which it, in turn, allocated, to local communities. These funds paid 75 per cent of the newly hired police officers' salaries for three years, after which local communities would be expected to foot the bill (Marks 2007). In 2009, Congress passed the America Recovery and Reinvestment Act (ARRA), which also provided "stimulus" monies to local communities to help pay for community and infrastructure development projects, to include public safety and security initiatives. The Department of Justice later determined that $3.7 billion in stimulus funds was available for local law-enforcement initiatives (Winesburg-Ankrom 2011). The justification given for the infusion of federal funding to pay for local law enforcement was the high levels of crime and drug-related violence, which were overwhelming local resources. During the Clinton administration (1992–2000), a number of programs to supplement police forces in major metropolitan areas, rural communities, and even tribal areas increased the nation's police forces by 18 per cent over 1994 figures (Marks 2007, 3).

After the terrorist attacks of 9/11, initial cost estimates for increased security were in the range of $200 billion annually (Zycher 2003, 32).

8 The Omnibus Crime Control and Safe Streets Act of 1968 was passed by Congress and signed into law by President Lyndon Johnson. The Act was created by Congress in response to the rising crime rates in the country at that time, which threatened the "peace, security and general welfare of the Nation and its citizens." As the result of limited resources available to local police forces, the Act provided the means for increased federal funding through grants to state and local police organizations (PLL 90-351 1968, 1).

This figure may seem exorbitant, but when the estimated expense of a nuclear terrorist attack was placed at $300 billion, such expenditures on preventive security measures appeared to be worth the cost (ibid.). Based on the concern of a catastrophic terrorist incident, in 2001 much of the federal grant money for community policing shifted to homeland security funding programs. Local communities were expected to fund basic public safety and security functions; however, grants could be requested to cover homeland security–specific needs such as drills and training exercises, disaster mitigation and response capabilities, physical security, information security, and cyber security initiatives, etc. On average, local communities would still pay for about 37 per cent of these associated public safety costs, but the state and federal governments would provide an additional 14 per cent each (Scavo, Kearney, and Kilroy Jr 2006).

Within the United States, an old adage is "While the president proposes, Congress disposes" (Haas 2011). In other words, policy is what gets funded. After 9/11, the Bush administration proposed the formation of a new Department of Homeland Security (DHS) to provide a coordinated federal response to domestic threats; however, DHS was not actually created until Congress passed the Homeland Security Act of 2002, which allowed for the largest reorganization of the federal government since the National Security Act of 1947 (CIA 2008). The original funding model for the Department of Homeland Security was to allocate 40 per cent of its funds equally to all fifty states. This later changed to allocations based on state population. The model was refined further to consider issues such as population density, and whether critical infrastructure that may be targets of terrorist attacks existed in certain states. When the Department of Homeland Security grants were first proposed, states and local communities developed lists of what they considered to be critical infrastructure, which may or may not have had the same sense of urgency of concern as those of federal officials. For example, the Corn Palace in Mitchell, South Dakota, was listed as "critical infrastructure" to South Dakotans, on the basis of tourism's economic impact on the community (Calvitto 2005).

The Homeland Security grant system is still in existence, and its impact on local communities remains controversial. Conventional wisdom would make one think that having access to new sources of external funding for public safety and security would free up funds at the local level for public services, such as education or health care. Ironically, since the Homeland Security grant system has been in effect, 18 per cent of local governments have reported budget shortfalls, leading to personnel reductions (Scavo, Kearney, and Kilroy Jr 2006, 23). The effect has been for local communities to become more dependent on state and federal sources of funding to carry more of the fiscal burden for security and safety-related public services. As with any federal funding program, there are always strings attached, which decrease local autonomy on how these funds may be allocated or employed.

Once federal bureaucracies are created by acts of Congress, its leaders feel obligated by taxpayers to determine whether those agencies are doing what they are being paid to do. The secretaries of defence and homeland security are called on routinely to testify before the appropriate committees of Congress with oversight authority over public safety and security. Congress members also have the service of the Congressional Research Service (CRS) and the Government Accountability Office (GAO), which provide research and produce studies on government agencies and their effective use of government funding.

State and local government agencies have similar oversight procedures and mechanisms provided by their elected government officials and executive agencies. In many counties within the United States, the sheriff is elected by popular vote, subject to being voted out of office if the people of that county do not feel that individual has lived up to expectations to provide public safety and security. Within police departments, internal affairs departments exist to conduct investigations against their own officers suspected of violating the public trust by using their positions for personal advantage or using excessive force in responding to a situation. When a local police department is found to be corrupt, or in violation of federal law, such as during the Civil Rights movement in the 1960s, then state and federal agencies can be brought in to investigate those departments and individuals if necessary. In a more recent example, President Clinton created the National Church Arson Task Force, a coalition of federal, state, and local law enforcement agencies focused on investigating a series of racially motivated church bombings in southern states from 1995 to 1998. The combined efforts of multiple agencies led to a higher arrest rate of 34 per cent, versus the national average of 16 per cent on arson cases (National Church Arson Task Force 1998).

Another means of funding for local policing involves the availability of excess military equipment through the Department of Defense Excess Property Program (1033 Program). The 1033 program was begun in the 1990s, as the U.S. military drew down its forces overseas as a result of the end of the Cold War. While much of the excess military equipment was provided to other nations' military forces, some items were made available to state and local police forces.[9] In August 2014, racial conflict in Ferguson, Missouri, following the acquittal of a white police officer for killing an unarmed black teenager, highlighted the program when police forces were seen responding to the violent protest with armoured personnel carriers and other military equipment, prompting a review by the Obama administration of the program (Condon 2014).

Intergovernmental Assessment

Within the United States, there is a hierarchy of public safety and security authorities. Most local, state, and federal government agencies work collaboratively, recognizing their own limitations and need for intergovernmental cooperation in response to routine public safety events. There are fifty-six FBI field offices in major cities throughout the country, along with 380 resident offices in small cities (FBI 2012b). The challenge often comes when the intergovernmental dynamics come to play in the face of an emergency or disaster that tests those governmental relationships. When events such as 9/11 or natural disasters occur, one of three different patterns tends to develop: a "top-down approach" where the national government takes control in response to the inability or unwillingness of state and local governments to do so; a "confusion approach" in response to the existence of little evidence of coordinated effort by government agencies; or the "shared-governance" approach, with the intergovernmental system working more "bottom-up," rather than "top down" (Schneider 1990). In the response to Hurricane Katrina, which

9 Equipment available to police forces under the Department of Defense's 1033 program include "aircraft (both fixed wing and rotary) and four-wheel drive vehicles (such as pickup trucks, blazers, ambulances and armored personnel carriers). The ambulances are used for mobile command vehicles and search warrant entry teams. The armored personnel carriers are used for SWAT teams along with victim and officer recovery. Ballistic helmets and vests are issued for officer safety. BDU clothing (including Nomex fire retardant), boots, wet weather and cold weather clothing, canteens, and web belts are some of the types of field gear items issued for marijuana eradication. Binoculars, radios, camcorders, and tv/vcr combinations are used for tactical and intelligence-gathering operations. Information technology equipment such as desktop and laptop computers, printers, and servers have also been issued" (MDPS 2014).

will be discussed later, it was evident that all three patterns of intergovernmental behaviour developed (Scavo, Kearney, and Kilroy Jr 2006, 84).

One means by which municipalities collaborate with state and federal agencies to deal with all kinds of hazards is through local Emergency Operations Centers (EOCs). On a daily operational basis, these are typically staffed by 9/11 emergency call workers, who can dispatch police, fire, and rescue units, depending on the emergency. During an extended crisis the EOC can be stood up and provide a facility with communications equipment, maps, computers, and other tools for community leaders to gather and exercise command authority. At the EOC, multi-level governmental interaction can occur, where liaison officers from other municipalities or state and federal agencies convene. Since 9/11, many EOCs have adopted the federal government's National Incident Management System (NIMS) as a means by which multi-level government representatives can speak the same language and understand the response mechanisms in place (or needed) to manage the crisis.[10] Local communities have tested the EOC and NIMS through exercises and drills to simulate a crisis and evaluate the means by which the municipalities are prepared to handle the event and what multi-level governance mechanisms may be necessary. These drills and exercises provide the means by which agency leaders can meet their counterparts at other levels of government and learn how to work these relationships during a crisis. As one participant in a national-level homeland security exercise once noted, the reason these exercises are so valuable is to establish relationships before a disaster occurs, so that leaders are not exchanging business cards during a crisis.[11]

A good example of agencies working across the local, state, and federal levels to provide public safety and security is the National Guard and the U.S. military. Each of the fifty states and territories (like Puerto Rico) has army and air force National Guard units. In peacetime the National Guard serves the state governor, providing a rapid response capability at the state level to respond to natural or anthropogenic disasters. Guard units have been called upon to respond to floods, fires,

10 The NIMS and the National Response Framework (NRF) were put in place by the George W. Bush administration after 9/11. Under President Obama, these programs were updated, to include the National Preparedness System (NRS), as a result of Presidential Policy Directive 8, issued in 2011 (National Preparedness System 2011).

11 Author's notes from meetings with personnel involved in such exercises.

hurricanes, tornadoes, terrorist incidents, and insecure borders. Members of the National Guard often work full-time in police, fire, and rescue organizations in local communities. They often have special training in hazardous materials (HAZMAT) removal or explosive ordinance disposal (EWOD), skills that serve their local government agencies, as well as Guard units. National Guard armouries are located in small towns throughout the country, where they serve as community centres where intergovernmental coordination takes place routinely. When the United States goes to war, the National Guard can be federalized and augment active duty forces as combat units. During the ten years of U.S. involvement with conflicts in Iraq and Afghanistan, National Guard units carried a large burden of responsibility, leading to long-term deployments of these citizen-soldiers. As a result, local police, fire, and rescue units (as well as schools, hospitals, etc.) were critically short of personnel.

Under the Clinton administration in 1998, the National Guard began to organize Weapons of Mass Destruction Civil Support Teams (WMD-CST) in every state. These specialized units were created to provide a federal first-response capability in the event of a terrorist incident in a local community, where the team members could augment local first responders and also help coordinate follow-on support from other federal agencies. After 9/11, formation of these units accelerated to include fifty-seven units, with some states, like California and New York, having two units (Viana 2012). The WMD-CSTs are also tied in closely to the new military command structure developed for Homeland Defence after 9/11, the U.S. Northern Command (USNORTHCOM), and its Joint Task Force – Civil Support (JTF-CS). USNORTHCOM provides military support to other government agencies at the federal, state, and local level. Through the leadership of the defence coordinating officer, this USNORTHCOM representative facilitates intergovernmental cooperation between agencies and the employment of both active-duty and National Guard forces to provide local security. An example of this role of the military in domestic security will be examined more fully later in the chapter, when discussing the case study of Hurricanes Katrina and Rita in 2005, and the impact on the federal response to Superstorm Sandy in 2012.

One area of increased tension between federal and local authorities that bridges the national and local security perceptions is immigration. After 9/11, public concern was high over the nation's inability to control its borders, which were viewed as conduits for terrorists to enter the United States illegally, despite the fact that all nineteen of the 9/11 hijackers had come to the United States legally, acquiring visas through the State Department (National Commission on Terrorist Attacks 2004, 4). Former Department of Homeland Security secretary Janet Napolitano admitted that terrorists have occasionally used the Southwestern U.S. border to infiltrate the United States, yet documented cases of terror suspects have been rare, with most recent Middle Eastern immigrants proving to be Iraqis, like Mexicans, trying to enter the United States illegally as undocumented workers (Chastain 2012).

Overall Assessment

As a federal republic, public security in the United States reflects the diversity of the nation when it comes to the nature of crime. On the one hand, national statistics reflect an overall decline in violent crime, yet do not reflect the reality of large cities like Chicago or Detroit, where gun-related deaths have increased. On the other hand, New York City has seen a decline in violent crime,[12] while rural communities, such as Newtown, Connecticut, or Blacksburg, Virginia, would evince a different narrative, as the result of their tragic school-shooting incidents.[13] A recent mass shooting in Orlando, Florida, in June 2016, with forty-nine killed and fifty-three wounded (Doornbos 2016). At the time it was the most deadly mass shooting in the United States. Since the killer targeted the LGBT community specifically, the attack further reflects the diversity of the target of violent crime in the country, as well.

From 2010 to 2011, violent crime incidents in the United States declined nationally from a rate of 404:100,000 to 387:100,000, reflecting a national decrease of 4.5 per cent (FBI 2011). There was a slight increase from 2012, with some individual states experiencing an increase in violent crime over the same time period, such as New York (2.4 per cent), Wisconsin (12.6 per cent), Alabama (7.6 per cent), and Nevada (8.5 per cent) (FBI 2012a). Since 2012, overall violent crime rates in the United States have continued in decline slightly.

---

12 Violent crime comprises murder and non-negligent manslaughter, forcible rape, robbery, and aggravated assault (FBI 2012a).

13 On 16 April 2007, thirty-two students and faculty members were killed by Seung Hui Cho, twenty-three, a student at Virginia Tech in Blacksburg, Virginia (FBI 2010). On 15 December 2012, twenty-six elementary students and staff members were killed at Sandy Hook Elementary School in Newtown, Connecticut, by Adam Lanza, twenty (Esposito 2012).

Figure 10.1. Violent Crime Offence

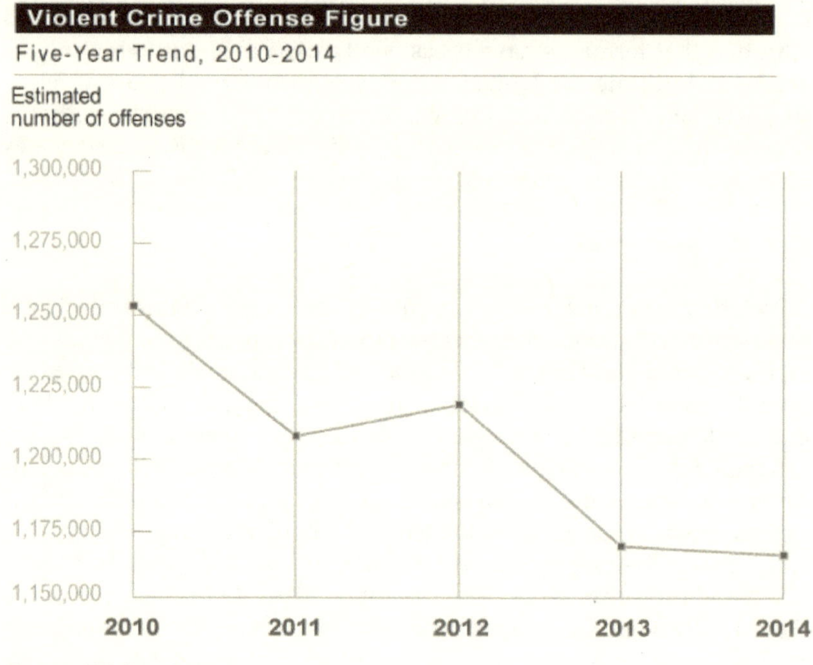

Source: FBI (2014).

In 2015, there was a sharp rise in homicide rates in major cities within the United States, with Washington, DC, and Baltimore, Maryland, accounting for over half the national increase in murders (Brennan Center for Justice 2015). While homicide rates have also remained steady with a rate of 4.5:100,000 nationally (FBI 2014), the average homicide rate for the nation's thirty largest cities is 10.1:100,000, an increase of 14.6 per cent in 2015 (Brennan Center for Justice 2015).

The irony is that, despite the overall decline in crime in the United States over the last decade, most Americans still have a view towards public security that reflects a fear that crime is actually on the increase in the United States. At the same time, Americans believe that crime within their local community has actually declined (Jones 2010), reflecting a duality of views on the nature of public security and threat perceptions.

Figure 10.2. National Murder Rate, 1970–2014

Source: Death Penalty Information Center (2016).

Table 10.3. Description of Seriousness of Crime Problem (%)

	Extremely serious	Very serious	Moderately serious	Not too serious	Not seriousat all
In the United States	20	37	39	2	*
In area where you live	5	10	34	34	17

* Less than 0.5%
Source: Saad (2007).

After the terrorist attacks of 9/11, 46 per cent of Americans viewed terrorism as the most significant threat to the United States (Newport 2010), precipitating a number of new federal laws and institutions to address this threat. Nine years later, less than 1 per cent viewed terrorism as the most serious threat to national security, yet 75 per cent still viewed terrorism as "an extremely or very important issue" (ibid.) and were willing to accede much more federal authority to this potential threat than they are to the threat of crime. The duality of these views is evident in the desire of Americans to protect their rights of gun ownership and support for local recourses to address the potential of violent crime, rather than accede to federal authorities' greater legal recourse to address the perceived criminal threat (e.g., through increased gun control legislation). At the same time, Americans are willing to grant the federal government increased power and the ability to curtail civil liberties to address the threat of terrorism, despite the low probability of such an occurrence within their communities.

Contrary to popular belief, domestic terrorism was a concern in the United States well before the events of 9/11. In the 1980s, the Federal Bureau of Investigation (FBI) established a number of Joint Terrorism Task Forces (JTTF) throughout the country to serve as the loci for federal, state, and local law enforcement counterterrorism efforts. The New York City JTTF was instrumental in the investigation involving the first World Trade Center bombing in 1993. In 2009, there were over 100 JTTFs in existence, providing an important function in information sharing and enhanced operational capacity to deal with terrorist threats (Mayer 2009, 131). In large metropolitan areas, such as New York City, an individual was also named as the deputy commissioner for counterterrorism, with a robust, dedicated staff of detectives assigned full-time to the JTTFs. In other locations, the JTTFs lacked dedicated full-time local law enforcement support and were more likely to be seen as crisis action centres where federal, state, and local officials would convene after an event occurred, rather than deterring terrorist attacks. In some locations, local law enforcement agencies saw little advantage to be gained from working in the JTTF with federal agencies (9/11 Commission 2004, 82). As a result, after 9/11, the Department of Homeland Security made a concerted effort to support the establishment of dedicated fusion centres apart from the JTTFs, staffed full-time to "coordinate the gathering, analysis, and dissemination or law enforcement, homeland security, public safety, and terrorism information" (White House 2007, 20). Yet DHS failed to provide these centres with actionable information, much less the requisite guidance and training of personnel necessary to be make this redundant federal effort necessary (Mayer 2009, 133).

State and local governments have varying degrees of counterterrorism capabilities. Given the nature of the threat, few small communities of twenty-five-member police forces (or fewer) have a dedicated counterterrorism capacity simply because they do not anticipate a terrorist incident. Large metropolitan areas, such as Los Angeles, have taken their own initiative to develop a counterterrorism capacity with or without federal support. The Los Angeles Police Department was prepared for terrorist attacks during the 1984 Olympics and thus developed its own task forces to deal with the potential threat then, and later created new units, such as the Terrorism Early Warning group to establish the infrastructure to work with and integrate involvement of federal agencies, such as the Secret Service, U,S. Coast Guard, and the Bureau of Alcohol, Tobacco and Firearms (Rust 2006, 21).

After the terrorist attacks on 9/11, the country's fixation on counterterrorism and preventing additional terrorist attacks created some internal tensions for public security officials at the local levels, particularly those responsible for policing communities with large Arab populations. Greater Detroit, Michigan, is one such community, with around 200,000 residents claiming to be of Arabic decent (Thacher 2005, 647). The largest concentration of Arab Americans in the greater Detroit area is Dearborn, Michigan, which prior to 9/11 had experienced conflict and racial tensions of its own. After 9/11, the Dearborn Police Department faced conflicting tasks of preventing hate crimes against the Arab population of the city, but also ensuring that it was supporting the country's new counterterrorism measures, by ensuring terrorist groups were not operating in the area (650). When the U.S. Department of Justice sought to interview 200 residents of Dearborn who were suspected of having ties to al-Qa'ida, the regional Anti-Terrorism Task Force (which included attorneys, FBI, and other police agencies) was brought in, adding an additional level of potential conflict between public safety and security officials responsible for counterterrorism activities (Thacher 2005, 656–657).

At the federal level, the National Counterterrorism Center (NCTC) was established in 2004 to provide a fusion centre between government agencies to analyse and share information about terrorist threats to the nation. It comprises members of intelligence, law enforcement, homeland security, and military agencies, with its director reporting to the director of national intelligence (NCTC 2012). It supports over seventy-five different government agencies with information on terrorist threats and "facilitates information sharing between the IC [Intelligence Community] and State, Local, Tribal, and Private partners – in coordination with DHS, FBI, and other members of the ITACG [Interagency Threat Assessment and Coordination Group] Advisory Council" (ibid.).

The National Strategy for Counterterrorism released by the Obama administration in 2011 focuses much of its attention on the threat posed by al-Qa'ida and its affiliated movements throughout the globe (White House 2011). To that end, the strategy discusses this terrorist group and its presence in various regions. It also addresses the importance of forming partnerships with other nations and cooperating in combating terrorism. However, the strategy makes scant mention of the plans needed for greater public safety and security cooperation domestically. In fact, the only reference to domestic counterterrorism efforts is in the following statement: "Integrating and harmonizing the efforts of Federal, state, local and tribal entities remains a challenge" (11).

Yet, despite these challenges, counterterrorism operations have thwarted suspected terrorists from carrying out attacks on the U.S. homeland. For example, on 25 December 2009, Umar Farouk Abdulmutallab (the underwear or Christmas Day bomber), attempted to blow up a Northwest Airlines jet en route to Detroit, Michigan (Ariosto and Feyerick 2012). On 1 May 2010, Faisal Shahzad attempted to detonate a vehicle laden with explosives in Times Square, New York (Adams and Nasir 2010). On 17 October 2012, Quazi Mohammad Nafis attempted to attack the Federal Reserve Building in New York City using a car bomb (Marzulli 2013). In many of these and other cases, effective counterterrorism "sting" operations were conducted by the FBI, state, and local police to prevent an attack.

Yet on 15 April 2013, two brothers, Dzhokhar and Tamerlan Tsarnaev, conducted a terrorist attack at the site of the Boston Marathon, killing 3 and wounding 260 people. In the subsequent investigation by the U.S. Congress, findings echoed those of the *9/11 Commission Report*, citing a failure to share information between federal, state, and local agencies. Despite the existence of the Boston JTTF and memorandums of understanding between agencies, as a result of the 9/11 attacks, there was still a general misperception of what classified intelligence information could be shared by whom and with whom. More troubling for the members of Congress was a general perception by law enforcement and intelligence agencies that the Boson Marathon attack could not have been prevented (U.S. House of Representatives 2014).

Although terrorist attacks and potential attacks will continue to occur on the U.S. homeland, the lessons learned from the Boston Marathon bombing are that the further away the nation is from the events of 9/11, the less emphasis is placed on counterterrorism and thus the need for greater public safety and security integration of effort between federal, state, and local agencies to respond to potential threats. This may be due to a level of complacency within bureaucratic structures, what Donald Kettl calls "punctuated backsliding," where after the initial rush of activity to address the crisis through major policy changes or creation of new institutions, government agencies eventually return to a previous equilibrium or stasis, until the new "policy lightning event" occurs (Kettl 2014, 159). In the United States, such was the case on 29 September 2005, when Hurricane Katrina made landfall in New Orleans, Louisiana. As a result of the focus on terrorism at the time as the main threat to public safety and security, the federal government was ill-prepared to deal with the consequences of a naturogenic event, which had the impact of a terrorist attack, due to the number of deaths and destruction, and the failure of public safety agencies to respond to the crisis. The impact of Katrina, and the subsequent policy changes that followed, was that the threat from natural disasters would increase the role of the federal government in areas of public safety and security that were primarily the domain of state and local governments. The result has been the development of a more inclusive view of homeland security in the United States to one that looks beyond terrorism to what is called an "all-hazards" perspective on threats to public safety and security (Kilroy 2007).

Public Security Case Study: Emergency and Disaster Response to Hurricanes Katrina and Rita and Superstorm Sandy

Prior to 9/11, local communities had the burden of responding to emergencies and natural disasters. The aforementioned EOCs coordinated the reaction of local first responders to an emergency. Only when the extent of the disaster exceeded local capacities did the community go first to the state, which then went to the federal agencies to provide support. The Stafford Act of 1985 established the means by which the president determines if a disaster warrants designation as a state of emergency and thus releases federal funds to support either public agencies or individual persons, or both. As originally envisioned, the Stafford Act puts the onus on state governors as the lead officials in determining whether local remedies have been exhausted and federal help is needed. The president and federal agencies, such as the Federal Emergency Management Agency (FEMA), would be in a reactive rather than a proactive role, awaiting the call from the governor's office (Kilroy 2007, 79).

Yet FEMA was often criticized for bringing too little, too late in disaster response. Its handling of the aftermath of Hurricane Andrew in 1992 in south Florida was a case in point, where President Clinton was compelled to fire the director (Kilroy 2007, 79). After 9/11, FEMA was placed under the new Department of Homeland Security. It lost its Cabinet-level agency status under the George W. Bush administration and was subordinated not only to new managerial positions within DHS, but also to the overarching mission of "homeland security" with its emphasis on terrorism as opposed to natural disasters. FEMA had its operating budget reduced, since it was no longer an independent federal agency, rather one of twenty-two federal agencies that now made up the new DHS. FEMA's director, Michael Brown, held the title of under secretary for emergency response; however, there were four other under secretaries in the DHS architecture competing for resources. That explains why FEMA was ill-prepared to respond to the devastating hurricanes that hit New Orleans and the Gulf states in 2005.

Hurricane Katrina, a category four hurricane, made landfall on 29 August in Louisiana, Mississippi, and Alabama, devastating communities in its path, with over 1,800 deaths reported. A month later, Hurricane Rita, another category four hurricane, came ashore in Texas and Louisiana, inflicting much larger economic damage to the nation's oil refineries in south Texas. As a result of the public and media criticism of the poor federal response to Katrina, President Bush prepositioned himself at U.S. Northern Command headquarters in Colorado Springs, Colorado, in order to exercise command over all federal relief efforts and demonstrate to the American public that federal agencies would not wait to be called on by state or local agencies for assistance (Kilroy 2007, 81).

After the hurricanes, the U.S. Congress took up the call to pull FEMA out from under DHS and restore it to its former independent agency status. Instead, DHS Secretary Michael Chertoff effectively argued for keeping FEMA under DHS, but removed some internal bureaucratic structures and changed leadership (like President Clinton), replacing a political appointee with a professional emergency responder. In 2006, President Bush signed a congressionally mandated change to the Stafford Act that gave FEMA a "quasi-independent" status under DHS, as well as opening the door for an expanded federal role in disaster response, at the expense of local and state agencies (Kilroy 2007, 82).

On 29 October 2012, Superstorm Sandy made landfall in southern New Jersey. Although it was no longer classified as a hurricane, the extent of its massive size and due to the nature of the high population areas impacted on the East Coast, it quickly became the second most costly storm in the nation's history with over $65 billion in damage in the United States alone (CNN 2014). As a result of lessons learned during Katrina and Rita, the federal government took a much more proactive role in providing support before the storm and relief after the storm to the states hardest hit by the natural disaster. President Obama sought to avoid the public relations mistakes of his predecessor, President Bush, who appeared disinterested in the fate of the people of the Gulf Coast states. Obama made a point of demonstrating the role and responsibility of the federal government to treat natural disasters as real threats to public security by proactively authorizing emergency declarations for states impacted by the storm, freeing up FEMA and other federal agencies to deploy their resources early to East Coast states, before the storm. President Obama also took unprecedented action after the storm to maintain federal commitment by signing two significant pieces of legislation increasing the amount of federal aid available, as well as creating a Hurricane Sandy Rebuilding Task Force (Ladislaw, Kostro, and Walton 2013).

The impact of these actions to help build resilient communities and protect critical infrastructure against natural disasters, like Superstorm

Sandy, is to expand the federal mandate in the areas of public safety and security beyond just the threat of terrorism. However, despite the lessons learned from Katrina and Rita, it is evident that increasing the federal role in disaster response as a public safety concern does not translate into immediate results. In the case of Superstorm Sandy, in the two years immediately after the storm there were still corrective actions by federal agencies (39 of 102 identified in a government accountability report) that had yet to be implemented, such as "improving emergency coordination with states; boosting training in the use of electronic medical records and other care; and ensuring adequate transportation of injured victims" (Yen 2014).

Conclusion

Federalism remains strong in the United States. U.S. states are still protective of what they consider to be federal intrusions in state affairs. New controversies evince a continuing intentional tension within the U.S. constitutional system, which originally leaned towards states' rights over federal rights. The contradiction, however, concerns public safety and security where states and local governments seek and expect increased federal expenditures to fund their public security–related expenses. This has accelerated after the events of 9/11 and Hurricanes Katrina and Rita, evidenced more recently in the federal response to Superstorm Sandy. In the 2005 National Action Plan on Safety and Security in America's Cities, produced after Hurricanes Katrina and Rita, Matt Mayer notes, "it is clear that mayors who contributed to the report believe that the federal government has primary responsibility to fix or fund every aspect of homeland security" (2009, 48–9). And that definition of homeland security has become more inclusive, taking an all-hazards perspective on public security.

During periods of insecurity, Americans are willing to concede more authority and discrimination to the federal government over the use of law and force to provide public safety and security. Since no large-scale terrorist attack has occurred on U.S. soil since 9/11, public attitudes towards security have been subsumed by economic factors, which are contributing to a public demand to reduce spending and cut the size of government. As a result, safety and security, along with the war on terror, fell further down in the polls as a factor in the 2012 presidential elections. However, when Superstorm Sandy hit the East Coast in November 2012, causing 186 deaths and over $65 billion in damage, states were quick to demand federal relief for clean-up efforts and remediation (Zerkel 2014).

Despite a change in public perception of the immediacy of terrorist threats, or even natural disasters, federal structures created to address public safety and security, such as the Department of Homeland Security, continue to grow. One area where DHS and the military have expanded their federal role is in cybersecurity and concerns over threats to the nation's critical infrastructures, from both state and non-state actors.

In a nation as large and diverse as the United States, it is evident that a federal system of government has served the people well in providing for both "domestic tranquility" and the "common defense," as stated in the preamble to the U.S. Constitution. Challenges to governance in the federal system in the United States occur when crises stress the system and those structures established to respond to threats, such as terrorist attacks or natural disasters, are found inadequate (Kettl 2014). Yet the federal system in the United States remains surprisingly resilient and flexible in responding to the challenges of governance from new threats to public safety and security. The reservation clause in the Tenth Amendment to the Constitution still provides a check on federal encroachment upon states and their authorities to provide for public security. However, a well-informed citizenry still remains necessary for maintaining such protections.

References

Adams, John Quincy. 1821. "Comments Made while Serving as President James Monroe's Secretary of State." In *The Future of Freedom Foundation Commentaries*. Accessed 4 January 2012. http://www.fff.org/comment/AdamsPolicy.asp.

Adams, Lorraine, and Ayesha Nasir. 2010. "Inside the Mind of the Times Square Bomber." *Guardian*, 18 September. https://www.theguardian.com/world/2010/sep/19/times-square-bomber.

Ariosto, David, and Deborah Feyerick. 2012. "Christmas Day Bomber Sentenced to Life in Prison." CNN, 17 February. http://www.cnn.com/2012/02/16/justice/michigan-underwear-bomber-sentencing/.

Ayers, Edwin, Lewis Gould, David Oshinsky, and Jean Soderlund. 2010. *American Passages: History of the United States. Vol. 1: to 1877*. 4th ed. Boston: Wadsworth.

Birkland, Thomas, D. 1997. *After Disaster: Agenda Setting, Public Policy and Focusing Events*. Washington, DC: Georgetown University Press.

Brennan Center for Justice. 2015. "Murder and Crime in 30 Largest Cities (2014–2015)." https://www.brennancenter.org/sites/default/files/publications/Crime_Data_Dec2015.pdf.

Bureau of Justice Statistics. 2017. "Federal Law Enforcement." https://www.bjs.gov/index.cfm?ty=tp&tid=74.

Calvitto, Celeste. 2005. "Homeland Security: South Dakota-Style." *Rapid City Journal*, 10 September. http://rapidcityjournal.com/news/local/article_2bfbc6ad-a860-5eaf-bafe-a4c52ed42694.html.

CBS SF Bay Area. 2013. "Cash-Strapped Cities Look to Sunnyvale for Cost-Saving Public Safety Model," 3 January. http://sanfrancisco.cbslocal.com/2013/01/02/cash-strapped-cities-look-to-sunnyvale-for-cost-saving-public-safety-model/.

Chastain, Mary. 2012. "Department of Homeland Security Secretary Janet Napolitano Told the House Homeland Security Committee That She Can Confirm Terrorists Enter America through the Mexican Border." Breitbart, 1 August. http://www.breitbart.com/Big-Government/2012/07/31/Napolitano-Admits-Terrorists-Enter-America-Through-Mexico-From-Time-To-Time.

Christie, Les. 2014. "Most Dangerous Cities." CNN Money, 17 December. http://money.cnn.com/gallery/real_estate/2014/02/03/dangerous-cities/.

CIA. 2008. "A Look Back … the National Security Act of 1947." https://www.cia.gov/news-information/featured-story-archive/2008-featured-story-archive/national-security-act-of-1947.html.

– 2016. "The United States." The World Factbook. https://www.cia.gov/library/publications/the-world-factbook/geos/us.html.

CNN. 2014. "Hurricane Sandy Fast Facts," 5 November. http://www.cnn.com/2013/07/13/world/americas/hurricane-sandy-fast-facts/.

Condon, Stephanie. 2014. "What Can Washington Do about Militarized Police Forces?" CBS News, 15 August. https://www.cbsnews.com/news/after-missouri-what-can-washington-do-about-militarized-police-forces/.

"Constitution of the United States." 1787. National Archives. https://www.archives.gov/exhibits/charters/constitution.html.

Department of Defense (DOD). 2012. "Defense Budget Priorities and Choices."

– 2016. Defense Manpower Data Center (DMDC). https://www.dmdc.osd.mil/appj/dwp/dwp_reports.jsp.

Department of Homeland Security (DHS). 2012. "Overview." https://www.dhs.gov/index.shtm.

Department of Justice (DOJ). 2011. "The Impact of the Economic Downturn on American Police Agencies." A Report of the U.S. Department of Justice Office of Community Oriented Policing Services, October.

Discoverpolicing. 2013. "Types of Law Enforcement Agencies." Discoverpolicing.org. http://www.discoverpolicing.org/whats_like/?fa=types_jobs.

Doornbos, Caitlyn. 2016. "Pulse Building Released Back to Owners." *Orlando Sentinel*, 13 July. http://www.orlandosentinel.com/news/pulse-orlando-nightclub-shooting/os-pulse-shooting-released-owners-20160713-story.html.

Esposito, Richard. 2012. "20 Children Died in Newtown, Conn., School Massacre." ABC News, 14 December. http://abcnews.go.com/US/twenty-children-died-newtown-connecticut-school-shooting/story?id=17973836.

Faragher, John Mack, ed. 1999. *Rereading Frederick Jackson Turner: "The Significance of the Frontier in American History" and Other Essays*. New Haven, CT: Yale University Press.

FBI. 2010. "Campus Attacks." https://www.fbi.gov/stats-services/publications/campus-attacks.

– 2011. "Crime in the United States 2011." http://www.fbi.gov/about-us/cjis/ucr/crime-in-the-u.s/2011/crime-in-the-u.s.-2011/tables/table-4.

– 2012a. "Crime in the United States 2012." https://www.fbi.gov/about-us/cjis/ucr/crime-in-the-u.s/2012/crime-in-the-u.s.-2012/violent-crime/violent-crime.

– 2012b. "Local Offices." https://www.fbi.gov/contact-us/field.

– 2014. "2014 Crime in the United States." https://www.fbi.gov/about-us/cjis/ucr/crime-in-the-u.s/2014/crime-in-the-u.s.-2014/offenses-known-to-law-enforcement/violent-crime/violent-crime.

Forbes. 2016. "Why Are Incarceration Rates in the US so High Relative to Other Countries?," 1 July. https://www.forbes.com/sites/quora/2016/07/01/why-are-incarceration-rates-in-the-us-so-high-relative-to-other-countries/#5013e686ce1e.

Governing. 2012. "Police Employment, Officers Per Capita Rates for U.S. Cities." http://www.governing.com/gov-data/safety-justice/police-officers-per-capita-rates-employment-for-city-departments.html.

Haas, Lawrence. 2011. "Follow the Leader: On Debt Talks, That's Congress." *Fiscal Times*, 20 July. http://www.thefiscaltimes.com/Blogs/Capital-Exchange/2011/07/20/Capital-Exchange-Follow-the-Leader-On-Debt-Talks-Thats-Congress.

Hamilton, Alexander, James Madison, and John Jay. 1961. *The Federalist*. Cambridge, MA: Harvard University Press. https://doi.org/10.4159/harvard.9780674332133.

Hawkins, Stephen. 2010. "Education vs Incarceration." *American Prospect*, 6 December. http://prospect.org/article/education-vs-incarceration.

Hughes, Zerline. 2012. "Release: United States Continuing to Overspend on Police, Despite Decreasing Crime Rates." Justice Policy Institute, 22 May. http://www.justicepolicy.org/news/3907.

International Association of Chiefs of Police (IACOP). 2011. "Police Officer to Population Ratios Bureau of Justice Statistics Data." *Perspectives.*

Jones, Jeffery M. 2010. "Americans Still Perceive Crime as on the Rise." Gallup News, 18 November. http://www.gallup.com/poll/144827/americans-perceive-crime-rise.aspx.

Kettl, Donald F. 2014. *System under Stress: The Challenge to 21st-Century Governance.* Washington, DC: CQ.

Kilroy Jr, Richard J. 2007. *Threats to Homeland Security: An All Hazards Perspective.* Edited by J. Richard. Hoboken, NJ: J. Wiley and Sons.

Ladislaw, Sarah O., Stephanie Sanok Kostro, and Molly A. Walton. 2013. "Hurricane Sandy: Evaluating the Response One Year Later," 4 November. Center for Strategic and International Studies. https://csis.org/publication/hurricane-sandy-evaluating-response-one-year-later.

Lipscomb, Andrew A., and Albert E. Bergh, eds. 1903–4. *The Writings of Thomas Jefferson.* Vol. 14. Washington, DC: Memorial Editions.

Marks, Audrey M. 2007. "Funding Squabble Reveals Stresses on Police Departments," 25 May. Boston University College of Communications. Accessed 6 January 2012. http://www.bu.edu/phpbin/news-cms/news/?dept=1368&id=46064.

Marzulli, John. 2013. "Thwarted Manhattan Federal Reserve Bomber Sentenced to 30 Years." *Daily News*, 9 August. http://www.nydailynews.com/news/national/thwarted-nyc-fed-bomber-30-years-article-1.1422360?barcprox=true.

Mayer, Matt A. 2009. *Homeland Security and Federalism: Protecting America from Outside the Beltway.* Santa Barbara, CA: ABC-CLIO.

Missouri Department of Public Safety (MDPS). 2014. "Department of Defense Excess Property Program (1033 Program)." Accessed 17 December 2014. http://www.dps.mo.gov/dir/programs/cjle/dod.asp.

National Church Arson Task Force. 1998. *Second Year Report for the President.* Department of Justice. https://www.justice.gov/crt/church_arson/arson98.php.

National Counterterrorism Center. 2012. https://www.dni.gov/index.php/nctc-home.

National Guard. 2014. "How We Began." http://www.nationalguard.mil/AbouttheGuard/HowWeBegan/.

National Preparedness System. 2011. Accessed July 14, 2016. https://www.fema.gov/media-library-data/20130726-1855-25045-8110/national_preparedness_system_final.pdf.

Newport, Frank. 2010. "Nine Years after 9/11, Few See Terrorism as Top U.S. Problem." Gallup News, 10 September. http://news.gallup.com/poll/142961/Nine-Years-Few-Terrorism-Top-Problem.aspx.

9/11 Commission. 2004. *The 9/11 Commission Report*. New York: W.W. Norton.
PLL 90-351. 1968. The Omnibus Crime Control and Safe Streets Act of 1968. 19 June. United States Congress.
Public Intelligence. 2011. "Global Private Security/Police Office Personnel Levels by Country/Per Capita 2011." https://publicintelligence.net/global-private-securitypolice-officer-personnel-levels-by-countryper-capita-2011/.
Rust, Sunchlar M. 2006. *Collaborative Network Evolution: The Los Angeles Terrorism Early Warning Group*. Monterey, CA: Naval Post Graduate School.
Saad, Lydia. 2007. "Perceptions of Crime Problem Remain Curiously Negative." Gallup, 22 October. http://www.gallup.com/poll/102262/perceptions-crime-problem-remain-curiously-negative.aspx.
Scavo, Carmine P.F., Richard C. Kearney, and Richard J. Kilroy Jr. 2006. "Local Government Managers' Views on Homeland Security." In *The Municipal Yearbook*, 19–26. Washington, DC: International Community Managers Association (ICMA).
Schneider, Saundra K. 1990. "FEMA, Federalism, Hugo, and 'Frisco.'" *Publius* 20 (3): 101–2.
Stockholm International Peace Research Institute (SIPRI). 2015. "SIPRI Military Expenditure Database." https://www.sipri.org/research/armaments/milex/milex_database.
Thacher, David. 2005. "The Local Role in Homeland Security." *Law & Society Review* 39 (3): 635–76. https://doi.org/10.1111/j.1540-5893.2005.00236.x.
U.S. House of Representatives. 2014. *The Road to Boston: Counterterrorism Challenges and Lessons from the Marathon Bombings*. House Homeland Security Committee Report. March (declassified document released on the House.gov website). Accessed 18 December 2014. https://homeland.house.gov/files/documents/Boston-Bombings-Report.pdf.
Viana, Liza Porteus. 2012. "Guard's WMD Civil Support Teams Can Respond Faster Than Other Federal Assets." Homeland Security Today, 14 May. http://www.hstoday.us/briefings/correspondents-watch/single-article/guards-wmd-civil-support-teams-can-respond-faster-than-other-federal-assets/af2160975c8dc3d4ab7f17f0942bdcdc.html.
White House. 2007. "National Strategy for Information Sharing." Washington, DC: White House.
– 2011. "National Strategy for Counterterrorism." Washington, DC: White House.
– 2012. "The Cabinet." https://www.whitehouse.gov/administration/cabinet.
Winesburg-Ankrom, Melissa. 2011. "Update on ARRA Funding for Police Departments." PoliceGrantsHelp, 29 September. https://www.policegrantshelp.com/news/1915903-Update-on-ARRA-funding-for-police-departments/.

Yen, Hope. 2014. "US Not Fully Prepared for Nuclear Terrorist Attack." Associated Press, 19 December. http://www.msn.com/en-us/news/us/us-not-fully-prepared-for-nuclear-terrorist-attack/ar-BBgZjWn?ocid=u143dhp.

Zerkel, Eric. 2014. "Superstorm Sandy Anniversary: Remembering Hurricane Sandy Two Years Later." https://weather.com/storms/hurricane/news/superstorm-sandy-anniversary-20141029.

Zycher, Benjamin. 2003. *A Preliminary Benefit/Cost Framework for Counterterrorism Expenditures*. Santa Monica, CA: RAND.

Further Reading

Birkland, Thomas. 1996. *After Disaster: Agenda Setting, Public Policy, and Focusing Events*. Washington, DC: Georgetown University Press.

Scavo, Carmine P.F., Richard C. Kearney, and Richard J. Kilroy Jr. 2007. "Challenges to Federalism: Homeland Security and Disaster Response." *Publius* 8 (1): 81–110. https://doi.org/10.1093/publius/pjm029.

11 Conclusion

CHRISTIAN LEUPRECHT AND MARIO KÖLLING

Like their unitary counterparts, the federal polities in this book struggle to adapt to deviant aspects of globalization that are fundamentally challenging the institutionalized security claim of the modern state: to renew, deepen, and expand control over transnational risk phenomena that seem impervious to state control. There is no ready formula to optimize efficient delivery and effective security outcomes in democratic federations. Rather, some federal systems appear to be more agile and adaptive than others. In the proliferation of federations as an antidote to state fragmentation and disintegration, no single template for nascent federations emerges as would-be federations such as Cyprus, Yemen, or Libya strive for a constitutionally viable consensus to reconcile freedom and security. Still, some variables and patterns emerge from the nine federal case studies in this comparative volume that should prove helpful to mature and maturing federations alike looking to improve their overall outcomes in this regard, and for deeply divided societies riven by conflict for whom federalism is the sole alternative to fragmentation and disintegration. The aim of this concluding chapter is to summarize these comparative findings. Given the limited sample of case studies, however, the conclusions in this volume are necessarily preliminary and meant to stimulate further empirical and comparative work.

The first section compares how responsive select federal case studies in this book are to anthropogenic threats. In particular, one would expect both the nature and extent of these threats to affect the nature of public security in a federal polity: the greater the stress and expectations vis-à-vis the state, the more centralized the system. The second section analyses the dynamics of centralization and decentralization, symmetry and asymmetry, as well as the necessary and sufficient conditions that underpin trends in one direction or another. Comparative empirical observations allow the formulation of some initial hypotheses for the role of and conditions of decentralization and asymmetry in public security in federal polities. If variation among subnational priorities, values, and interests matters, then one would expect decentralized and asymmetric systems to prove more adaptable and thus effective at ensuring public security – but also at greater risk of inefficient delivery and ineffective outcomes due to greater potential for controversy and outbidding. The third section gauges institutional path-dependency of a regime's institutions, horizontal and vertical intergovernmental relations, and legitimacy as independent and intervening variables in public security in federal polities. The final section discusses these observations in light of the initial hypotheses and research questions by identifying the institutional logic that underpins the observed trends, and how these findings inform the nexus between security and federalism.

Anthropogenic Threats to Public Security

Anthropogenic risks can be endogenous and exogenous. Endogenous anthropogenic threats in Canada, Germany, and Switzerland tend to be latent (in the sense of unintentional and non-criminal), primarily taking the form of technological risk. Now that the risk from the terrorist group ETA has subsided, Spain might be classified in this group as well. The United States faces a moderate risk, largely as a result of rates of violent crime that are above average among democratic federations. Several federations in the sample face high risks: Brazil and Mexico from drug-related homicides and organized crime, South Africa from disproportionate rates of murder, rape, and robbery that are exacerbated by xenophobia and socio-economic conditions, and India from high levels of homicide and persistent political violence in different parts of the country.

Only South Africa and India confront manifest exogenous anthropogenic threats. South Africa faces a steady influx of economic migrants from countries in southern Africa, especially from Zimbabwe, which has had, and still has, a destabilizing effect on public security by fostering xenophobia. While refugees and migration pose an ongoing challenge to India, as a result of both political instability and the impact of climate change in its vicinity, India is the only country in our sample with festering territorial disputes, notably with Pakistan and China.

Several of the countries in our sample confront the threat of transnational terrorism, but it remains modest and isolated. India, by contrast, continues to confront regular challenges from domestic, international state-sponsored, and transnational terrorism. Given this panoply of challenges, security theory would predict that we would expect to find a more centralized approach to security in India and, to a lesser extent, South Africa, than among the remainder of the sample. Analogous dynamics informed the latent centralization of security measures in many countries in our sample in the aftermath of 9/11 that resulted in a recalibration of shared-rule and self-rule with respect to public security. However, the nature and magnitude of public security challenges faced by India, coupled with less state capacity among constituent units to respond to these challenges, both explains why India is an outlier in its centralized approach to public security, and why it is likely to remain so for the foreseeable future.

Division of Powers: De/centralization

Some federations take a top-down approach to security, others a bottom-up approach. But is this a reflection of the fact that the former were once unitary states, or that they are more homogeneous, or both? Table 11.1 summarizes the division of power over security matters across the nine federal polities in this volume.

While security has tended towards greater centralization since 9/11, the vectors driving a federation's approach seem to be a function of both path-dependency and diversity. On matters of public security, heterogeneous federations are more centralized than homogeneous ones, likely because of a latent threat that heterogeneity is perceived to pose to territorial integrity of the federation as a whole.[1] India and South Africa stand out for their centralization on matters such as policy, investigation, arrest, and public order. In India, this is manifest in the emphasis on the Indian *Union* as opposed to its federal aspects. The emphasis on the Indian *Union* seems to

1 A developing country, also called a less-developed country (LDC), is a nation with a lower living standard, underdeveloped industrial base, and low Human Development Index relative to other countries. There is no universal, agreed-upon criterion for what makes a country developing versus developed, and which countries fit these two categories, although there are general reference points such as a nation's GDP per capita compared to that of other nations.

Table 11.1. Constitutional Allocation of Security Capacities

Country	Levels of government among which the Constitution divides power	Relevant constitutional provisions governing the separation of power	Residual powers	Are powers of constituent units enumerated?	Federal security responsibilities	Federal ministries and agencies	Security responsibilities of constituent units	Security agencies and services of governments of the constituent units	Responsibilities, agencies, and services provided by municipalities
Brazil	3: federal, state, and municipal	Title III, Articles 18–38	States	Yes	Land/air/sea borders; crimes against political order; crimes against Federal institutions or interests; drugs and contraband; railroads; highways.	Ministry of Justice; Polícia Federal; National Secretariat for Public Security; National Public Security and Citizenship Program; National Public Security Force	States are primary and residual bearers of responsibility for public security broadly writ: patrolling, investigation, etc. Also responsible for social side of integrated initiatives like UPPs.	Polícia Civil; Polícia Militar; state Security Secretariats	May create municipal guards with restricted powers
Canada	2: federal and provincial; municipalities fall under provincial jurisdiction	Sections 91 and 92	Federal	Yes	Crime,* disaster assistance under certain conditions, border safety, national security, emergency management and mitigation	Public Safety Canada, Department of National Defence, Royal Canadian Mounted Police, Correctional Services of Canada, Canadian Security Intelligence Services, Canadian Border Security Agency, Parole Board of Canada	Crime,** provincial fire safety, disaster relief, hazard elimination, workplace safety, highway/transport safety	Responsible ministries and agencies vary by province. Large ones have ministries for public/community safety and correctional services; Ontario Provincial Police and Sûreté du Québec, other provinces RCMP	As delegated by the province, including municipal policing

India	Federal, state, and municipal	Articles 245, 246, Schedule 7 (Lists I, II, III), Parts IX and X (Articles 243–243ZG; XI & XII Schedules), Article 244(1) Schedule V, Article 244 (1) and 275 (1) Schedule VI	Federal	Yes	National security, defence forces, deployment of federal forces to aid civil powers in a state, disaster management, legal and penal codes, nuclear power, preventive detention, railways	Ministry of Home Affairs, Ministry of Law and Justice, Central Police Organizations (nearly 12)	States: public order and police, criminal codes and procedures	Police	None
Mexico	3: federal, state, and municipal governments have constitutional powers	Articles 73 and 124; also Articles 115 and 117	States (Article 124)	Yes	Federal crime investigation and prosecution (organized crime, drug traffic, possession of firearms) Disaster relief operations Border safety, airport security, port security	Secretariat of Public Safety (Secretaría de Seguridad Pública)* National Attorney General (Procuraduría General de la República) Secretariat of National Defence (Secretaría de la Defensa Nacional) Secretariat of the Navy (Secretaría de Marina) National Security and Investigation Centre (Centro de Investigación y Seguridad Nacional) Civil Protection (Coordinación Nacional de Protección Civil) * SSP disappeared on 1 December 2012, and the federal police became part of the Secretariat of the Interior	Local crime investigation and prosecution State highway safety Correctional services Emergency management	State police: in charge of security and traffic enforcement in state highways; special tactical teams; correctional services State attorney: local crime investigation and prosecution State civil protection agency: emergency management at state level	Municipal police: traffic enforcement, incivilities and response to emergency calls Municipal civil protection agency: emergency management at local level

South Africa	National government Provincial government Municipalities	Sections 205–8 Constitution of 1996	National	Yes	Policing, preventing, investigating crime, apprehending suspects	South African Police Service (SAPS)	Provinces have limited oversight role over SAPS; Control over provincial roads	Highway traffic police officers	Metropolitan police forces Policing municipal by-laws
Spain	Central government and Autonomous Communities, provinces and municipalities Only the central government and the autonomous communities have political autonomy	Art. 149	Constituent units	No	Civil Guard Highway patrol Counter drug operations Anti-smuggling operations Customs control Weapons licences and arms control Security of border areas and coast guard Environmental law enforcement National Police Force Issue identity documents Control receipts and outgoings of foreign people and Spaniards Immigration asylum, extradition and expulsion Gaming enforcement Drug enforcement Collaboration with Interpol and Europol Control of private security companies		Asymmetric responsibilities Basic responsibilities: Protect the buildings and institutions of the AC Coordinate local police forces		Basic responsibility: urban traffic control

Switzerland	Cantons primarily, federal authorities subsidiarily (except defence: only responsibility of federal authorities)	Articles 3, 42, 43, 47, 52 of Federal Constitution	Federal authorities in emergencies	No, yet the cantonal powers comprise maintaining and restoring of public security and safety Re safety, particular fields are within the federal responsibility (legislation), but enforced mostly by the cantons	(Military) Defence. Federal *responsibility* for the protection of people and representations according to international law (execution by cantons) Several federal competences re criminal justice (prosecution and judgment) as well as international cooperation (mutual judicial assistance)	Department of Defence and Population Protection (with Army, Fed. Office for Population Protection, and Intelligence services), Department of Justice and Police (with Federal Office of Police (fedpol) incl. fed. criminal police, Fed. Office for Migration. Federal Attorney General's Office ("autonomous" authority with separate monitoring body reporting to federal Parliament)	Main responsibility for maintaining and restoring public security. Mutual assistance among cantonal police services if necessary. Cantons can delegate limited police powers to communities	Political level: Cantonal Department of Police (or home affairs etc.); administrative level: cantonal police service, cantonal office for civil protection	Political level: municipal police or security/ safety directorate. Administrative level Municipal police services where foreseen by cantonal law Municipal fire brigades and ambulance services. Municipal civil protection office

United States	Federal, state governments only in the Constitution Local governments are considered subordinate to state governments In practice, local governments exercise great autonomy from state and federal government	Articles I, II, and III lay out roles of federal government and separation of powers Within first 10 amendments, called the Bill of Rights, the Tenth Amendment contains the "reservation clause," which leaves all powers not enumerated in the Constitution to federal government to state governments	States	Yes	Specific crimes (e.g., treason), disaster assistance under certain conditions, border security, national security, federal emergency management and mitigation	Department of Defence, Department of Homeland Security, Department of Justice, Federal Bureau of Investigation, U.S. Customs and Border Patrol, U.S. Marshals, Drug Enforcement Agency, Bureau of Alcohol, Tobacco, and Firearms	Most criminal cases, fire safety, disaster relief, hazard elimination, workplace safety, highway/transport safety	Responsible agencies vary by states and metropolitan areas. State Highway Patrol, State Bureaus of Investigation, tribal police, county sheriffs, local police forces	As determined by state and local legal jurisdictions
Germany	2: federal and state (Länder); municipalities fall under Länder jurisdiction	Articles 30, 70–2, 74	Länder	No	Protection against dangers of international terrorism or when a threat affects more than on Land	Department of the Interior; Federal Criminal Police Office; Federal Police; Federal Office for the Protection of the Constitution		State Departments of the Interior; State Criminal Police Offices; State Police Forces; State Offices for the Protection of the Constitution	Municipal offices of public order (Ordnungsamt) are responsible for public order, safety, and security on the local level; no municipal police

be driven by a concern about territorial integrity, heightened by the experience and aftermath of Partition. In South Africa, the centralized approach to security is a lag effect of the centralized security apparatus under the apartheid regime, but is also indicative of the centralized institutional security culture that is prevalent throughout much of Africa. Mexico and Brazil show similar patterns of centralization but more moderately than the high degree of centralization found in India and South Africa. In Mexico, the legacy of decades of authoritarianism continues to shape public security. However, the Mexican regime is more centralized than it appears on paper. The centralization of resources and powers with the army and federal police run counter to a more balanced approach in the Constitution. Such centralization may thus be temporary in response to pressing acute existential domestic security concerns, in contrast to which the Constitution holds out the possibility of a return to a more decentralized approach. That possibility is confirmed by the oscillation between decentralization and centralization found in Brazil. While the centralization of public security correlated with authoritarianism, constitutionally the federal government's control over security in constituent units is actually relatively weak. De facto, however, the federal government has control over powerful civil and military police forces and intelligence agencies, which it is at considerable liberty to deploy because of areas of shared jurisdiction with the constituency units. That is emblematic of a general trend in federalism studies where federal governments have a propensity to crowd constituent units out of areas of concurrent jurisdiction.

By contrast, centralization in matters of public security among the sample of homogeneous federations is relatively low. The German arrangement is quite decentralized – right down to domestic security intelligence agencies under the purview of each Land – but happens to be structured in such a way as to produce symmetric outcomes. Legislative capacity and the implementation over matters of public security resides largely with the Länder governments. This is less by intentional institutional design than by dint of strategic interests of strong local bureaucracies and predates the current constitutional arrangement by several decades, autocratic interludes in the first half of the twentieth century notwithstanding. Competencies of the federal government are limited largely to overcoming collective-action problems, such as national criminal investigations, counterterrorism, or the armed forces.

Insofar as Switzerland had hitherto lacked a federal police, it is even more decentralized than the German system but has been subject to some centralizing security trends as of late. In fact, the Swiss system takes the opposite approach: only those powers clearly vested in the federal authorities by the federal Constitution, requiring a double majority by voters and cantons, are areas of federal competence. Switzerland's approach relies heavily on cooperation among cantons that enjoy substantial autonomy, particularly in matters of public security. (Military) defence, however, falls exclusively under federal jurisdiction, with a militia army minimizing the amount of necessary (or rather indispensable) military professionals.

In Spain, the legacy of decades of authoritarianism prompted a gradual process of decentralization that included public security, but the balance between central and sub-state power remains hotly contested. Constituent units with a long legacy of some degree of linguistic and cultural autonomy, notably in the Basque country, Navarre, and Catalonia, were especially proactive in demanding their own security forces: the Basque Ertzaintza and the Catalan Mossos d'Esquadra date back well into the eighteenth century. These regions' long-standing autonomy in public security seems to be path-dependent. It has waxed and waned over the centuries, despite more centralized interludes. Regaining autonomy over security that these regions had traditionally enjoyed as a result of the decentralization process seems to have had a contagion effect. Other autonomous communities where the main obstacle is not de jure constitutionally but the de facto ability by the central government also sought a transfer of more resources to realize and expand some degree of autonomy over public security. For autonomous communities that do not yet have their own police force, the recent economic and financial crisis has, for the time being, halted their ambitions.

Federal countries with vast territories, such as the United States and Canada, have historically taken a more decentralized approach to matters of public security. However, in the United States that mindset is driven by scepticism of government in general, and of central government in particular, as exemplified by *Posse Comitatus*, which explicitly restricts the involvement of the armed forces in domestic law enforcement operations, along with other limitations on domestic operations (such as intelligence gathering) by organizations such as the Central Intelligence Agency and the National Security Agency. In Canada, by contrast, decentralization is more a matter of administering and delivering public security equitably and effectively across large swathes of territory with linguistically and ethno-culturally diverse populations. Both federations resolve concerns over the delivery and administration of security resources by granting constituent units sufficient powers of taxation to raise the resources necessary to cover their respective public-security obligations. Nonetheless, both countries – heterogeneous by virtue of their vast territory – retain important, well-resourced federal domestic security capacities.

Conversely, then, homogeneous countries in our sample show a pattern of decentralization of public security, whereas decentralization seems to have its limits in heterogeneous countries. In South Africa, the provinces are limited to oversight, consultation, and social services; municipalities, by contrast, have limited powers of arrest, along with control over policing traffic and by-laws. In all cases, suspects are handed over to national authorities for detention and prosecution. Similarly, Indian states have few formal powers over public security, although, constitutionally, they have control over police and law and order. In fact, the Indian Constitution even allows the president to dismiss and dissolve elected constituent units' governments in a case of emergency and bring them under direct central rule, as happened in Punjab, the North East, and Kashmir. Since these constituent units straddle an international border, it stands to reason that concerns about territorial integrity continue to outweigh their autonomy in the delivery and administration of public security. Mexico is similarly becoming more centralized. Previously constituent units and the federal government had their own criminal codes (thirty-three), but since 2014 there is now a unified criminal code. Spain's central government contributes funding to constituent units as well as municipalities for public security; by virtue of the German federal (tax) system, the federal government provides funding neither to the Länder, nor to municipalities. Assessing the merits of one model over another, however, requires more data, since the experience of federations that have granted municipalities constitutional status and where municipalities receive direct federal funding seems to suggest that this may exacerbate collective-action problems across the federal systems. Whether this is a function of institutional design or of other endogenous factors is unclear. In Canada, the United States, Germany, and Switzerland constituent units enjoy considerable autonomy over public security, with limited leeway for the federal government to control public security directly, other than through targeted financial incentives as well as some law enforcement and intelligence capacity at the federal level. Indeed, all four countries have seen sub-state autonomy compromised in the aftermath of 9/11 through anti-terrorism legislation with latent centralizing tendencies, including the creation of federal police forces in Germany and Switzerland and more sweeping powers for security services in general and federal police in particular in the United States and Canada. In all four federations, however, constituent units retain a substantial degree of autonomy in the application and execution of public security. Add to that variegated tendencies towards decentralization of public security in Spain, in Mexico and in Brazil and the book's initial hypothesis that public security is, ultimately, a sub-state matter seems to be confirmed.

For decentralization to materialize, however, certain conditions seem to be necessary. Detailed constitutional provisions alone are insufficient and, as the Spanish case suggests, may not even be necessary. Rather, a commitment to a balance between shared rule and self-rule as well as adequate resourcing through own-revenue or transfers are necessary. However, the contrast between Germany and Spain (with the exception of the Basque country and Navarre) on the one hand, where transfers are based on shared tax revenue, own resources, and transfers, and the United States and Canada on the other hand, where fiscal autonomy in own-source revenue plays a significant role, suggests that the mechanism by which public security is financed in decentralized systems is somewhat immaterial. As in any other policy field, systems with a greater degree of own-source revenue may be prone to unjust outcomes because the federal government has less leverage. Yet the American and Canadian experience suggests that even under conditions where constituent units raise most of the revenue to pay for public security, equitable outcomes across large, heterogeneous territories with considerable variation in conditions are readily achievable. In other words, as long as resources are adequate, the mechanism by which they are provided seems secondary to an overall commitment to administering and delivering public security autonomously.

A/symmetry

While political and economic development emerge as determinants of dynamics of centralization and decentralization in federal polities, that is not the case for proclivities towards symmetry and asymmetry. Federations where the administration of public security is decentralized, such as the United States and Germany, can nonetheless decentralize symmetrically. In Germany, this is by design, in the United States it is the result of the federal government gradually acquiring more expansive powers to encourage or coerce convergence at the level of constituent units. Resources play a considerable role in the degree of symmetric development in public security. In South Africa especially, public security resources accrue predominantly to national agencies. Similarly, in Brazil and Mexico federal agencies are better resourced than those of constituent units, and there is considerable variation in spending on public security among constituent units in both federations. As a result, in Mexico, for example, both the quantity and quality of police forces vary considerably across Mexican states and constituent units.

Yet resources alone are not deterministic: despite being well-resourced with relatively similar levels of per-capita spending by constituent units, public-security actors at the level of constituent units in the United States and Germany generate equitable outcomes. But this is, of course, precisely what one would expect to find in a modern state whose sovereignty is defined in part by its ability to assert the monopoly of violence over a given territory. In other words, the sign of maturity of public security in a federal state is the extent to which it is able to generate comparable levels of public security across a single territory. In Canada, Switzerland, and Spain, territory, language, culture, political culture, and history have preconditioned and possibly even necessitated asymmetry to just ends. By contrast, in federations with highly disparate levels of public security, such as India, Brazil, or Mexico, or federations where public security remains more elusive, such as South Africa, a greater degree of federal intervention is perceived to be necessary to achieve more just outcomes. In Mexico, that intervention goes so far as the General Law of the National System of Public Security that deliberately legislates intergovernmental mechanisms to improve the efficient delivery and just administration of security.

On the one hand, asymmetric approaches to public security may be more tolerable where public security is already inequitably distributed (e.g., India and South Africa). On the other hand, asymmetry may actually be necessary to achieve just outcomes under certain conditions, including linguistic, cultural, ethnic, or national diversity (India, South Africa, and Spain). India – and to a lesser extent South Africa or Spain – is somewhat of an outlier in this regard: large, diverse countries, especially India, with a highly centralized approach to public security have little tolerance for asymmetry in its delivery. Neither decentralization nor asymmetry is a sufficient condition to generate effective public security outcomes; but the observations in this study suggest that they may be necessary, especially in diverse federations.

Drivers of Intergovernmental Dynamics

Table 11.2 summarizes intergovernmental coordination mechanisms across the nine federal polities discussed in this volume.

Table 11.2. Intergovernmental Coordination Mechanisms Related to Public Security (without Switzerland)

	Intergovernmental mechanism	Levels of government involved	Effectiveness
Spain	Bilateral mechanisms	2	Weak
	Safety Boards	3	
Canada	Ministers' Conference (participation by provincial and federal governments is discretionary)	2	Weak: mechanism has not been used to coordinate security policy
	Canadian Association of Chiefs of Police, Police Information and Statistics Committee, which liaises with Statistic Canada's Canadian Centre for Justice Statistics	Multiple: federal, provincial, municipal, Aboriginal	Medium: strong, long-standing association but weak ability to influence policy
United States	Formal structures through joint task forces (e.g., terrorism, counter-drug, etc.) or other ad hoc arrangements. Informal through law enforcement associations and organizations (e.g., Fraternal Order of Police, National Sheriffs' Association, etc.)	Multiple: federal, state, local, tribal	Medium to strong: varies by agencies, locations, and size of communities
Brazil	SENASP PRONASCI National Public Security Fund	Multiple	Weak to medium*
South Africa	Intergovernmental forum (MinME) – national minister with nine provincial ministers	National and provincial governments	Weak due to limited role of provinces in policing

India	Inter-State Council Secretariat	Multiple	Weak
Mexico	National Public Safety System (and council) Public Safety Ministers' Conference Attorney General Offices' Conference Municipal Public Safety Conference Civil Protection System (and council)	3 2 2 2 3	Weak to medium: somehow has been effective to coordinate national projects and programs, but has failed to improve security and safety Medium: coordination has improved among civil protection municipal, state, and federal agencies, but the system has failed to strengthen local capacity
Germany	Political level: Conference of Federal and State Ministers of the Interior; Administrative level: joint institutions of the federation and the Länder (like the Joint Terrorism Prevention Center or the Joint Internet Surveillance Center)	2: Federal and state	Medium: sometimes lack of cooperation between security services of the federation and the Länder Strong: Conference of Ministers of the Interior serves as effective instrument of the federation for security policy cooperation with the Länder and a way for the Länder's interests to be represented vis-à-vis the federation

* It depends on how effectiveness is measured. They have coordinated fairly well, but the outcome for citizens has been negligible.

Regime

Scholars of federalism are heavily invested in historical institutionalism and, indeed, path-dependency seems to play an important role in explaining observed patterns. On the one hand, authoritarianism, in one form or another, has shaped experiences in most of the countries in our sample. The political experiences of Brazil, Mexico, South Africa, and Spain seem to reverberate in today's network of federal structures and processes. In all four federations, federal security actors continue to play a large role in the delivery of public security. Although that role has diminished somewhat in Spain, multilevel governance of public security in Spain aggravates operational overlap and redundancies that have proven difficult to disentangle, largely because of a public-security tradition premised on an expansive role for central institutions. Germany's authoritarian legacy is more distant but shaped an institutional design premised on thwarting the centralization of authority but has given rise to problems of transparency and cooperation. Germany's federal institutional design, especially in public security, is strongly influenced by the American model. The nuance, of course, is that American institutions are the result of scepticism of central government that sprang from a war of independence against colonial rule, as opposed to Germany's authoritarian past. In India, a similar reaction against colonial rule gave rise to the opposite result: centralized security institutions. This suggests that exogenous anthropogenic threats, in India's case notably the threat of Partition, trump concerns over strong government in the form of a centralized security apparatus. Canada's experience is somewhat analogous, with an arguably more centralized approach to public security ceding way to decentralization and asymmetry as the initial external threat emanating from the United States subsided. Switzerland is the outlier. The last international conflict in which it participated (as an entity) was the battle of Marignano (1515); except for the two world wars, the greatest risk to its sustainability has since been the threat of internal strife. Switzerland's decentralized, asymmetric approach to public security is thus a combined function of reconciling unity in diversity and diminishing external threats to its territorial integrity.

Intergovernmental Relations

Our sample divides into cases where intergovernmental relations in public security are heavily politicized (and thus arguably more subjective) and those where they are less politicized (and thus arguably more objective). Politicization seems to be more determined by institutions than political development. Relations in Brazil, India, and South Africa are heavily politicized; relations in Mexico less so. In Spain, dynamics between police forces are highly politicized. Controversy over public security, the level at which it should be delivered, and the way public security is resourced among constituent units is widespread. This lack of consensus is apparent in the lack of formal mechanisms of cooperation and the difficulty of making the ones that do exist, such as the Council for Security Policy and Security Boards, work. The South African Police (SAP) is heavily influenced by a federal government that is controlled by the African National Congress. Its "tough-on-crime" rhetoric legitimates the central government's heavy-handed approach and resonates with the electorate. Ergo, oversight through politically neutral organizations and the provinces – that technically have responsibility for oversight – as well as intergovernmental coordination is limited and ineffective. In South Africa especially, public-safety resources accrue mostly to national agencies. However, limited collaboration between the SAP and municipal forces shows that the relationship may become less politicized as South African politics matures and security institutions professionalize. Analogous security rhetoric has served to legitimize strong centre federalism in India, much to the chagrin of the constituent units – and to the detriment of intergovernmental cooperation. However, politicization is not as much a function of federal political parties as of resentment among minorities who militate against perceived oppression by the central state and its security agents. That sentiment is prominent in Kashmir but similarly prominent in support for the Naxalite rebellion in Bihar, Jharkand, and Andhra Pradesh as well as Karnataka, Chhattisgarh, Orissa, Maharashtra, Uttar Pradesh, and West Bengal. In Brazil, regional elite interests and concomitant corruption reinforce lingering paternalism and clientelism from its oligarchic past. Although not partisan per se, these dynamics complicate intergovernmental relations and the intergovernmental effort that does exist such as the Integrated Management Committee and the National Public Security Force tend to operate on the operational and tactical rather than the strategic level.

In other words, politicization of intergovernmental relations tends to be driven by grievances over the use, provision, and resourcing of public security at the level of constituent units and the lack of institutionalized cooperation bodies at the vertical and horizontal level. But politicization takes different forms: in South Africa especially and to a lesser extent in Spain, where it is driven by partisan politics, as opposed to Brazil and Mexico where it is not. Ergo, partisan politics is neither a necessary nor a sufficient condition for the politicization of intergovernmental relations. Conversely, however, the absence of such partisan politics may not be a sufficient condition, but appears to be a necessary one, for objective intergovernmental relations. As in Brazil and Mexico, the administration and delivery of public security in Canada, Germany, and Switzerland is largely beyond the fray of partisan politics. In the United States local sheriffs are elected officials, and that can place them within the political fray.

The Canadian and American experiences in particular suggest that lapses in public security are prone to exploitation for partisan gain by local and opposition politicians. Similarly, ideology has an impact on intergovernmental relations, as some parties see more or less of a role for the state in public security. Essentially, however, intergovernmental relations on public security in these federations tend to be fairly objective insofar as the institutional mechanisms to work out horizontal and vertical differences tend to be quite mature.

A key difference in the way these mechanisms operate is the role and importance of politicians vis-à-vis bureaucrats. In Germany and Switzerland, for instance, strong horizontal and vertical institutional structures are pivotal to intergovernmental relations and often see relatively little political involvement. Swiss intergovernmental relations on public security matured over a long time without significant disruption that in part accounts for their strong institutionalization within a robust rule-of-law framework. Germany's Conference of Interior Ministers is a highly institutionalized and effective intergovernmental mechanism, but its name belies the fact that its primary purpose is as a vehicle for horizontal and vertical coordination and cooperation among the bureaucracies of the Länder and the federal government. Intergovernmental relations in Mexico are equally institutionalized, but mechanisms such as the National Public Security Council, the Attorneys General Conference, the Minister of Public Security Conference, the Prisons Conference, and the Municipal Public Security Conference operate primarily at the political rather than bureaucratic levels.

In Canada, by contrast, intergovernmental relations on matters of public security tend to be fairly ad hoc and premised on political involvement, with bureaucracies usually acting at the behest of politicians rather than on their own initiative. The United States and Spain are outliers: formal vertical intergovernmental institutions are all but non-existent, and horizontal ones are ad hoc and often bilateral ones holding relatively little sway. Of course, that applies only to the strategic political level; there are plenty of contacts at the operational and tactical levels. Trust and communication among bureaucrats and operators emerges as a hallmark of maturity in intergovernmental relations in federal systems. That is, most intergovernmental aspects do not actually require much political involvement, because civil servants already cooperate well and mutually respect each other's competence and jurisdiction. This is one of the problems to which a centralized approach to public security seems to give rise: hierarchical suppositions engender an undue sense of importance among federal security actors and a consequent disrespect for security services at "subordinate" orders of government. That federal forces and intervention in local security matters is required thus becomes a self-fulfilling prophecy, but one that runs counter to the premise that security is local and one that asserts national security priorities over subnational security interests.

Legitimacy

In federations where paternalism is prevalent, institutional capacity and legitimacy along with judicial efficacy tend to be low to begin with, and even lower at the levels of constituent governments. Where people feel least secure, government and especially its related security institutions enjoy the least legitimacy. In Brazil, India, and South Africa, for instance, corruption is endemic, and partly as a result, public-security actors of the constituent units are widely condemned as inept and ineffective. Under these circumstances, central institutions seem to enjoy a relatively greater degree of trust than sub-state ones: in the relative scheme of things, where central institutions have legitimacy deficits, sub-state and local appear to have even less legitimacy. In Mexico and India, for instance, the armed forces consistently enjoy considerable trust, in contradistinction to state police. In Brazil, perception is widespread that police repression is applied unevenly, and there is a large gap between formal structures and the implementation of security provisions: whilst Brazilians have apprehensions about federal security actors, they are even more apprehensive about most local ones. While institutional legitimacy and state capacity tend to be high among other federations in the sample, Spain is an interesting anomaly. The convoluted relationship between autonomous communities and the central government, and the entangled diversity of police forces to which it gives rise, makes it difficult for citizens to hold any one level of government accountable for criminality and policy. Low levels of transparency and accountability thus make Spain comparable to Brazil, India, Mexico, and South Africa. But in Spain, where crime rates are below average, citizens tend to perceive public security positively. However opaque, then, ultimately what matters is not the structure of the system, but the efficiency and equity of the outcomes it generates.

Proactive versus Reactive Policymaking

The major difference here is between intergovernmental systems that are sufficiently robust to prioritize prevention. In the absence of robust intergovernmental relations, there is a tendency to resort to reactive public security measures. India and South Africa dedicate few resources to prevention. They rely instead on central enforcement measures. Brazil's "institutional duplicity" overlays an egalitarian political system with a stratified social structure in order to ensure that prescribed means rarely accomplish intended ends, because legitimate and illegitimate institutions operate side-by-side, and occasionally in concert. Change and intervention by the centre are occasioned by policy shocks, while the fundamental structure of the public-security system remains unchanged. By contrast, ambitious judicial and security-sector reform in Mexico is an impulse for greater prevention, but neither reaction nor prevention thus far appears to have generated tangible improvements in public safety and in stemming the spread of violence.

By contrast, the high degree of trust, confidence, and legitimacy in public security in Canada, Germany, Spain, Switzerland, and the United States is the direct result of a functional federal/decentralized system (or positive outcome). In the federal approach to dividing power, the resources and surge capacity to react, especially on a large, coordinated scale, are vested with the federal government. By contrast, preventive measures, such as social, education, and health-care policy – or, as in the case of administrative federations, at least their implementation – is vested with constituent units. Ergo, proactive, preventive measures are difficult to operationalize, let alone sustain, in federations whose constituent units lack the necessary capacity, resources, or competencies and the concomitant intergovernmental relations and mechanisms.

Their absence causes federations to default to a Hobbesian mode where the federal government becomes the sole guarantor of public security, but at the cost of being able to tackle only symptoms of public insecurity, not their roots. And when it does so, federal priorities, values, and interests are frequently misaligned with local ones. That is, ultimately, why decentralization is integral to public safety. Decentralization is not a normative preference per se. Rather, the ability to be proactive about implementing preventative public-security measures to sustain an environment where people feel safe and confident about their security hinges on harnessing strategically (1) the broad set of policy tools that are often conceived of as public safety and go beyond mere public security and, in circumstances that require reactive measures as a fallback position, (2) public-security resources and actors that know and understand their communities and will put the community's priorities, values, and interests first.

Closing Remarks

Federal institutional design thus affects public security; so do a plethora of endogenous effects whose impact on the performance of a federal polity's spatial strategy and capacity to generate public security cannot always be readily disentangled. That makes it difficult to control systematically for vertical and horizontal effects, such as decentralization and asymmetry, on security outcomes. Inherently, federal security institutions, practices, and outcomes appear to be more a result of federalism per se than other general governance and societal factors in mature federations. Yet mature federations are also mature democracies. While federal versus democratic effects are difficult to disentangle, the observations do support the thesis that federal and democratic commitments go hand-in-hand, and that democratic governance and a federal political culture are necessary – albeit not perforce sufficient – conditions for federal security institutions, practices, and outcomes. That may explain why federal polities that face challenges in delivering and administering security seem to rely heavily on a centralized approach.

Federal approaches to security seem to work best where the principle of subsidiarity prevails, along with a consensus on the levels of government best suited to different security challenges. By their very nature anthropogenic threats, for instance, transcend sub-state jurisdictions and thus involve collective-action problems that require federal coordination. Yet if one reason for a federal system is to reconcile self-rule and shared rule in societies across whose territory priorities, interests, and values vary considerably, then central and constituent governments are perforce likely to differ in their security priorities, interests, and values. Similar to other policy areas, the greater the variance among priorities, interests, and values, the greater the incentive for decentralization and asymmetry to reconcile unity in diversity. In fairly homogeneous cooperative federations, such as Germany, delivering and administering security is a matter of intergovernmental coordination. In diverse or heterogeneous federal polities, by contrast, horizontal and vertical competition among governments of constituent units generates different objectives and practices. In the absence of effective intergovernmental mechanisms to reconcile these differences, delivering and administering security risks become subject to a zero-sum game dominated by the federal government as the best-resourced and most powerful player. The less optimal the performance of the federal system, the more security is likely to be under-delivered, and the scarcer it is, the more contentious its delivery and administration become, by virtue of spawning opportunistic behaviour by competing governments within the federal polity.

Public security outcomes, then, are as much a function of institutional design and operational differences as they are of the nature of the security threats as well as federal and democratic culture and commitments. The challenge in institutional design on the one hand, and the way the network of intergovernmental institutions functions on the other, is an equilibrium that optimizes the efficient delivery and effective administration of security across a federal polity. That seems difficult to accomplish when there are looming threats to territorial integrity or a path-dependent institutional culture of centralizing security. The ability to reconcile shared rule with self-rule is as important for public security as it is for other policy arenas in federal polities. How they are reconciled is a function of the types and intensity of the threats to public security a country faces, the nature and diversity of society and the federal territory, and the path-dependent trajectory that constrains and conditions institutional development.

The nature and territorial concentration of distinct linguistic, cultural, and ethno-national groups is likely to influence the need and extent of asymmetric public-security arrangements. Irrespective of the degree of asymmetry, however, decentralization emerges as a determinant of the legitimacy and efficacy of public security. The institutional logic is informed by territorial differentiation of security priorities, values, and interests across constituent units on the one hand, and subsidiarity on the other. The more collective conceptions vis-à-vis the administration and delivery of public security are de-aligned, the more public security is likely to diverge from local priorities, values, and interests. And the greater this de-alignment, the less objective and functional the intergovernmental relations needed to shift from immediate Hobbesian concerns about order to a more holistic approach to public security that follows when federal polities can optimize in the way they reconcile freedom and security.

Aside from identifying best practices and lessons learned, this study set out to understand the extent to which decentralization and asymmetry are driven by heterogeneity in values and preferences. Such heterogeneity also increases political opportunism across sovereign jurisdictions, thus making it more difficult to arrive at an intergovernmental consensus about the division of labour between the central and sub-state governments. Where public security is controversial, the overall efficiency in delivery and effectiveness in outcomes is reduced. Owing to social, political, economic, ethnic, cultural, religious, linguistic, and regional diversity, security priorities, interests, and values at the subnational level may diverge substantially from those of other constituent units as well as federal ones. Ergo, strategic rational actors within the horizontal and vertical webs of intergovernmental institutions have different interests and incentives to pursue different paths of (in)action. Inherent in a federal approach to public security, then, is the potential for considerable tension in the way public security is conceived at different levels of government, and how it is delivered. However, structural and institutional factors may combine to reconcile or aggravate such tensions.

This volume sought to draw a systematic and methodical link between a set of federal polities on the one hand, and competing approaches to a core mandate of the modern state on the other: reconcile domestic security with fundamental democratic norms. To this end, it reviewed constitutional, institutional, and legislative frameworks that underpin public security across nine federations, and the implications that follow for institutional design, public administration, and public policy. In the process, the volume sought to make a contribution to the way policy choices and performance are mediated by federal structures and processes and to innovate federal security policy, administration, institutional design, and processes through the comparative study of the state's monopoly of force in federal polities.

Contributors

Todd Hataley is adjunct professor at the Royal Military College of Canada and research fellow at the Centre for International and Defence Policy at Queen's University. His research interests include extremist violence, management of international boundaries, regional security, and security reform. Dr Hataley is the author of over twenty scholarly publications. His most recent publications include *North American Regional Security: A Trilateral Framework* (Lynne Rienner), and *Evolving Transnational Threats and Border Security: A New Research Agenda* (CIDP, Queen's University).

Kai Michael Kenkel is associate professor at the Institute of International Relations at the Pontifical Catholic University of Rio de Janeiro and associate researcher at the German Institute of Global and Area Studies in Hamburg. He was trained at the Graduate Institute in Geneva and Johns Hopkins University. He has published extensively on security issues, focusing most recently on humanitarian intervention and the responsibility to protect, as well as United Nations peace operations, especially Brazil's role therein. His recent publications have centred on the normative debates surrounding intervention. He has been managing editor of *Contexto Internacional* and recently served on the board of the Brazilian Defence Studies Association.

Richard J. Kilroy Jr is assistant professor of politics at Coastal Carolina University in Conway, South Carolina. He teaches courses in intelligence studies, homeland security, and Latin American politics. His publications include *Threats to Homeland Security: An All Hazards Perspective* (Wiley 2008, 2018), *North American Regional Security: A Tri-*

lateral Framework? (Lynne Rienner, 2014), and *Colonial History and Territorial Issues in Africa and Latin America* (Northeast Asian Historical Foundation, 2010). His PhD is in foreign affairs from the University of Virginia.

Mario Kölling is assistant professor at the Department of Political Science at the Spanish National Distance Education University and senior researcher of the Manuel Giménez Abad Foundation, Zaragoza. From 2011 to 2014 he was Garcia Pelayo Researcher at the Centro de Estudios Politicos y Constitucionales in Madrid. He graduated from the University of Potsdam (Germany) and holds a PhD from the University of Zaragoza in public law.

Christian Leuprecht is the Class of 1965 University Professor in Leadership at the Royal Military College of Canada, Matthew Flinders Fellow at Flinders University in South Australia, cross-appointed to Queen's University, and Munk Senior Fellow in Security and Defence at the Macdonald Laurier Institute. He is an elected member of the College of New Scholars of the Royal Society of Canada and a recipient of RMCC's Cowan Prize for Excellence in Research.

Ajay K. Mehra is a professor in the political science faculty of the University of Delhi and coordinates activities of the Centre for Public Affairs, a forum of concerned citizens. He has worked extensively on Indian democracy, institutions, internal security (comparative policing, terrorism, Naxalism), and politics of urbanization. He has over three decades of experience of research and teaching in these areas. He has authored, co-authored, and edited over a dozen books and contributed over sixty scholarly papers in journals and books.

Edgar Mohar is executive director for ANPC, an emergency managers association in Mexico, and an independent public safety consultant. Edgar Mohar holds a master's degree in public administration from the Monterrey Institute of Technology and Higher Education, Mexico. He worked in the public safety sector for several years, first as municipal public safety director in the city of Queretaro, and then as secretary of citizen security and safety for the state of Queretaro, Mexico. As a consultant, he has worked for the Mexican federal government, the World Bank, and several NGOs in Latin America and the United States.

Markus H.F. Mohler was prosecutor in 1971–9, and in 1979–2001 was commandant of the Cantonal Police of Basel-Stadt; meanwhile in 1984–98 he was director of the Swiss Senior (commissioned) Officers Courses; on behalf of the Swiss Federal Department of Foreign Affairs (FDFA) he was head of teams to consult Hungary and Czechoslovakia on police reform (1991–4). In the military (militia Swiss type) his last assignment was colonel in the Armed Forces Joint Staff for internal security. In 2001–11 he was consultant and trainer on behalf of FDFA in African and western Balkan countries, and in 2005–11 he was lecturer on public law, especially safety/security, and police law at the Universities of Basel and St Gallen. He has written numerous publications on these topics.

Lukas Muntingh is co-founder and Project Coordinator of Africa Criminal Justice Reform (ACJR), formerly the Civil Society Prison Reform Initiative (CSPRI), as ACJR was known from 2003 until 2017. He holds a PhD (Law) from UWC and an MA (Sociology) from Stellenbosch University. He has been involved in criminal justice reform since 1992 and was Deputy Executive Director of Nicro prior to joining UWC. He has worked in Southern and East Africa on child justice, prisoners' rights, preventing corruption in the prison system, the prevention and combating of torture, and monitoring legislative compliance. He has published extensively and presented at several conferences. His current focus is on the prevention and combating of torture and ill-treatment of prisoners and detainees.

Rainer J. Schweizer is professor of public, European, and international law at the University of St Gallen, permanent visiting professor at the University of Lucerne, the Military Academy of the Swiss Federal Institute of Technology Zurich, as well as the Università Carlo Cattaneo, Milan. He is a member of the European Academy of Sciences and Arts, Salzburg, and co-editor of several scientific law journals in Switzerland, Germany, and Austria.

Nico Steytler is South African research chair in multilevel government, law and policy, Dullah Omar Institute of Constitutional Law, Governance, and Human Rights of the University of the Western Cape, Cape Town, South Africa. He was a member of the Municipal Demarcation Board (2004–14) and is a commissioner of the Financial and Fiscal Commission (2013–18). He was the president of the International Association of Centers for Federal Studies (2010–16).

Klaus Stüwe is professor and chair of comparative politics at the Catholic University of Eichstaett-Ingolstadt, vice president for international relations of his university, and member of expert committees worldwide. He has authored and edited eighteen books and published more than 100 articles that concentrate on comparative politics, constitutional courts, political communication, federalism, family policies, and public security.

www.ingramcontent.com/pod-product-compliance
Lightning Source LLC
LaVergne TN
LVHW090152080826
844660LV00013B/781/J

* 9 7 8 1 4 8 7 5 0 2 6 7 6 *